Thomas Rawlings

The Confederation of the British North American Provinces

Thomas Rawlings

The Confederation of the British North American Provinces

ISBN/EAN: 9783337141196

Printed in Europe, USA, Canada, Australia, Japan

Cover: Foto ©ninafisch / pixelio.de

More available books at **www.hansebooks.com**

TO THE

HONOURABLE WILLIAM NAPIER.

MY DEAR SIR,

During my sojourn in England the past two years, circumstances have caused me to seek many interviews with you. And during those interviews I have always been impressed with the profound interest you manifested in all that concerned the welfare of the British North American Colonies, and the future development of the Hudson Bay Territory. You have done me the honour on one or two occasions to say that you thought a pamphlet, which would carry to the public a general idea of that whole territory, and impress upon the Government at home the importance of uniting by iron bands the Atlantic with the Pacific Ocean, would be a task pleasing to me, who had lived in America so many years. Acting upon that suggestion, I have compiled, from the best authorities, all the information which I thought bore upon the subject. You will find the work fragmentary and disjointed, but a merchant lays no claim to the dignity of a *littérateur*.

Faithfully yours,

THOS. RAWLINGS.

HAMPTON VILLA, PEMBRIDGE PLACE,
London, February 16, 1865.

PREFACE.

I PURPOSE, in the following pages, to treat of the migratory movements of the human race chronologically—of the discoveries on the continent of America—of the early history, progress, present condition, and future prospects of all that territory lying north of the 49th parallel, the Lakes and the St. Lawrence, and extending from the Pacific to the Atlantic Ocean, and which will constitute the proposed British North American Confederacy.

I desire to prove by that history, that progress, that prosperous present, and by that prospective future, what a splendid territory Great Britain possesses, and how proud she should be of so thriving, so energetic, so ambitious a people.

I shall devote a few chapters to the consideration of the Western States of the United States; I shall show by statistical tables their progress, their development, and their inherent agricultural and mineral wealth.

The subject of a railway communication between the Atlantic and Pacific Oceans will also claim attention; and it will be my endeavour to point out that route which, by its natural advantages, offers the most feasible and least expensive means of crossing the continent.

It will be my aim to gather, select, and compile every item of interest, every recorded experience in pioneer life, every statistical fact of importance, and every suggestion which may tend to the instruction or guidance of the Emigrant.

I shall not hesitate to quote largely from works which chorographically treat of America, and whose authority may substantiate my statements, or whose author's language will make more clear the subjects I wish to illustrate, or the ends at which I aim.

If the facts and observations contained in these pages add somewhat to the general information of the public in reference to the Transatlantic World, or if the emigrant who has determined upon a new sphere of action shall find any remarks which may assist in guiding him in his judgment, and result in ameliorating the early hardships of his new career, my object is accomplished.

T. R.

CONTENTS.

CHAPTER I.
INTRODUCTION.

The British Colonies; their Extent, Population, Imports and Exports—The proposed British North American Confederation; their Extent, Population, Imports and Exports; their prospective Wealth—Confederation a Means of Security—The Great Railway Route from the Atlantic to the Pacific Ocean—The Duty of England in reference to the Colonies . . .   1

CHAPTER II.
MIGRATORY MOVEMENTS OF THE HUMAN RACE.

Early Efforts of the Explorer, Geographer, and Navigator—America in its Primitive State—The Causes which operated to develop the Migratory Movements of Mankind, and the Progress in Discovery made by various Expeditions 9

CHAPTER III.
THE DISCOVERY OF AMERICA.

Scandinavian Records—Eric the Red—Speculation of Europeans—Columbus and his Voyages—Balboa, Magellan, Cortez—Pizarro and his Comrades—Sir Francis Drake—Expeditions to the Arctic Ocean and their Result . . 15

CHAPTER IV.
THE PROGRESS OF COLONIZATION.

The Colonization of Newfoundland, New Brunswick, Prince Edward's Island, Nova Scotia, and the Canadas (Upper and Lower). 25

CHAPTER V.
STATISTICS OF NEWFOUNDLAND, PRINCE EDWARD'S ISLAND, AND NOVA SCOTIA.

Newfoundland : Agriculture; Government; Fisheries; Shipping; Imports and Exports; Population—Prince Edward's Island : Industrial Resources; Imports and Exports; Counties, Towns, and Population; Education; Government—Nova Scotia : The Seasons ; Botanical Productions ; Shipping; Agriculture; Fisheries; Commerce; Population; Quadrupeds, Birds, and Fish; Crown Lands; Education; Government; Halifax; Gold-Fields; Minerals 31

CHAPTER VI.

DESCRIPTION OF NEW BRUNSWICK.

New Brunswick—Rivers and Counties—Capabilities of the Province—Forests—Fisheries—Minerals—Fruit and Vegetables—Manufactures—Counties—Commerce—Finances—Government—Public Schools—Militia—Census of 1861—Agriculture 46

CHAPTER VII.

THE CANADAS.

The Lakes, Rivers, and Canals—The Pictured Rocks—The Great Lakes—Mineral Wealth—Commerce, Shipping, Trade, and Statistics—Rivers—The Rapids—Canadian Song—Emigration—Montreal, Toronto, Quebec, Kingstown, Hamilton, Cobourg, &c.—The Farming Interest of Canada—Agricultural Statistics and Tables 54

CHAPTER VIII.

HUDSON'S BAY TERRITORY.

The Hudson's Bay Company: its Charter, its Profits, its Furs—The Fur Trade: its Extent and Value—The Territory: its Government, its Physical Features, its Plains, Lakes, and Rivers—The Saskatchewan Valley—Testimony of Captain Blakiston, Captain Palisser, Sir George Simpson, Monsieur Bourgeau, Father De Smet, Professor Hind, and others in reference to its Agricultural Resources—The Railway Route—Its Minerals, Grass, Fish, Animals, Birds, Roots, Berries, &c.—The Red River Settlement—American Trade—Homes for the Emigrant—The Company's Lands in the Market—Crossing the Rocky Mountains—Progress of the West—The Future Policy of the Hudson's Bay Company 85

CHAPTER IX.

BRITISH COLUMBIA AND VANCOUVER'S ISLAND.

The Rocky Mountains: their Extent, their Altitude, their Passes—British Columbia: Early Discovery, Boundary-line, Lakes, Rivers, &c.; Gold and the Gold-mines; Discovery of the Gold; Testimony of Governor Douglas, G. Forbes Macdonald, Esq., and the *Times* Correspondent—Gold on Fraser River—Richness of the Mines—Mines on Thompson River—Lillooett Gold-mines—Cariboo Gold River—Steele's Company—Labour in British Columbia—Export of Gold in 1863—Fertility of Soil in the Gold Neighbourhood—Progress of the Colony—Vancouver's Island: its Agricultural Resources, Coal-beds, Importance as a Naval Station, Imports and Exports; Prospecting, Panning, and Washing Gold 105

CHAPTER X.

THE RAILWAY SYSTEM OF NORTH AMERICA.

Early Travelling—Steam a Revolutionizer—Length of Railway in England, France, and the United States—Opening of the Ohio and Mississippi Railroad—Professor Mitchell's Testimony as to their Value—Increase in Traffic of American Railways—Railway System of Nova Scotia and New Brunswick—Canadian Railways—The Inter-Colonial Railway—General Review of the Subject—The Duty of England towards the proposed British North American Confederacy 127

PART II.

CHAPTER I.

THE UNITED STATES OF AMERICA.

Progress and Extent of Territory—Her Natural Beauties, Lakes, Rivers, Prairies, and Mountains—English Appreciation of America, and her Sympathy—Her Poets, Orators, Historians, and Artists—Peace and Reciprocity—The Blessings of Peace—The Reciprocity Treaty—Its Results and Mutual Benefits—Its Continuation desirable 138

CHAPTER II.

THE UNITED STATES.

Primary Object of the Book—Captain Palisser's Testimony—Route wholly through British Territory impossible—The only feasible Route, by way of Michigan and Minnesota to Hudson's Bay—Wealth of the Western States —OHIO: Products of Agriculture; Railways—INDIANA: Area, Population, Progress of the State, Agricultural Products, Manufactures, and Railways —MICHIGAN: General Statistics, Products of Agriculture, the Cereal Products, Miscellaneous Crops, and Railroads—WISCONSIN: Topographical Features, Railroads, Products of Agriculture, Valuation and Taxation— IOWA: Agricultural Wealth, Increase, Railroads—ILLINOIS: Agricultural Progress, Valuation and Taxation, Railways, and Number, Extent, and Cost of all the Railways in the United States 149

CHAPTER III.

MINNESOTA.

Extent of Territory—St. Paul, the Capital—Physical Districts—Falls of St. Anthony and its Water Power—Mineral Resources—Sandstone, &c.—Salt

CONTENTS.

Springs—The Relations of Minnesota in Reference to Internal Commerce—Rapid Progress of Cultivation—Agricultural Productions—Progress of Population—The Future of Minnesota—Testimony of Hon. W. H. Seward—Conclusion—Railway through Minnesota—Illinois Central Railroad—The Value of the Lands—Value of the Illinois Lands 165

CHAPTER IV.
EMIGRATION.

Advice to Emigrants to Canada or the United States—Progress of Emigration to America—Comparative Increase in Immigration from 1861 to 1864—Emigration from Germany—Laws of Migration—Inducements to Settle in America—Stock-Breeding and Raising in Illinois 193

CONTENTS OF APPENDICES.

APPENDIX "A."

The British American Federation—Resolutions Adopted at a Conference of Delegates from the Provinces of Canada, Nova Scotia, and New Brunswick, and the Colonies of Newfoundland, and Prince Edward's Island . . . 205

APPENDIX "B."

Increased Production of Cultivated Plants near the Northernmost Limit of their Growth—Extracts from an Article upon the "Acclimating Principle of Plants," by Dr. Forry 212

APPENDIX "C."

Professor M. F. Maury and Pacific Railroads—The Physical, Commercial, and Military Necessity of two Railroads, one North and one South 217

APPENDIX "D."

Table of Distances, Fares, &c., between Great Britain and North America—Distances to Chicago, Illinois, from Quebec, New York, Boston, and New Orleans—Table of Distances and Fares in the United States and Canada, *viâ* Grand Trunk Railway 223

APPENDIX "E."

Itineraries of Routes from St. Paul to Pembina, Fort Garry, Fort Ellice, Edmonton House, and the Gulf of Georgia, British Columbia—Table of Distances from St. Paul to Pembina: From St. Paul to Lake Floyd; Lake Floyd to Pembina; Red Lake River to Pembina—Plain Trail: Route of Woods and Pope; Route of Ellis Smith and Party—Various Routes: Saux Rapids to Sioux Wood River; St. Cloud to Georgetown; St. Cloud to Goose River; Detroit Lake to Georgetown, &c.—Railroad Lines—Table of Distances from Breckinridge to Pembina—Routes and Portions of Routes to the North and North-West of Pembina 226

APPENDIX "F."

St. Paul and Pacific Railroad—Statement of the Hon. E. Rice, State Senator. 233

APPENDIX "G."

Value of Moneys in Canada—Colonial, British, American—Value of English Coin throughout Canada 239

THE CONFEDERATION

OF THE

BRITISH NORTH AMERICAN PROVINCES.

CHAPTER I.

INTRODUCTION.

The British Colonies; their Extent, Population, Imports and Exports—The proposed British North American Confederation; their Extent, Population, Imports and Exports; their prospective Wealth—Confederation a Means of Security—The Great Railway Route from the Atlantic to the Pacific Ocean—The Duty of England in reference to the Colonies.

THE BRITISH COLONIES.

THE gradual development, continued progress, and sure, but increased prosperity of England's possessions, dependencies, and colonies, should ever be a matter of careful consideration, study, and deliberation, by the Government of Great Britain, her statesmen, and her people.

When we consider their number, their extended and yet widely-separated distribution, geographically and climatically; the variety of their productions; the material contributions which they make to our unsurpassed wealth; the deep interest they have in maintaining and extending our religious, commercial, and political influence; how largely they share in the splendour of our prosperity and the solidity of our power; that, in a great degree, they are the reservoirs and granaries from which we draw those materials which ultimately clothe and feed our millions; that they are large consumers of our varied products and fabrics; that in many of their harbours our fleets find a safe refuge from hostile foes; and that, while travelling through them, or passing over their lakes and rivers, there is a feeling of consanguinity and love for all that surrounds us, and the old flag still waving above to shield and protect us: considering these things, should we not watch over them with parental care, support them while struggling through their days of experimental existence, and foster every attempt which they make to enlarge their sphere of action, extend civilization and commerce, and assist them in developing their various elements of innate wealth?

EXTENT, POPULATION, IMPORTS AND EXPORTS.

Each of our various possessions in different quarters of the world contributes its quota towards the full measurement of our greatness. Our colonies in 1862 imported a total of £45,423,903, and exported £65,283,251.

British India, comprising Bengal, North-West Province, Punjaub, Madras, and Bombay, extends over 933,722 square miles, and a population of 135,634,200. Her revenue in 1863 amounted to £36,662,867.

In Africa we have Sierra Leone, Gambia, Gold Coast, Cape of Good Hope, Natal, Lagoo, and St. Helena, comprising an area of 240,000 square miles, and a population of 500,000.

The Australian Colonies and New Zealand consist of New South Wales, 323,437 sq. miles; pop. (1861), white, 351,046, coloured, 14,589; total, 365,635. Imports (1862) £4,019,482. Exports £2,234,592. Queensland, 678,000 sq. miles; pop. (1862) 70,000; 8,063,612 lbs. of wool were exported. Victoria, 86,831 sq. miles; pop. (1862) 555,744. The imports were £6,073,951, while the exports were £2,870,715.

Western Australia, 978,000 sq. miles; pop. 10,000. Southern Australia, 383,328 sq. miles; pop. (1862) 140,329. Export of wool 13,229,009 lbs. Imports £950,637. Exports £866,583. Tasmania, 26,215 sq. miles; pop. 100,000.

New Zealand, 106,259 sq. miles; pop. 165,364. Imports £1,364,935. Exports £611,445, Total imports Australia (1862) £12,847,325. Exports £7,109,809.

Then we have Gibraltar, with a population of 15,462. Imports (1862) £1,144,699. Exports £97,559. Malta, pop. 141,000. Heligoland, pop. 2172. The Bahamas, pop. 35,287; territory 2921 sq. miles. Bermuda, pop. (1861) 11,918.

In the West Indies we have Antigua, pop. (1861) 36,000. Barbadoes, pop. 152,727. Dominica, pop. 25,065. Grenada, pop. 31,500. Jamaica, 6400 sq. miles; pop. (1861) 441,255. Montserrat, pop. 7645. Nevis, pop. 9822. St. Christoph.'s and Anguil, pop. 20,741. St. Lucia, pop. (1862) 27,141. St. Vincent, pop. 31,755. Tobago, pop. 15,410. Trinidad, pop. 84,067. Turk's Island, pop. 4372. Virgin Island, pop. 5000.

In South America we possess British Guinea, 76,000 sq. miles; pop. 155,066. Imports £524,021. Exports £1,561,543.

In Honduras we have a territory of 13,500 sq. miles; pop. 25,620. Imports £118,504. Exports £299,746.

How all these petty islands combine to form vast territory; how the thousands of populations aggregate; how the separate millions in money make a balance-sheet in the aggregate! These oases in the desert of waters consume much and contribute much; they furnish rich woods, sugars, spices, and tropical fruits; and they absorb the superabundant articles which encumber, and accumulate in, our manufactories and warehouses.

PROPOSED BRITISH NORTH AMERICAN CONFEDERATION.

We next approach the colonial possessions of North America. The individualism of the Newfoundlander, Nova Scotian, Prince Edward's Islander, New Brunswicker, and Canadian, will soon become obsolete; that vast region of territory which stretches in magnificient breadth from the Atlantic to the Pacific Ocean, and from the 49th parallel, the lakes, and the St. Lawrence River to the boundaries of Russian America and the Arctic Ocean, is soon to become united in one confederacy and under one representative of Her Majesty.

If the reader will examine the map of North America, he will perceive what an extent of territory British North America occupies, and how unrivalled are its lines of intercommunication by sea, lake, and river. He cannot fail to appreciate the momentous issues which are involved in uniting under one authority and power the whole of this portion of the continent.

In North America, the authority of Great Britain extends over Canada, with 350,000 square miles and a population of 2,571,000.

New Brunswick, containing 27,700 square miles, and a population of 200,000.

Nova Scotia, with 18,725 square miles, and a population of 300,000.

Prince Edward's Island stretches over 1,365,400 square acres, and contains a population of 80,856.

Newfoundland, within its ocean-girt banks, is 36,000 square miles, and its population exceeds 120,000.

The Hudson Bay Territory stretches over an area of 2,700,000 square miles, and contains a population of 120,000.

British Columbia and Vancouver's Island together cover 295,000 square miles of territory, and contained a population, on the 10th of May, 1864, of 64,000.

BRITISH NORTH AMERICA—EXTENT, POPULATION, IMPORTS AND EXPORTS.

The whole of the British North American Territory contains 3,429,555 square miles, being greater in extent than Great Britain and Ireland, France, Russia, Austria, Prussia, Spain, Turkey, Denmark, Sweden, and Norway, together with Belgium, the Netherlands, Switzerland, and all the minor German States combined, while her population exceeds that of either Portugal, Denmark, Hanover, Saxony, Switzerland, or the Netherlands, being 4,000,000. Newfoundland produces over £1,000,000 a year from her fisheries. Prince Edward's Island exports over £300,000 annually, besides contributing a fleet of splendid clippers to the mercantile marine, whose reputation for strength, symmetrical proportion, and swiftness is unsurpassed by any in Aberdeen or Boston. Nova Scotia exported (1863) 6,546,488 dollars or £1,350,000, while her imports amounted to 10,201,191 dollars or £2,050,000. Over 7000 vessels entered her ports during the year. The imports of New Brunswick during the same year were 7,658,642 dollars or £1,595,513, while her exports during the same period, including the value of the ships built in her dockyards, were 8,841,936 dollars or £1,842,079. The exports from Canada, including the new shipping, were 41,831,532 dollars or about £8,200,000, while her imports were 45,964,493 dollars or £9,192,000. The quantity of new shipping built in all the North American Colonies in 1863 was 645 vessels, measuring 219,763 tons register, and of the value of £1,758,104. The customs and excise revenue of the five North American Colonies was 8,149,329 dollars, or 2 dollars 47 cents per head, or about 10s. sterling.

The value of the furs exported for the past year from Hudson's Bay amounted to £200,000. The export of gold from Vancouver's Island, British Columbia, for 1863 was 6,000,000 dollars.

PROSPECTIVE WEALTH.

When we consider the annual product of the American fisheries; that they give employment to 40,000 seamen (useful as auxiliaries in time of emergency); the vast tracts of land as yet uncultivated, and only waiting for the coming emigrant to develop their resources and increase the already teeming products that load their granaries; the splendid fleets conveyed as it were from the forests to the ocean, changed as if by magic from the lofty green-clad tree to the graceful lines of the barque that bears her riches to the Old World; the splendid cities, that for architectural beauty and advancement compare favourably with any on the American Continent; the wealth of minerals—coal, copper, iron, and gold—that lie embedded in the mines of Nova Scotia and the Canadas, the borders of Lake Superior, the valleys of the Saskatchewan, the sands that lie at the foot of the Rocky Mountains and permeate the bed of British Columbia—how unbounded are the resources of the American Continent!

Then contemplate for a moment the extended watercourses and outlets to the ocean—lakes vast as seas, where the commerce of the world may sail; rivers stretching from the ocean until their delicate arteries are lost in the pearling cascades of the far-off mountains; noble harbours plentifully distributed on the Atlantic and Pacific coasts, each a haven for the weary voyager—and then consider how bravely the people have fought their way into the proud position they now occupy. Perilous obstacles that thwart the irresolute and damp the ardour of the timid, have been but incentives to impel them forward. How proudly must they contemplate their marvellous increase in population, in agriculture, in mechanics, and in commerce! Surely the consolidation of these various provinces, the blending of interests, the political affinity, the commercial relationship, the social commingling, and the unity of action which a federation would enjoin, would give them a unity of purpose which they would not otherwise possess. Old names, old parties, old jealousies, old feuds, and bitter memories would cease to exist; and thus, by uniting the various interests, instead of a group of petty states, powerless against aggression, they become by consolidation a great power, with an extended territory, and a population which will form the nucleus of a future mighty empire. Remember that England, at the time of Charles II., contained a population of only 5,000,000, or 1,000,000 more than the present British American Confederation; but what a territory have they in comparison with England upon which to erect their nation! Power demands respect, and they should have a military, naval, and civil force, to defend and protect themselves against all aggressive assaults.

CONFEDERATION A MEANS OF SECURITY.

We are all aware that nothing tempts an ambitious people so much as opportunity, such as the discovered weakness of a neighbouring power. History inculcates the lesson that the strong and the many overrun the weak and the unarmed. Nothing contributes so greatly to the continued harmony of commercial relationship as mutual respect, and the knowledge that both are ready and possess the means to resent insult or resist aggression. We do not for a moment suggest the consolidation of the British Provinces on military grounds, or as a menace to their neighbours; but rather it seems a judicious and politic move, which may place them in such a position that, in any emergency, they may be prepared to defend their territory from any sudden attack.

Lawless and armed, but unauthorized men, who recognize neither national comity, legal rights, nor personal honour, oftentimes imperil the peace of nations by their thieving and murderous acts, committed under the high-sounding name of war. Disbanded armies, having no occupation, degenerate into bands of brigands, which are alike dangerous to friend as to foe.

The great objects to be obtained by confederation should be commercial, and, if possible, reciprocity of trade should be always maintained with the United States. The deplorable and unfortunate war that for the present necessarily retards the progress of that portion of America (and which God grant may soon cease!) has of necessity affected materially all countries who hold commercial relationship with her. But through the Reciprocity Act the trade of the British Provinces with the United States has doubled. During the year 1863, 3,050,369 tons of freight arrived in the United States from the Canadas. ⸱ Besides this fact, they are so narrowly separated by natural lines of demarcation—the iron, steam, and bridge links of travel are so numerous and continuous along and across both the river, lake, and recognized treaty lines; the constant current of human life, agricultural, mechanical, and manufactured products is so continuous and unceasing; in fact, in a mercantile aspect the Canadas and the United States are married one to the other, and there can be no cessation of peaceful and commercial relationship, unless it is brought about by political demagogues desirous of inflaming the vulgar passions, or diplomatists who hold not the welfare of the human race as a primary consideration. Macaulay remarks ("History of England," vol. i., p. 370): "The chief cause which made the fusion of the different elements of society so imperfect, was the extreme difficulty which our ancestors found in passing from place to place. Of all inventions, the alphabet and the printing-press alone excepted, those inventions which abridge distance have done most for the civilization of our species. Every improvement of means of locomotion benefits mankind morally and intellectually as well as materially, and not only facilitates the interchange of the various productions of nature and art, but tends to remove national and provincial antipathies, and to bind together all the branches of the great human family." There is another aspect of the question.

RAILWAY ROUTE FROM THE ATLANTIC TO THE PACIFIC.

We are well aware that the subject of a road from the Atlantic to the Pacific Ocean, and the creation of a direct route for traffic and passengers from India, China, Japan, California, Australia, and all the islands in the Pacific Ocean, across the American Continent, has for many years occupied the attention of various Governments. The attempts to find a northern, or Arctic oceanic passage, have resulted in misfortune and disaster. Their history is that of individual heroism, of self-sacrificing devotion to a purpose, of cruel hardships bravely borne, of dreadful terrors coolly met, of determined will and tenacious purpose overcoming many obstacles, but ending in disappointment and failure, and too often in misery, despair, privation, a lonely death, and a monument of snow.

Topographical engineers, scientific explorers, and itineraries, have explored the American Continent from end to end, and the conclusion arrived at is that the most feasible route to the Pacific is through the Fertile Belt of the Hudson's Bay Territory, and over the Rocky Mountains north of the boundary-line; and as it is the purpose of the proposed confederation of the British Territories to complete, at an early period, the intercolonial line, uniting Nova Scotia to the Canadas, with the splendid system of railway which constitutes the Grand Trunk Railway and its connexions, we shall have already completed one-half of the passage across the American Continent, and opened a through line which, at all seasons of the year, will draw the products of the West through British Territory to the sea; starting from La Crosse to St. Paul, Minnesota; from Fond du Lac, at the head of Lake Superior; and from St. Paul we have a system of railways, which are partly built and which 'are now under contract and construction, to Pembina, on the boundary-line and on the Red River Settlement. This will open the whole of 80,000 square miles of rich prairie land in Hudson's Bay Territory to the emigrant. But from Pembina the great Fertile Belt offers every facility to build the Pacific Railroad; the lands themselves will eventually pay for it. For the present we have a waggon-road passing over these prairies, and across the Saskatchewan Valley to the foot of the Rocky Mountains. Carry out the project of a railroad to the Pacific Ocean, at whatever cost to the British Government or people, and the future of that country will present a panorama of magnificence unexampled in history, and before which the splendour of Roman wealth, in the days of Augustus, will sink into insignificance. The silks, teas, and opium of China will swiftly speed over the Rocky Mountains to the warehouses of Europe; the spices and Oriental luxuries of India will be transported over lands where the red race but an age since had trapped the beaver and the ermine; the re-awakened commerce of Japan would find a way across the prairie land of Hudson's Bay Territory; the gold of California, or British Columbia, and the Saskatchewan Valley, would find a safe passage by the great lakes to the Atlantic; the wool of California would find a more direct route to England; and the homeward and the outward bound would cross the Atlantic on their way to India, China, Australia, California, British Columbia, British North America, and the United States, in social companionship. What scenes would be witnessed on their route! What a continent to journey over! What mountains—what lakes—what rivers—what mighty cataracts—what lovely prairies—what splendid forests—and what a world of knowledge would daguerreotype itself upon the brain! Remember British Columbia is teeming with gold, but its distance and the difficulties attendant upon reaching it, preclude thousands from doing so, who would, were the journey expeditious, cheap, direct, and feasible. Hudson's Bay, though controlled by a company, that even in the days of Charles II. and James I. could entertain the king in sumptuous magnificence, yet till a recent period has shut out by selfish laws all emigrants, and closed the doors of admittance to her hidden treasures. The Canadas, with millions of acres of rich land uncultivated, and with the surroundings of civilization attendant on them, would offer their attractions to the exodus of people that swarm from the Old World. New Brunswick would open her grand old forests, that in autumn are robed in colours bright as the rainbow, and gemmed with sparkling icicles in the long winter, when the axe lays them low for the raftsman and the lumberer; Nova Scotia and Prince Edward's Island would alike offer a home and a bright picture for the sober, industrious emigrant and the hardy pioneer; while all along the coasts of Labrador and Newfoundland there is employment for thousands upon thousands who love a sailor's life.

ENGLAND'S DUTY TO HER AMERICAN COLONIES.

The provinces are loyal to the British Crown; they have with firm resolution and steadfast faith clung to the power that fostered them when weak and sheltered them in danger; they now combine to consolidate their interests and power and better to prepare for the future. They can subsist a hundred millions of inhabitants. Not a tithe of their wealth has been brought to light or discovered; their resources cannot be even conjectured—a fit jewel to decorate a crown. New born, with every element of strength, with every prospect of a splendid future, and with every basis for a permanent and lasting Government.

CHAPTER II.

MIGRATORY MOVEMENTS OF THE HUMAN RACE.

Early Efforts of the Explorer, Geographer, and Navigator—America in its Primitive State—The Causes which operated to develop the Migratory Movements of Mankind, and the Progress in Discovery made by various Expeditions.

EARLY EFFORTS OF THE EXPLORER, GEOGRAPHER, AND NAVIGATOR.

THE present chapter will be devoted to an historical *résumé* of the migratory movements of the various patriarchal families, nomadic tribes, and peoples who have from time to time spread and extended their dominion, influence, and power over the then known world during the different decades.

All sciences and discoveries possess an individual history, and the continual additions made to this history serve as landmarks for the future guidance of the explorer, the geographer, the astronomer, the philosopher, and the student of the different sciences. To trace the gradual progress and development of any particular branch of knowledge; to watch the slow but sure elimination of light and truth out of darkness and ignorance; to appreciate fully the boon conferred upon the present by the laborious studies, speculations, explorations, and deductions of those antecedent to our own time; we must consider the difficulties which attended every step in progress and science in the earliest periods. The modern geographer commences his studies with a recognized doctrine of the astronomical circles or divisions of the sphere; the philosopher possesses certain recognized truths upon which to found his theories and speculations; the astronomer possesses the celestial map, with the locality of certain planets and stars clearly defined; the traveller going forth to journey and to discover, finds highways and pathways marked out upon the map for his guidance—the labours of those who have preceded him have left a trail which he may follow. The ocean has been mapped—its distances from shore to shore, its currents, its depths, its shoals, and its hidden dangers, are partially known. The passes of the mighty mountains—

"Rock-ribb'd, and ancient as the sun"—

are marked out for the traveller; their comparative height, their distinctive features, the difficulties to be surmounted in traversing them, and their applicability for commercial highways. The illimitable deserts that spread vast and desolate, without tree, shrub, plant, or cereal to welcome the traveller, have yet been explored by the heroic adventurer. The jungles of India, breathing disease and death from her miasmatic swamps, echoing with the roar of wild beasts, and loathsome with the hissing snake, have yet been penetrated by the fearless hunter. The almost interminable woods that impeded the advance of the pioneer, gradually fell prostrate and disappeared before the persevering energy and hardy strokes of the woodman with his axe. The frail barque has battled with the tempestuous hurricane, the angry and maddened waves, the overtopping, freezing, and frowning iceberg, and the endless dangers of the sea, guided by the cool navigator who bore a few brave hearts towards a new and undiscovered world. No obstacles that nature presented; no privations attendant upon voyaging; no sufferings, however appalling in their nature; no torture that the vindictive and merciless savage could invent; no uncertainties or doubts as to the fate of pioneers who had preceded them, or even the pitiless tale of survivors who had left their comrades unburied in an unexplored land; no warnings of certain death as the *dénouement* of an expedition. The burning heat of the tropical sun, and the intense cold of the frigid zone, have failed to deter the brave, the unselfish, the worthily ambitious, or the resolute from attempts to extend the dominion of the flag and the nation which they so nobly represented; thus opening a new and congenial sphere for the emigrant, and mapping out a new path for the mariner and the trader.

AMERICA IN ITS PRIMITIVE STATE.

As America four centuries ago was unknown to the dwellers of the eastern hemisphere, so at one time was Asia unknown to the dwellers of Africa and Arabia and the inhabitants of Europe. How well-regulated have been the discoveries of new regions to the increase of population, and its pressure upon circumscribed territory. While Pharaoh, Augustus, Hannibal, Constantine, Anthony, and Cæsar were battling for the possession of increased territory, and for the supreme dominion of the world, they remained in ignorance of a continent, the relation of whose wealth and extent would have inflamed their ambition a thousand fold. Niagara poured her ocean of waters in tumultuous roar as grandly and as loudly then as she does now. The auriferous valleys of California and Columbia were as ready then as now for the miner and the sand-washer—ready to give their endless and incalculable wealth to the first hand that sought for it. The unmatchable prairies were gorgeous then as now, with a royalty of beauty glowing in the flowers that defied the imitative pencil of the artist to depict, or the pen of the writer to describe. Forests of oak and pine rose spire-like from the earth, and covered the mountains almost to their topmost peaks, while they spread dense and luxurious over plain and valley. Marbles of every hue lay buried in their richness with a wealth of quantity that would have built Constantine, Herculaneum, Pompeii, Athens, and Rome with ten thousand Colosseums and

Vaticans. Yes, the palaces of the earth. Were there famine?—the rich lands of the unknown continent, uncultivated and unploughed, would have given free estates to armies of stalwart men, and produced corn enough to fill the granaries of all countries. While Europe warred—while new dynasties were rising to again decay and give place to others; while cities were extending their boundaries, their wealth, and their grandeur till they became the seats of vast dominions, so that for a time they were the wonder of their age, and then, by natural or artificial convulsions, their noble temples, their architectural columns, their splendid palaces, and their wealthy inhabitants were overwhelmed in ruin and death, so that fragments and hieroglyphics only remained to tell their story to some traveller who, like Caius Marius at Carthage, might weep over their ruins, and deplore the loss of their former splendour—America, in all her wealth of treasure, her magnificence of proportion, and her loveliness of apparel, slept in her undiscovered beauty beyond the eye of the European. Spring came budding in emeraldic hue; summer threw her flowery and luxurious mantle over tree, shrub, and plant; autumn glowed with her rainbow-tinted foliage; and winter bared the naked arms of the trees, stripped the dead and drooping branches of decaying leaves, and buried bleak mountains, vast prairies, hill and vale, river and lake, beneath a mantle of profound snow. The echo of the woodman's axe disturbed neither the merry warblers nor the timid game; the roar of trade had not as yet obtained a whisper; the silent arrow was the only instrument winged with death; the stealthy tread of the Indian alone broke the silence, which was vast and measureless; the wigwam was the only abode that approached the modern mansions and city villas of the opulent.

"This is the forest primeval. The murmuring pines and the hemlocks,
Bearded with moss, and in garments green, indistinct in the twilight,
Stand like Druids of old, with voices sad and prophetic—
Stand like harpers hoar, with beards that rest on their bosom."

The world moved on in ignorance, and so was satisfied.

But if America thus continued to remain in its primitive state for so many ages, it must be remembered that the people of the Old World made but little progress in discovery, despite of their restlessness and wanderings. Even to this day the geography of Africa is being made known to the world, through the instrumentality of heroic spirits like Livingstone, Speke, Grant, and Burton.

We will now diverge somewhat from these general remarks and endeavour to give a concise and succinct history of the progress and discovery made from time to time in various lands, describing the manner and the date of their peopling and settlement, and consider for a moment what are the causes which operate as a stimulus and incentive to force people to leave home and country in search of an uncertain future.

The love of power inherent in the human race; the desire

manifested in all ages for extended dominion; the restless ambition of discontented and grasping sovereigns; the tyranny and oppressive terrorism exercised over the subjugated and the weak by both conquerors and rulers; the visionary hopes of adventurers in search of auriferous wealth; the earnest desire evinced by scientific navigators and explorers; the speculations and prophecies of astronomical and geographical *savans;* the wanderings of nomadic tribes; and the continued pressure of a cumulative population within certain circumscribed limits: have each and all combined to enlarge, extend, and complete our geographical knowledge by the discovery of new countries whose existence remained for ages a matter of speculation and conjecture.

THE PROGENITORS OF THE HUMAN RACE.

Tracing our way through the dark labyrinth of antiquity, we perceive that the progenitors of the multitudinous races that people the earth were but little nomadic populations, who wandered from place to place till they found a congenial climate, when they settled; and in process of time, from families they became tribes, and at length they grew into great nations, that founded empires and built stately cities on the spots where their progenitors had pitched their simple tents and tended their flocks and herds. As time progressed, they changed their simple and peaceful habits: the herdsman, the shepherd, and the hunter, became the trader, the merchant, and the warrior; and then strifes breaking out between adjacent countries, through various influences, aggressive action was soon taken by the stronger—their domain was extended by conquest, while the weaker were compulsorily forced to migrate to other lands. We read also that as the different countries became densely populated, it was customary to select representatives from various tribes, who were required to go forth and travel, and by lengthened journeys endeavour to discover new countries which might become the nurseries for branches of the various increasing tribes. Josephus, the Jewish historian, relates that in the days of Noah, and in consequence of the confusion of tongues at Babel, the people were dispersed abroad, and went out by colonies everywhere, and each colony took possession of such lands as they lighted upon, so that the whole continent was filled with them, both the inland and maritime countries; there were some also who passed over the sea in ships and inhabited the islands. "Abraham advised his sons also to go forth and establish colonies in Arabia, Africa, and Assyria." Joshua conducted the Israelites, after many years' wandering, into the land of Canaan. By the dispersion of the various peoples at Babel, and their compulsory wanderings and voyagings, we trace directly the foundation of the aboriginal inhabitants who occupied the country when the first European navigators appeared on the newly discovered shores of the American Continent.

MIGRATORY JOURNEYS OF THE PEOPLE OF WESTERN ASIA.

When the Mesopotamian plain and Western Asia became filled with a numerous, powerful, and warlike people, which they soon overran, they determined to extend their influence and power by migratory journeys and conquest. First, Upper Armenia, then Caucasus, then Scythia; after which we find migrations were made round and into the interior of Africa. We are informed by Herodotus, surnamed the "Father of History," and who wrote the first real and authentic history of Greece, that Necho or Pharaoh Necho (one of the kings of Egypt, who flourished in the seventh century before Christ) manned a small fleet with Phœnicians, and gave them directions to steer their course down the Red Sea and endeavour to double the land, so as to return into the Mediterranean by the Atlantic Ocean and the Pillars of Hercules. Steering into the Southern Sea, the Phœnicians, when autumn approached, drew their vessels to shore, and having landed and built temporary abodes, they sowed crops; and having reaped them, they put to sea again. In this wise they toiled onward for two years. In the third year they passed the Pillars of Hercules and reached Egypt. Thus the whole of Africa had been circumnavigated. Yet all the discoveries made at that period were mere itineraries. Geography without astronomy could never expect to rise above a chaos of empirical systems; without a knowledge of the spherical figure of the earth, of the stellary arrangement of the heavens, and the application of the stellary latitudes and longitudes to the various corresponding points of the earth, no correct or precise geographical knowledge could be attained. It is only by slow degrees that geography has struggled out of the slough of error into genuine scientific truth; and so long as we were left ignorant of the phenomena of the heavens which affected the globe as to its various climates, its seasons, and the different productions which are severally peculiar to different regions—so long as we were ignorant of the true figure of the earth, its magnitude, the relative position on the surface of continents, isles, oceans, seas, lakes, rivers, mountains, countries, and peoples—so long we were compelled to rely on the veracity of adventurous and enterprising voyagers, and the deductions of empirical philosophers. The continued additions of patient and laborious astronomers; the accumulation of statistics furnished by military surveyors; the dry details collected by missionaries, and too long buried in the archives of monasteries; the different wars which mark the various epochs—all lent their aid; for the moment lands were conquered the regions were mapped and surveyed, and every distance traversed was described with accuracy. Thus, as we before remarked, war, science, religious fanaticism, compulsory migration, the extension of commerce, political necessity, and individual curiosity and enterprise, have contributed their share towards the exploration and discovery of distant lands.

CELEBRATED ASTRONOMERS, GEOGRAPHERS, AND TRAVELLERS.

As astronomers and geographers who have eliminated truth and knowledge out of the chaos of incongruous systems, and whose contributions and researches have gradually developed the various erroneous systems into a recognized science, dissipating ignorance, and separating the false from the true, we have the names of Eratosthenes, Hipparchus, Pliny, Ptolemy, Sebastian Munster, Artelius, and Mercator: in more modern times, we have Cassini, Picard, La Hire, Herschel, and Humboldt.

Of travellers who have attained celebrity, we may mention Necho, who sent the expedition round Africa; Carpini and Rubruquis, who travelled by the north of Russia, along the shores of the Black Sea and the Caspian, to the central plain of Asia Minor; Marco Polo, a Venetian, who travelled through Tartary to China, and spent over twenty years in exploring the least known regions of Asia, and who afterwards glowingly described the barbaric wealth and splendour which he had seen. Louis the Fourteenth, of France, at a later day, sent Maupertius and Condamine, the one to explore the regions of the Arctic Circle, and the other the Equator. But a volume would not contain a tithe of the history of modern explorations in different parts of the world; we have, therefore, not attempted anything beyond a mere outline of the various geographical discoveries and migratory movements which have marked the extension of the influence of civilization.

CHAPTER III.

THE DISCOVERY OF AMERICA.

Scandinavian Records—Eric the Red—Speculation of Europeans—Columbus and his Voyages—Balboa, Magellan, Cortez—Pizarro and his Comrades—Sir Francis Drake—Expeditions to he Arctic Ocean and their Result.

SCANDINAVIAN RECORDS—ERIC THE RED.

THE discovery of a New World, with all its attendant novelties, must certainly form an epoch in the history of the times when it was made known. To trace the progress of its discovery and the gradual advancement made in exploring the various regions and their peopling, must prove of interest to those who purpose to follow the footsteps of countless thousands who reclaimed the woods and the prairies from the savage.

If the reader will take a cursory look at the map, he will perceive the close proximity of Norway, Sweden, Iceland, and Greenland, and the various groups of islands in the north-east, while upon the north-west he will find that Asia and North America are only separated by a narrow strait, called Behring Strait. It will at once be obvious that the peopling of North America from both Asia and Europe by this route, is not only within the bounds of possibility, but probability. The adventurous spirit of man would lead him to at least venture a few miles from his own coast in order that he might understand the nature of those boundaries or surroundings which were peculiar to his abode; and, therefore, while remaining ignorant of the history of America previous to the year 986, A.D., and only partially and meagrely being able to trace any history up to the time of the discovery by Columbus, yet we have sufficient evidence furnished by Scandinavian records to prove that America was known to the inhabitants of Iceland and Norway long anterior to the voyages of Columbus. It is' true these discoveries were made of no practical utility to the inhabitants of the Old World, but it is undeniable that adventurers who had been nurtured amidst the perils and hardships of a seafaring life did penetrate into the American Continent and establish commercial relationship to a limited extent with the natives. Iceland was discovered by some Scandinavians in 861, A.D., and circumnavigated within three years afterwards; at a later date a Norwegian colony was established there. We next find these colonists proceeding towards the south as far as Greenland, where it is related that Eric the Red established a colony which he christened Erico-Fiord, and which continued to exist for nearly four centuries. During the whole of this time constant communication and intercourse was held with Norway. Large quantities of whale oil and seals were transmitted to the parent country, while in return the settlers received their necessary supplies.

In the same year in which Eric the Red migrated to Greenland, Biarne, the son of one of his companions, sailing in a similar direction, was carried by northerly winds out of his intended course and beyond his destined point. He reached a land which was without mountains, exhibiting only gentle elevations covered with wood, and still further to the southward another land which was flat and also overgrown with wood. Standing thence out to sea, and sailing for three days with a south-west wind, Biarne and his companions arrived at a large island, the shores of which were high and covered with icebergs. From this last-discovered land they returned by four days' sailing to the colony of Greenland. The discoveries of Biarne were speedily followed up. Lief Ericson— that is, Lief, son of Eric the Red—in the year 1000, A.D., came to the same land which Biarne had seen, and to which he gave the name of Helluland. He next met with a country which he called Woodland; from thence he continued to journey to the eastward till he discovered an island where they found many vines and grapes. To this island they gave the name of Vineland, and here he and his companions spent three winters, and during that time explored the adjacent country; but afterwards falling into a difficulty with the natives (Esquimaux), Thomald, the brother of Lief Ericson, being slain, the remainder of the expedition returned to Greenland in 1005. The observations they made, and the descriptions which they gave upon their return of the country they had visited, soon prompted others to undertake voyages in the same direction, in hopes of making still further discoveries. The King of Norway himself seems to have been impressed with the story related by the returned adventurers, and he therefore authorized Thorform, surnamed Karisfene (one who is destined to be an able or great man), and related to the king, as well as Snorre Thorbrandsen, a noted geographer—both of whom were men occupying exalted and influential positions in their country— to form an expedition, and endeavour to reach still further south, and if possible establish a colony as a nucleus from which explorations might be made into the interior of the country. In the spring of 1005 the expedition, which consisted of two ships, and contained one hundred and sixty men, with all the attendants of such scientific instruments as were then known, with many of the party who had accompanied the former expeditions, and with ample provisions and all the necessaries for a three years' voyage, left Greenland. They found the first part of their journey both dangerous and tedious, and the navigation intricate, in consequence of the great icebergs and immense fields of ice which impeded their progress; they, however, soon passed Helluland, discovered by Lief

Ericson, and Markland, discovered by the same explorer. Next they reached Kialarnes, inhabited by the Esquimaux. They continued their journey southward, passed numerous islands near the mouth of a river, and finally reached Vineland, where they landed. They found a country more beautiful to the eye than their own, and rich in trees, corn, and flowers. They record that cattle could feed without being housed, and that fruit, delicious to the palate, but new to them, grew in abundance; that there were vast mountains luxuriant with great forests; that they were full of deer and game, and that the rivers were full of fish. But although they spent three winters in this attractive land—although they found that the seed which they had brought with them, and which they sowed, thrived wonderfully, and the climate was healthy and pleasant—yet unfortunate bickerings and quarrels with the natives soon brought about discord and war, and they were compelled to depart to their own homes after a three years' sojourn. Still the intercourse between Greenland and Vineland did not cease, but on the contrary it was carried on for over a century, that is, to 1121.

The testimony here given is taken from the Scandinavian records, and is most particular in the relation of details; and there can be no doubt that the Helluland of the Northmen was our present Newfoundland, with its naked and rocky approaches; Markland answers to Nova Scotia and the adjacent forest-covered regions; the keel-shaped Cape Kialarnes is the well-known Cape Cod, with its deserts and long narrow beaches of sand; in the island between which and the neighbouring mainland Biarne sailed, we recognize Nantucket, with its adjacent shoals; and the pleasant Vineland is the region beyond the Connecticut and neighbouring New England States of our modern maps.

SPECULATION OF EUROPEANS.

But from the year 1121 to 1492 we have a blank in the progress of discovery. No tales had ever reached the nations of Southern Europe of the adventures of the hardy Northmen —not a whisper of the existence of a territory that was to be the theatre of actions so marvellous, and of a progress so unparalleled, that in its contemplation the mind is lost in wonder—not a fugitive leaf from the Scandinavian records ever found its way into the libraries of Southern Europe, to tell the enthusiastic dreamers that their mental visions were but the positive reflex of a living, moving world—no wanderer ever made his way to England or Spain to guide the barques of Columbus over the unfathomable deep. The currents of the ocean might fill the mind with speculation and conjecture; the shipwrecked mariner washed on some desolate shore pauses, and starts with mingled fear and amazement, when for the first time he sees clearly defined upon the sand the outline of the human foot; he knows at once he is not alone—that there before him is palpable evidence of the existence of a being like unto himself; and though he may doubt whether he be friend or foe, yet he is convinced that there must be within his reach the means of sustaining human life. Did the idle wanderers, as they strolled along the Atlantic shore, toying with the glistening pebbles in the sunshine, gathering the floating seaweed that had journeyed over many thousand miles, or examining the strange natural curiosities that were wafted to them by wave and tide, ever pause to reflect from whence they came? Did they think that the ocean swept onward without boundary and beyond the navigator's reach? Did the rich and rare fruits, perhaps half decayed, that were left by the waves upon the sandy shore, never create conjectural thoughts as from whence they came? In shape, in taste, and in colour they were strange to the eye and to the palate. Did they not wonder at the beauty and newness of the flowers that grew from the seeds they gathered from the faded and drooping plants that lay upon the wave-washed beach? Did the botanist never gaze with delight on the branches of trees whose formation puzzled his intelligence—on trees whose character differed from those indigenous to his own soil, whose trunks were greater in circumference, whose wood was rich in colour and beautiful in grain, and whose branches were arranged with marvellous beauty? What more perfect to his eye than the expanding fan-like leaf of the palmetto, or sweeter to the taste than the stately sugar-cane? There were branches of innumerable and yet unknown varieties of trees; there were weeds of exquisite and delicate texture and form; there were images quaint, grotesque, and peculiar; there were, finally, the poor silent bodies of the dead of an unknown race (that peopled not their own land) found lying on the rugged rocks and bare sands where the receding waves had left them. Was it to be wondered at that men of a contemplative and reflective character conjectured that these were the evidences of a land peopled beyond the Atlantic—that they interpreted it to mean that these were signs to tell them that if they would but venture they might discover "a land flowing with milk and honey." The spherical nature of the earth had become a positive belief in the mind of Columbus; the marvellous narrative of Marco Polo had strengthened his belief in a Western World, or at least in a passage to India and China—the fond hope of the explorer to discover. All the evidences which the shore could give, all the theories he could build up from the study of the map of Ptolemy, the golden-tinted pictures of Marco Polo, and the fond hopes of his own buoyant nature, assisted him in battling against every obstacle, every disappointment, and every opposing force that seemed to delay the accomplishment of that which had now become to him the dream of his life. It is said that "all great discoveries, whether in the physical or the moral world, are the consequences of prior trains of thought and events." The classic fable of a Minerva springing full armed from the brain of Jupiter, has no parallel in the actual world of human nature. The dreams of the visionary enthusiast point towards the conclusions which a later age carries into active being—the loose and scattered events which, taken singly, point to no conclusion, are combined by the philosophical observer into a connected train, and important consequences educed from the consideration to which they lead. All the signs on the sandy shores—all the fervid belief of the age was in favour of the existence of a great western region; and Columbus, besides this, believed that, by philosophic induction, he was certain of its existence. Once convinced, and his whole soul was in his dream of success. He petitioned Ferdinand and Isabella—he conversed with the most celebrated *savans* of Spain upon his projects—he endeavoured to obtain the assistance of all who had power within the magic circle of the Court—he tried to enlist the sympathies of the rich and the influential. Long were his delays and patient were his endeavours, but he never faltered. Ever earnest, ever steadfast, and ever hopeful of success, despondency never claimed him as a victim for an hour. The day of triumph came—the day when the means were to be placed at his disposal for the fulfilment of his project had arrived. A generous and noble Castilian lady, with a crown upon her brow, became his patron, and through her agency Columbus was provided with an armament sufficient, with good fortune and fair winds, to accomplish his desire. To Isabella of Spain is the honour due of encouraging with her money, her good wishes, and her smiles, the expedition which discovered America; and yet in all that land no single monument is erected to her honour and her glorious memory.

COLUMBUS AND HIS VOYAGES.

Three small vessels carrying ninety men set sail from Palos, on the coast of Spain, on a bright September morning. The shores were lined with a noble concourse of spectators. Proud Castilian maidens and noble Spanish cavaliers cheered Columbus as he departed, though they looked upon his errand as madness. A long and stormy passage ensued, dissention and mutiny broke out amid the crew, and all the anticipations of a successful issue seemed gradually passing away; but the heart of the bold and heroic navigator was true as steel, and his resolution never faltered. Firm in the conviction that ere long he would descry the wished-for land—strong in the belief that a glorious conclusion would be the result of his laborious journey—he sailed on; and as the sun went down, crimsoning the west, on the 11th day of October, 1492, a new world, and the home of future millions, dawned upon his delighted eye.

The spot on which Columbus landed was the small island of Guanahani, or San Salvador, one of the Bahama Archipelago. After visiting Hayti, or Hispaniola, where he left some of his crew who desired to settle, he returned to Europe to report the result of his discoveries, and to receive the congratulations of his sovereign.

Columbus made four voyages to America. The second was in 1493, when he discovered Jamaica. The third in 1498, when Trinidad and other islands were added to his previous discoveries. In his fourth and last voyage, in 1502, he visited the western shores of the Caribbean Sea, and then explored the coasts of Central America.

Among those who formed the second expedition of Columbus was Alonzo de Hojeda. This individual, impressed with the belief that Columbus had neither realized the true value nor vast extent of the territories lying in the western hemisphere, determined upon following up the discoveries of his former master. He, in conjunction with Amerigo Vespucci, a Florentine pilot, set out upon their voyage of discovery, the result of which they gave to the world in a series of volumes. All the discoveries of Columbus were confined to Central and South America, and the existence of North America was unknown to him, so that he died in ignorance of the full value of his discovery, he believing he had arrived at the verge of the Indies. To Amerigo Vespucci, who gave his name to the New World, we contend, belongs the honour. "History presents elsewhere no example of the universal excitement which the discoveries of Columbus awakened, and of the sustained enthusiasm by which they were followed up. The young, the adventurous, the needy, the discontented of every grade—those who felt the pressure of social wrong (real or imagined), under whatever form, in the countries of Europe—hastened to amend their lot in the newly-found lands beyond the Atlantic. The cry of 'Westward, ho!' became the rallying signal for people of every class, and of every age; and still, after the lapse of nearly four centuries, the fervour called into being by Columbus maintains its existence, and produces its active fruits. Visions of El Dorado glittering in their golden wealth floated before the eyes of the earlier and more sanguine adventurers from Spain, and lent their charm to not a few of those bold spirits who ere long hoisted the flag of Britain above the western waters. To discovery, and the first fruits of discovery —reaped amidst ferocious and unrelenting barbarity practised by the early Spaniards towards the simple and unoffending natives of the New World—succeeded permanent settlement, with its attendant commerce and social polity; and cities grew up beside the coasts and rivers of the newly-colonized regions of the West." The works of the European race supplanted those that already existed ere the white man had placed his foot on the American shores; the native erections, abandoned to neglect, became buried amidst the thick overgrowth of the forest and the tropical jungle, to be rediscovered in the present time, and to excite regret that they alone remain to tell of the partial civilization which the Indian population had attained, and which the tide of Spanish conquest so ruthlessly destroyed. Prescott and Squier in their laborious history have preserved descriptions of the magnificent ruins that attest the mighty splendours that adorned the Montezumas and the palaces of Central America.

BALBOA, MAGELLAN, CORTEZ, PIZARRO AND HIS COMRADES.

In 1513, Nunez Balboa crossed the isthmus that divides the Gulf of Darien from the Pacific. Seven years later Fernando Magellan, who believed in the existence of a continuous ocean round the southern half of America, determined on attempting its discovery. He sailed from San Lucar, on the coast of Spain, in 1519, and having wintered at Port San Julian, in latitude 49°, early in-the spring, he pursued his way until he passed though a strait, which he named Magellan, and then entered the Pacific Ocean. In three months and twenty days Magellan crossed the immense sea and reached the Philippine Islands. Here he engaged in a conflict with the natives, when he lost his life. His companions, with the *Vittoria*—the only remaining ship of the five comprising the expedition—returned to Europe, having passed across the Indian Ocean and round the Cape of Good Hope; and thus, in three years and fourteen days, had achieved the remarkable and memorable accomplishment of the first circumnavigation of the globe.

Pursuing in chronological order the advancement in discovery, we next meet with the stories of Cortez and Pizarro. Fernando Cortez landed on the coast of Mexico in 1519; with a few hundred followers he overthrew the empire of Montezuma, and conquered Mexico. A few years later, Peru and the sovereignty of the Incas were conquered by Francisco Pizarro. Almagro, a companion of Pizarro, about the same period made himself master of Chili. Next we hear of Francisco de Orellana, who accompanied Gonzales Pizarro across the mountain ranges of the Cordilleras. After leaving Pizarro, who became disheartened, he built boats and canoes, and having launched them on the river which crossed his path, he descended its current until he reached the Atlantic Ocean, having travelled over a thousand leagues. This was in the year 1541.

In the year 1500, Pedro Alvarez Cabral, a Portuguese, while making a voyage to the Indies by the way of Good Hope, discovered Brazil. In 1514, Juan de Solis discovered the river La Plata. This river was christened La Plata, or the "River of Silver," by Sebastian Cabot, who ascended it in 1526.

SIR FRANCIS DRAKE.

In 1577 Sir Francis Drake sailed from Plymouth, and having passed through the Strait of Magellan, carried the banner of England into the Pacific Ocean. He explored the coasts as far up as 28° N., and returned to Europe after an absence of two years and ten months.

Sir Francis Drake was followed by the expedition of Sarmiento, A.D. 1581, and the Dutch expedition under Schonter in 1615, both of which sailed along the extreme southern extremity of the New World.

EXPEDITIONS TO THE ARCTIC OCEAN.

While the minds of so many were directed to the southern and central regions of America, and seemed to rest self-satisfied with the conviction that they had discovered the track to India, others believed in the existence of a north-western passage, and turned their energies in a northern direction, in hopes of crossing from the Atlantic to the Pacific by the Arctic Circle.

"When we contemplate," says Cooley, in his "History of Maritime and Inland Discovery," "the early discoveries of the Spaniards and Portuguese, we see needy adventurers and men of desperate character and fortune pursuing gain or licentiousness with violence and bloodshed. But the English navigators who, in the reign of Elizabeth, sought to extend our knowledge of the globe, were men of a different stamp, and driven forward by motives of a more honourable nature. They undertook the most difficult navigation through seas perpetually agitated by storms and encumbered with ice, in vessels of the most frail construction and of small burthen; they encountered all the difficulties and distresses of a rigorous climate, and in most cases with a very distant or with no prospect of ultimate pecuniary advantage."

Among these was John Cabot, a native of Venice, but who had settled in Bristol, in England, during the reign of Henry VII. In 1496 a patent was granted to Cabot and his three sons, Louis, Sebastian, and Sansius, giving the right to acquire and settle in the unknown lands which they were in search of. Sebastian Cabot " understanding," says the chronicler, " by reason of the sphere, that if he should sail by way of the north-west, he should by a shorter track come to India, he thereupon caused the king to be advertised of his device." Setting out accordingly in two small " caravels " furnished for the purpose, he sailed to the north-westward from the English coast, " not thinking to find any other land than that of China, and from thence to turn towards India." Thus was the famous search after the " north-west passage " inaugurated.

On the 24th of June, in 1497, they arrived at the banks of Newfoundland, where they landed. During the autumn of this year and the spring and summer of the following year they explored a great part of the coast of North America. In 1576-7-8, Martin Frobisher made three voyages, and reached as far north as Frobisher's Strait in 1585-6-7. John Davis made three attempts to discover the north-west passage. Henry Hudson followed, 1607 to 1610, and discovered Hudson's Bay. Thomas Britton entered Hudson's Bay and crossed to the extreme western side in 1613. William Baffin, in 1615, though he failed to find a north-west passage, added largely to the geographical knowledge of the day; the highest point reached by him was the immense inlet which is called Baffin's Bay. In 1728, Behring, a Pole, in the employ of Peter the Great of Russia, crossed over from Asia, and discovered Behring's Strait, proving the separation of the American and Asiatic continents. In 1762, Captain Cook passed through this channel and coasted the Arctic shores as far as Icy Cape, under the meridian of 162° W. In 1669, the Hudson's Bay Company was established. In 1771, Samuel Hearne discovered and traced the course of the Coppermine River. In 1789, Alexander Mackenzie traced the Mackenzie River to its source. In 1818, another attempt was made to find an opening to the Western or Pacific Ocean. The expedition consisted of two vessels, the *Isabella* and the *Alexander*, under the command of Captain (afterwards Sir John) Ross and Lieutenant (afterwards Sir Edward) Parry. This expedition proceeded as far as Lancaster Sound, and proved comparatively a failure. Parry, in a second voyage, however, passed through Lancaster Sound, Barrow's Strait, and wintered at Melville Island, at the meridian of 113°, having advanced over half the distance towards Behring's Strait—600 miles. At the same time that Parry was sailing through Lancaster Sound, Lieutenant (afterwards Sir John) Franklin, Doctor (afterwards Sir John) Richardson, and Mr. (afterwards Sir George) Back, passed overland and traced the Coppermine River to its outlet in the Arctic Ocean. During this journey they explored many thousands of miles of the Hudson's Bay Territory.

SECOND EXPEDITION BY FRANKLIN, RICHARDSON, AND BACK.

In 1825, Franklin, Richardson, and Back undertook a second expedition overland, and through the dreary regions of the frozen north, and again explored the territory between the Coppermine and the Mackenzie rivers. In 1826, 1837-8, 1838-9, other expeditions through these regions were made by Beechey, Dease, Simpson, and Back, who went as far as the meridian 148° 52', and to the Icy Cape, discovered by Captain Cook. In 1845, the spirit of Polar adventure awoke with renewed ardour, and Sir John Franklin set out upon that journey which has thrown such a lamentable cloud over all connected with that region, and which for so many years excited the sympathy of the world, and the noble efforts of brave souls to trace his wanderings, his sojournings, and his grave. In May, 1845, the *Erebus* and *Terror* set sail from Sheerness, and the last ever seen of them was near Baffin's Bay, by the Esquimaux, on the west coast of King William Land, in 1850. We know that Franklin died in the summer of 1847. The survivors abandoned the ships, and started for the Great Fish River. Exhaustion and intense severity of climate must have completed the work which prior suffering had already commenced. "They dropped by the way" (to quote the expressive words of the Esquimaux), and not one of the brave adventurers who composed Franklin's party ever returned within the confines of civilized life. The names of Rae, M'Clintock, M'Clure, Penny, Inglefield, Belcher, Herne, Hall, and others, are indissolubly connected with the history of Arctic discovery; they enlarged and extended our geographical knowledge, and the continuity of an icy channel between the two oceans was proved conclusively through their researches. Their unselfish heroism—their noble tenacity of purpose, manifested during unexampled hardships and sufferings—their earnest devotion to science, and their contributions to our geographical knowledge, have crowned their names with imperishable glory.

CHAPTER IV.

THE PROGRESS OF COLONIZATION.

The Colonization of Newfoundland, New Brunswick, Prince Edward's Island, Nova Scotia, and the Canadas (Upper and Lower).

NEWFOUNDLAND.

NEWFOUNDLAND was discovered on the 24th of June, 1497, by John Cabot, who attempted its colonization in conjunction with his sons and those of his companions who were desirous of settling with him. He bore a charter and grant from Henry VII. of England, giving him the right and title to all such lands as he should discover. The aborigines who dwelt upon the island were, however, of a most savage character; and, after suffering severe hardships, and engaging in hostile conflicts with them, they finally abandoned the attempt, and sailed for Nova Scotia. In 1576 Sir Humphery Gilbert, a half-brother of Sir Walter Raleigh, made an attempt to colonize the island, but it proved equally unsuccessful. In 1583 he made another attempt, landed at St. John's, and took formal possession in the name of his mistress, Queen Elizabeth. He was accompanied by two hundred adventurers, whom he left there, and departed for England, but on the voyage the ship in which he had embarked foundered at sea. In 1620 Lord Bacon and others established a colony at Conception Bay. In 1617 Captain Whitbourne established a settlement at Little Britain; they found the land sterile and uncultivated, abounding in great white bears and elks. The discoverers called this country by a name signifying "rich in fish," from the numbers which swarmed in the rivers and along the sea-coast. The inhabitants were wild and unfriendly, clothed with the skins of beasts, and painted with a reddish clay.

In 1623 Sir George Calvart (Lord Baltimore, who settled Maryland) formed a settlement here. In 1631 Lord Falkland sent a number of Irish families here, and, providing them with every means necessary for fishing and agriculture, they obtained a permanent footing on the island, and for a long while prospered harmoniously. In 1646 there were sixteen settlements flourishing on the coast of Newfoundland; there were at that time over 350 families of British extraction, a large addition to which was made by Sir David Kirk in 1654. But after years of toil, suffering, and hardship, the British Government, whose duty and interest would seem alike to extend their protection and fostering care, commenced that mistaken policy towards the colonists which in the end cost us so dearly on the American Continent. An edict, cruel in its nature, impolitic in principle, and insane in its intent, was promulgated by the "Lords of Trades and Plantations." They seemed afraid that the colonists might succeed; they systematically discouraged agriculture, and finally entirely prohibited it. The colonists who rebelled at this edict were expelled from the territory, their lands confiscated, their houses destroyed, and in some instances death was inflicted upon them. It was the policy of the British Government at that time to force the colonists to occupy themselves with the fisheries, and to draw their supplies from the old country. In 1696 the French seized the English settlements, and from this period till the year 1815 the whole island was a scene of bloody conflict, atrocious cruelty, and inhuman oppression between the French and the English. The treaties of Utrecht, 1715; of Paris, 1763; of Versailles, 1783; and of Paris, 1814 and 1815, finally settled the right of possession, and it was adjudged to be the property of Great Britain.

The natives met with in the first discovery of Newfoundland were supposed to be the descendants of Biorn, a sea-king of Iceland, who took possession of this island in the year 1001. The author of "Hochelaga" gives the following history of the natives found here by the European settlers:—"They were fierce men, of stalwart frame, and intractable disposition; their complexion was of a dark red; they were bold fishers and hunters, and of courage in battle. From the first, they and the white men were deadly foes. The Mic-Mac Indians of Nova Scotia and these red men carried on a war of extermination against each other for centuries; each landing with destructive swoop on the other's coasts, scalping the men, and carrying the women into slavery. The Esquimaux warriors were more frequently victorious, till, in an evil hour, they provoked the wrath of the pale-faces. The rifle and the bayonet soon broke their spirit. Abandoning the coasts and the hunting-grounds of their fathers, they fled into the dreary forests of the interior. Sometimes, in the long winter nights, they crept out from their wild fastnesses, and visited some lonely hamlet with a terrible vengeance. The settlers in return hunted them down like wolves. In the course of years their life of misery reduced their numbers and weakened their frames so much that they never ventured to appear. It was known that some few still lingered, but they were almost forgotten.

"The winter of 1830 was unusually severe in this country, and prolonged beyond those of former years. Towards its close, a settler was hewing down trees at some distance from one of the remote villages, when two gaunt figures crept out from the neighbouring 'bush;' with sad cries and imploring gestures, they tried to express their prayer for help. The white man, terrified by their uncouth and haggard looks, seized his gun, which lay at hand, and shot the foremost; the other tossed his lean arms wildly into the air—the woods rang with his despairing shrieks as he rushed away.

Since then none of the fallen race have been seen. The emaciated frame of the dead man showed how dire had been their necessity. There is no doubt that the last of the red men perished in that bitter winter."

NEW BRUNSWICK.

New Brunswick, now a distinct colony, formed a part of Nova Scotia till the year 1785. It was first settled in 1762, by a party from Massachusetts. When the independence of the United States was declared in 1783, numerous bodies of Royalists sailed from New York and settled in New Brunswick. Most of these were the men and their families who had joined the British army during the revolutionary struggle. For two or three years they were greatly assisted by the Government until they had cleared sufficient land, erected houses, and gathered in crops, and were prepared alike to resist the inclemency of the seasons, the rigours of the climate, and the assault of savages. From the time that New Brunswick was separated from Nova Scotia, in 1785, until 1803, the province was governed by Sir Guy Carleton, under whose paternal, firm, and judicious administration the country gradually advanced from a rude wilderness to a permanent and prominent position among its sister colonies. In 1815, on the conclusion of the second war with the United States, another large body of disbanded military was added to the inhabitants. From this time forward the population steadily increased—in 1824 it being computed at 80,000.

PRINCE EDWARD'S ISLAND.

This island was discovered by Sebastian Cabot in 1497. It was first used by the French as a fishing-station, in 1663; they began to colonize it about the beginning of the eighteenth century. The settlers evinced a great interest in the continual wars between the French and English, and took an active part in the contests that were waged. In 1752 the population was estimated at 1354. In 1758, in consequence of the expulsion of the Acadians from Nova Scotia, the population nearly doubled. By the treaty of Fontainbleau in 1763, it became a dependency of Great Britain. In 1764, the whole territory was surveyed and divided into sixty-seven townships. "These townships or lots, or parts of them, with certain reservations, were to be granted to parties having claims upon the Government, upon certain conditions of settlement, and the payment of quit-rents. Lot 66, about six thousand acres, was reserved for the Crown; lots 40 and 59 had already been promised to parties who had made improvements on them. Sixty-four townships or lots remained to be disposed of. There were more applicants than lots; so they were disposed of by means of the ballot-box. When an individual was to receive a whole lot, his name alone appeared on the slip of paper;

in other cases, two and sometimes three names were inscribed on one paper, as sharers in one lot. Upwards of one hundred individuals participated in these grants, which were made in 1767.

The quit-rents were of three rates: six shillings, four shillings, and two shillings annually per hundred acres. The grantees were to settle on each lot—a settler for every two hundred acres. This arrangement proved a failure, for in 1781 nine whole and five half townships were sold for the payment of .quit-rents. The nonresidence of the proprietors, the coercive measures adopted by the Home Government (which compelled the emigrants to be Protestants who were not from Great Britain), and the pressure of the quit-rents, combined to retard emigation. It was not until these burdensome conditions were removed, and the Earl of Selkirk settled eight hundred Highlanders there in 1803, that the first permanent impulse to settlement was given. The settlers who now took up their homes were a frugal and industrious class of small farmers, and soon advanced in comfort and wealth. Since this time, with the natural increase of population and the importations from Great Britain, the colony has flourished and prospered; and in 1832 the population had increased to 32,292,

NOVA SCOTIA.

The attempts to colonize Nova Scotia date back to an early period. In 1598 Henry IV. of France empowered the Marquis de la Roche to make a settlement; in 1613 the governor of Virginia, Sir Samuel Argall, broke up this settlement. In 1621 James I. of England granted the whole country, by letters patent, to Sir William Alexander, a Scottish nobleman. A large fleet of vessels, with several hundred hardy pioneers, soon set sail for the colony, whose name had been changed from French Acadia to Nova Scotia. In 1632 Charles I. ceded both Acadia and Canada to France. In 1654 it was captured by the British. In 1677 it was again ceded to France by the treaty of Breda. In 1690 it was recaptured for the British by Sir William Phipps. By the treaty of Ryswick in 1696 it was restored to France. In 1710 the people of Massachusetts conquered a portion of Nova Scotia; but by the treaty of Utrecht in 1713 "all Nova Scotia, with its ancient boundaries, as also the city of Port Royal and the inhabitants of the same," were ceded to Great Britain.

In 1749 the Hon. Edward Cornwallis was appointed governor, and he sailed for Nova Scotia with 3760 families. He landed, and commenced the erection of a city, which he named after his patron, the Earl of Halifax. The French settlers in New Brunswick, Nova Scotia, and Cape Breton, caused the new comers great trouble and annoyance. They allied themselves with the Indians, and made continual depredatory excursions, which resulted in a succession of conflicts and disasters. In 1755 the French (Acadians) were removed to the number of nearly seven thousand. In 1763 Cape Breton was annexed to Nova Scotia—separated in 1784—and finally, in 1819, they were permanently joined. In 1784 New Brunswick was separated from Nova Scotia and erected into a separate province. Nova Scotia owed much of her early advancement to the Royalists from the American Colonies, who, during and after the War of Independence, emigrated there to the number of twenty thousand.

THE CANADAS, UPPER AND LOWER.

In the month of May, 1535, Jacques Cartier, having visited Newfoundland, set sail again westward, passed the north side of Anticosti, and ascended the St. Lawrence River until he reached the mouth of a river which he called the Saguenay. The country round about he christened Hochelaga. In a work called "Hochelaga; or, England in the New World" (London, 1846), we find many interesting and pleasing descriptions of the early history of the British Colonies of North America. Speaking of Jacques Cartier's early voyage, it says: "During the voyage up the stream they passed shores of great beauty; the climate was genial, the weather warmer than that of France, and everywhere they met with unsuspicious friendship. They found Hochelaga a fortified town among rich corn-fields, on an island under the shade of a mountain, which they called Mont Royal. Time has changed it to Montreal. The old name, like the old people, is long since forgotten. The inhabitants had stores of corn and fish laid up with great care; also tobacco, which the Europeans saw here for the first time. The natives were courteous and friendly in their manners—some of them of noble beauty. They bowed to a great Spirit, and knew of a future state. Their king wore a crown, which he transferred to Jacques Cartier. But when they brought their sick and infirm, trusting to his supernatural power to heal, the Christian soldier blessed them with the cross, and prayed that Heaven might give them health." Soon after this the adventurers returned to France, carrying with them one of the kings or chiefs, who soon died of melancholy and grief. Four years later, another adventurer, the Sieur de Roberval, landed at the mouth of the St. Charles River, but, instead of being met in the same friendly spirit the Indians had received Jacques Cartier and his compatriots upon the former visit, they at once declared them invaders, and threatened their extermination. To protect themselves against the hostility and vengeance of the justly offended Indians, who remembered the forced extradition of their king, they erected a strong fortification at the village of Charlesbourg. In 1549, after a few years of internal contention and external violence with the savages, they returned to France. Many years—in fact, nearly half a century—elapsed before any attempt was made to extend French sway in this territory. Some few individuals succeeded in trading and bartering with them for fur to a limited extent, but no combined attempt to colonize was made until De Mont, with a great piratical fleet, made his appearance, and marked his path with crime, cruelty, bloodshed, devastation, and extermination. Next came Champlain, who sailed up the St. Lawrence River, and founded the city of Quebec ; and, after cultivating for a time the rich valleys of the St. Charles, he, in company with many of his followers, set out upon an exploring expedition to the great Western Lakes. All the territory north of the St. Lawrence River and the lakes he called Canada, or New France. The new settlers met at the outset with the same obstacles to the peaceful pursuit of their voyage which had marked the history of all attempts at settling or permanently occupying the country. The Indians attacked them vigorously and continuously, and often with the most deplorable results ; in the end, however, they were compelled to succumb to their less numerous but more civilized opponents, and after a time they sought their alliance. But other antagonistic elements were at work to retard their progress—other agents, which are ever the accompaniments of civilization, quickly decimated their numbers, and the pale-face soon domineered as lord and master. The continuous wars, too, that were desolating Europe found their dark shadows sweeping over the young colonies in the New World. The blood of England and France had been transplanted to these shores, and, instead of the emigrant pursuing his peaceful occupation and reclaiming the soil, he seized the flint-lock instead of the pruning-hook. The Indians were invited to display, in all its merciless and horrible aspect, their mode of warfare upon the English, who occupied the southern banks of the St. Lawrence. Success alternately smiled upon the fortunes of both parties, but the atrocities that were committed on the defenceless and the helpless, the uncalled-for cruelties that characterized that long period of warfare which culminated in the battle on the heights of Abraham and decided the supreme sovereignty of Britain, is one of the darkest pages in the history of that period. Still emigration did not flourish, or the settler make much progress in penetrating the dense forests, for we read that " Upper Canada, only eighty years ago, was a wilderness from the Ottawa to the St. Clair." Despite the attempts which had been made so continuously by the French, this great province seemed to have remained in almost its primeval purity, vastness, and extent. About 1783, the British settlement commenced, and a revolution of progress was at once apparent. In 1791, Upper Canada was made a distinct province, and divided into four districts —the Eastern, Midland, Home, and Western. In 1782, Upper Canada had only 10,000 inhabitants; in 1824 she had 152,000; while in 1829 she possessed a population of 225,000. In the year 1829, agricultural societies were introduced in the several districts of the province, and the Imperial Government lent every assistance to promote the cultivation of the lands.

CHAPTER V.

STATISTICS OF NEWFOUNDLAND, PRINCE EDWARD'S ISLAND, AND NOVA SCOTIA.

Newfoundland: Agriculture; Government; Fisheries; Shipping; Imports and Exports; Population—Prince Edward's Island: Industrial Resources; Imports and Exports; Counties, Towns, and Population; Education; Government—Nova Scotia: The Seasons; Botanical Productions; Shipping; Agriculture; Fisheries; Commerce; Population; Quadrupeds, Birds, and Fish; Crown Lands; Education; Government; Halifax; Gold-Fields; Minerals.

NEWFOUNDLAND.

NEWFOUNDLAND embraces 36,000 square miles. It lies upon the eastern side of the Gulf of St. Lawrence; the Strait of Belleisle divides it from the coast of Labrador. The coast is open to the Atlantic on three sides—north, south, and east. The shores are exceedingly rugged and irregular in outline, and exhibit a succession of deep bays and estuaries, with peninsulas and headlands between. Many of the inlets form good and commodious harbours. The principal bays are the Bay of Conception, Bonavista, Notre Dame, Trinity, White, and Hare upon the eastern and northern coasts; of St. George upon the western side; and of Fortune, Placentia, and St. Mary upon the south.

Newfoundland is a series of barren and rocky districts, with here and there a few tracts of alluvial soil along the rivers. But few cattle are reared, and the crops of barley and oats scarcely ripen. The interior is hilly and swampy, and traced and dotted with many lakes and rivers.

The winter is long and very severe. Fogs are prevalent during many months of the year. The summers are dry and the heat intense. In winter the snow-storms are violent and accompanied by hurricanes.

The following statistics show the progressing increase in agriculture and neat cattle:—

In 1845 there were 83,435½ acres of land in possession, and 29,656¾ acres under cultivation, the value of which was 2,990,625 dollars; horses, 2409, valued at 120,450 dollars; neat cattle, 8135—value, 203,375 dollars; sheep, 5750—value, 23,750 dollars; goats, 5791—value, 28,955 dollars; hogs, 5077—value, 39,075 dollars; bushels of potatoes, 853,352½; bushels of grain, 11,695; tons of hay and fodder, 11,013.

In 1857 (the latest census taken) the whole of the improved land of the island was 46,616¾ acres. Tons of hay cut, 16,250; bushels of oats raised, 9438; bushels of wheat and barley, 1932¾;

bushels of potatoes raised, 571,480; bushels of turnips, 12,832; bushels of other roots, 3502; bushels of clover and timothy seed, 731½. Number of neat cattle, 12,962; milch cows, 6924; horses, 3509; sheep, 10,737; swine and goats, 17,551. Butter made, 134,968 lbs.; cheese, 158 lbs. There are a few factories, which are principally devoted to the manufacture of cod-liver oil.

In 1857 there were 80 vessels built, of the combined tonnage of 2427; there were also 630 boats built, besides which the island owned 212 vessels, the tonnage of which was 6229.

GOVERNMENT.

The Government of Newfoundland is conducted and controlled by the Lieutenant-Governor, appointed by the Home Government, and he is assisted by the Legislative Council and the House of Assembly. Every male member of the population being twenty-one and renting a house is entitled to a vote for any elective officer. The Judiciary consists of a Supreme Court, with a Chief Justice and two Assistant-Justices. There is also a Central Circuit Court and a Court of Vice-Admiralty. There are five hundred and fifty miles of electric telegraph laid, as well as a submarine line from Aspy Bay, Cape Breton, to Cape Ray, Newfoundland. The tariff is three dollars, or twelve shillings sterling, for ten words.

FISHERIES.

The Fisheries are of course the principal source of income to Newfoundland, and we shall, therefore, give a somewhat detailed description of them. They are of great value, and comprise salmon, cod, herrings, mackerel, caplin, and seal.

The banks of Newfoundland are of submarine elevation, and spread over an area of six or seven hundred miles in length. The Great Bank is 300 miles from north to south and 250 miles from east to west. The depth of the water is various, in some places being only fifteen fathoms, in others eighty fathoms; and the temperature is lower by 10° than that of the surrounding ocean. The abundance of codfish which are found here is extraordinary and unparalleled.

The fishermen who are usually engaged in cod-fishing, employ the early months of the year in catching seals, which they find in great quantities upon the floating ice; early in June this occupation is changed for cod-fishing. In a commercial sense there are three qualities of cod—first, the best and largest fish, called *merchantable* fish; second, the *Madeira* fish, a medium variety, which serves to supply the Spanish or Portuguese markets; third, the inferior qualities, which are exported to the West Indies for the use of the negroes.

In 1849 the dried codfish exported was valued at 2,825,895

dollars; in 1857 the value was over three millions of dollars, or £600,000.

In 1852 there were 367 vessels, of 35,760 tons, manned by 13,000 men, which took 550,000 seals. In 1857 there were 802 vessels, with a tonnage of 57,898; men on board, 14,442; number of seals taken, 428,143.

In 1857 there were 157,354 barrels of herrings cured, 2940 tierces of salmon cured, and 913 of fresh salmon disposed of at St. John's.

IMPORTS AND EXPORTS.

No better idea can be formed of the increase and progress of Newfoundland than by presenting a tabular view of the imports and exports for a series of years. The whole of the exports may be said to consist of fish:—

Year	Imports.	Exports.
1829	4,006,650 dollars	4,697,190 dollars
1846	4,011,435 ,,	3,795,515 ,,
1847	4,217,045 ,,	4,032,825 ,,
1848	3,848,140 ,,	4,187,905 ,,
1849	3,700,912 ,,	4,207,521 ,,
1850	4,163,116 ,,	4,683,676 ,,
1851	4,609,291 ,,	4,293,876 ,,
1852	3,857,468 ,,	4,306,376 ,,
1856	6,356,830 ,,	6,693,985 ,,
1857	7,067,160 ,,	8,255,855 ,,
1858	5,864,310 ,,	6,594,180 ,,
1859	6,620,680 ,,	6,785,565 ,,
1860	6,270,640 ,,	6,358,560 ,,

In 260 years there has been shipped from Newfoundland, fish and oil to the value of £130,000,000. The revenue of the colony for the year 1862, was £116,929, and the expenditure for the same year was £138,058. The revenue is derived entirely from customs, there being no other tax of any kind. The colonial debt is £173,642. The value of the exports from the colony (1862) was £1,171,723, and of the imports, £1,007,082. The number of ships owned and registered in Newfoundland (1863) was 1386, measuring 87,030 tons. The number of arrivals was 1345; departures, 1159; vessels built during the year, 26. Of the imports in 1862, the value of £345,797 was from the United States; and of the exports, £47,729 was to the United States. There are two banks at St. John's—the Union Bank, capital £50,000, and the Commercial Bank, capital £50,000. The number of schools in 1857 was 280, attended by 10,266 pupils. The number of inhabited buildings in 1857 was 18,364.

POPULATION—DESCRIPTION OF ST. JOHN'S.

The population in 1785 was 10,000; in 1845, 96,295; in 1851, 101,600; in 1857, it was 122,638. The increase of population cannot be attributed to immigration, but simply to the natural increase of the inhabitants. The soil offers no inducement to the settler, and it is only the hardy mariner and fisherman who can expect to find a sphere of employment suitable for them. Mr. Warburton thus humorously describes St. John's, the capital of Newfoundland :—" Round a great part of the harbour are sheds, acres in extent, roofed with cod split in half, laid on like slates, drying in the sun, or rather in the air, for there is not much of the former to depend upon. Those ships, bearing nearly every flag in the world, are laden with cod ; those stout, weatherly boats, crowding up to the wharves, have just now returned from fishing for cod ; those few scant fields of cultivation, with lean crops coaxed out of the barren soil, are manured with cod ; those trim, snug-looking, wooden houses—their handsome furniture—the piano, and the musical skill of the young lady who plays it—the satin gown of the mother—the gold chain of the father—are all paid for in cod ; the breezes from the shore, soft and warm on this bright August day, are rich, not with the odours of a thousand flowers, but of a thousand cod. Earth, sea, and air are alike pervaded with this wonderful fish. There is only one place which appears to be kept sacred from its intrusion, and, strange to say, that is the dinner-table. An observation made on its absence from that apparently appropriate position excited as much surprise as if I had made a remark to a Northumberland squire that he had not a head dish of Newcastle coals."

PRINCE EDWARD'S ISLAND.

Prince Edward's Island is on the southerly side of the St. Lawrence. It is 140 miles in length and 34 in breadth. It occupies an area of about 2000 square miles. The features of this country are softer than those of its neighbours ; there are no mountains, but gentle and fertile undulations, clothed to the water's edge with valuable woods and rich verdure. The north shore is very beautiful—many cheerful villages and green clearings, with small lakes, shady arbours, and numerous streams, diversify its scenery. The land is admirably adapted for pastoral and agricultural purposes. Crops are produced almost immediately after the land is redeemed from the forest. The island was at one time crowned with a complete and continuous canopy of trees, such as the elm, ash, maple, spruce, pine, cedar, birch, hemlock, juniper, and beech. The rivers abound with an excellent variety of fish, such as the mackerel, salmon, trout, eels, flounders, and lobsters ; while the coast is alive with cod, oysters, halibut, and sturgeon. Game is also very plentiful, such as wild duck, pigeons, brandt, and geese.

INDUSTRIAL RESOURCES.

The census of different dates gives the following statistics in reference to the industrial resources of the province:—In 1846, 82 vessels were built, the tonnage of which was 12,012, valued at 330,000 dollars. In 1847, 96 vessels were built; tonnage, 18,445; value, 553,350 dollars. In 1860, 66 vessels were built; value, 309,225 dollars. In 1861, there were 89 fishing establishments; 1239 boats, employing 2318 persons. Lieut.-Governor Dundas, in his annual report for 1863, says: "There is one great source of wealth round the coasts of the island, which is almost neglected by the inhabitants; I allude to the fisheries. During the summer months hundreds of schooners are attracted to the shores of this island from the neighbouring provinces, and from the United States, while it is the exception to find a vessel belonging to the island engaged in this occupation.

"The inhabitants are chiefly engaged in agriculture. Sudden vicissitudes of fortune do not, therefore, frequently occur; but there appears to be a gradual improvement in the culture of the soil, and new farmhouses and buildings are invariably of greater pretension than those which preceded them—signs, I trust, of increasing prosperity."

The census of 1861 gives the following agricultural returns:— Wheat, 346,125 bushels; barley, 223,195 bushels; hay, 31,100 tons; potatoes, 2,972,335 bushels; oats, 2,218,578 bushels; buckwheat, 50,127 bushels; turnips, 348,784 bushels; horses, 18,765; neat cattle, 60,115; sheep, 107,242; hogs, 71,535.

In 1861 there were 350,000 acres under cultivation. The population in 1822 was 24,600; in 1833 it was 32,292; in 1841, 47,034; in 1851, 55,000; and in 1861, 80,856.

IMPORTS AND EXPORTS.

The value of the imports in 1847 was 718,270 dollars; the exports, 356,130. In 1850 the imports were in value 630,475 dollars; of exports during the same period, 325,990 dollars. The value of the exports for 1860 was 1,015,970 dollars. The value of the imports for the year 1862 was £211,240. 18s. 6d., an increase of £1305. 2s. 7d. on the value of 1861. The value of exports was £150,549. 2s. 1d., £12,565. 5s. 9d. less than that of the preceding year. The value of 57 vessels of 7715 tons transferred to other ports is not taken into consideration. The revenue of the colony for the year 1862 was £25,861. 13s. 6d.

The public debt of the island on the 31st of January, 1861, was 155,324 dollars.

COUNTIES, TOWNS, AND POPULATION.

The island is divided into three counties—Queen's County, Prince's County, and King's County. The whole population of the colony, according to the census of 1861, was 80,857, of whom 40,880 were males, and 39,997 were females. Divided according to their religious faith, there were 44,975 Protestants, and 35,882 Catholics. The population of Charlottetown was, by the same census, 6706. Georgetown, in King's County, has a population of about 800.

EDUCATION.

The Prince of Wales College, established at Charlottetown in 1860, is the most important educational institution of the colony. It is supported from the public revenue. St. Dunstan's College is a private establishment near Charlottetown. In 1856 a normal school for the training teachers was established. The number of schools in the same year was 260, and of pupils 11,000. In 1861 there were 302 public school-houses, and 280 teachers; but we have no returns of the number of scholars for that year. The amount of money disbursed from the Colonial Treasury, in 1862, for public education was £11,000 sterling, or 55,000 dollars. In 1863 an Act was passed by the Legislature transferring a portion of this expense to the people individually.

GOVERNMENT (JANUARY, 1864).

Lieutenant-Governor, Commander-in-Chief, Vice-Admiral, &c., his Excellency George Dundas, Esq., appointed January, 1859. George Dundas, Esq., formerly an officer of the Rifle Brigade; retired from the army 1844; represented Linlithgow in Parliament 1847—1858.

Executive Council, or Ministry.—Hon. Hamilton Gray, President; Hons. Edward Palmer, James Yeo, John Longworth, James C. Pope, David Kaye, James M'Laren, Daniel Davies, and William Henry Pope. Clerk of the Executive Council, Charles Des Brisay, Esq. Assistant-Clerk, Donald Currie, Esq.

Principal Executive Officers.—Colonial Secretary, Hon. Wm. H. Pope; Colonial Treasurer, George Wright, Esq.; Attorney-General, Hon. Edward Palmer; Comptroller of Customs, Hon. Francis Longworth; Commissioner of Crown Lands and Surveyor-General, Hon. John Aldous; Postmaster-General, Lemuel C. Owen, Esq. The Lieutenant-Governor is appointed by the Crown, and is the royal representative in the colony. The Executive Councillors are appointed by the Lieutenant-Governor from the majority side of the Colonial Parliament, and they are responsible for the Government while in office.

Colonial Legislature.—The legislative power of the colony is exercised (subject to the revision of the Crown) by a Legislature composed of a Council and a House of Assembly. Formerly the members of the Legislative Council were appointed by the Crown for life, but they are now (since Feb., 1863) elective. They are thirteen in number, chosen by the property-holders of the colony for a term of eight years; six of those now in office to retire at the end of four years, so that one-half of the Council may be renewed every fourth year. The members of the House of Assembly are thirty in number, and are chosen by the qualified electors of the colony, by districts, to serve for a term of four years. No property-qualification is required to enable persons to vote for members of the Assembly. Officers of the Legislative Council—Hon. Donald Montgomery; Clerk, James Barrett Cooper, Esq. Officers of the House—Hon. T. Heath Haviland, Speaker; Chief Clerk, John M'Neill, Esq.

Judiciary: Court of Chancery.—Chancellor, the Lieutenant-Governor; Master of the Rolls, Hon. James H. Peters; Registrar, Charles Des Brisay, Esq.

Supreme Court.—Chief Justice, Hon. Robert Hodgson; Assistant-Judge, Hon. James H. Peters; Puisne Judge, John Barrow, Esq.; Clerk and Prothonotary, Daniel Hodgson.

Besides the foregoing tribunals, there is an Instance Court of Admiralty, of which the Chief Justice of the Supreme Court is Judge; a Court of Probate of Wills, &c., of which Hon. Charles Young is Surrogate; and a Court of Marriage and Divorce, composed of the Lieutenant-Governor and Executive Council. The terms of the Supreme Court commence on the first Tuesday in January and May, and on the last Tuesday in June and October.

Ecclesiastical.—Church of England: the Lord Bishop of Nova Scotia, Rt. Rev. Hibbert Binney, D.D., has jurisdiction of the island. Catholic Church: Rt. Rev. Peter M'Intyre, D.D, Bishop of Charlottetown.

NOVA SCOTIA.

Nova Scotia and the island of Cape Breton form one province. Nova Scotia is a peninsula, and has an area of 15,600 square miles, being 256 miles in length by 100 miles in breadth. Cape Breton is 100 miles in length, and 72 in breadth, and possesses an area of 3000 square miles. The two conjoined present a surface of 18,600 square miles, or 12,000,000 acres. The interior of Nova Scotia forms a table-land, some parts of which are rather hilly, and abounds in lakes. Cape Breton is generally hilly in the interior. The climate resembles that of Lower Canada, the winters being severe and the summers hot, but the air is generally healthy. Fogs are experienced along the Atlantic coast. The harbours, bays, lakes, and rivers are numerous and extensive.

The harbour of Halifax is pronounced "one of the best in the world." It is easy of access for the largest ships, and is capable of floating the combined fleets of Europe. It is protected against the winds, and after narrowing itself just above the city, it expands itself into a lovely basin, called the Bedford Basin, which covers an area of nine square miles; this basin is from four to thirty fathoms in depth. We have never sailed round a more beautiful sheet of water; the shores crowned with forest-trees, and interspersed with snow-white cottages and flowering orchards, lend a charm to it that is not easily to be forgotten. The coast-line of Halifax extends a distance of 1000 miles.

The principal bay is the Bay of Fundy. "This remarkable bay is fifty miles in width, and after extending a hundred miles inland divides into two branches. The northern branch is called Chiegnecto Bay, the southern branch, the Basin of Minas. The extraordinary height and rapidity of its tides are famous. At the mouth of the Minas Channel the tide rises to about fifty feet, while at the mouth of the Shubenacadie, near the head of Cobequid Bay, at the spring-tides it obtains the height of seventy-five feet.

The principal rivers are the Shubenacadie, the Avon, and the Annapolis, flowing into the Bay of Fundy; the St. Mary's, Musquodoboit, La Have, and Liverpool, flowing into the Atlantic.

THE SEASONS.

Spring commences in Nova Scotia with the beginning of April. Seed-time and planting continue till the middle of June. Summer begins with the latter part of June, and embraces July and August. Vegetation is very rapid in the middle and western parts of the province, where the hay crop and usually all the grain crops, are harvested by the last week of August or first week in September.

Autumn is the finest season in Nova Scotia. It is mild, serene, and cool enough to be bracing, and the atmosphere is of a purity that renders it peculiarly exhilarating and health-giving. The "Indian summer" occurs sometimes as late as the middle of November, and lasts from three to ten days.

The winter in Nova Scotia may be said to comprise about four months. It begins, some seasons, with the 1st of December and runs into the month of April. Other seasons it begins in the middle of December and ends with the last of March.

BOTANICAL PRODUCTIONS.

Nova Scotia is remarkably rich in her botanical productions, the principal of which are the white and red pine, the hemlock, the black, red, and white spruce, the fir, and the juniper; these are the *soft wood*. The *hard woods* are the white soft maple, the white sugar maple, the black sugar maple, the red maple, the striped maple, the mountain maple, the white ash, the black ash, the white beech, the red beech, the white oak, the black oak, the yellow, the white, the canoe, and the poplar-leaved birch, and the hazel. The principal ornamental trees are the sumach, the wild pear, the mountain ash, the wild hawthorn, the wild red cherry, the willow, the aspen, the poplar, the white-leaved poplar, the acacia, the black cherry-tree, and the sarsaparilla. The wild plants are numerous, and some of exquisite beauty; the May flower, the white pond lily, the wild rose, the Indian cup, Solomon's seal, the tree cranberry, the pigeon berry, the Indian hemp, the wild pea, the star flower, and the violet. The fruit-bearing trees are the raspberry, blackberry, strawberry, blueberry, whortleberry, cranberry, and gooseberry. The various products of the forests gave employment in 1862 to 1401 saw-mills, 130 shingle-mills, and 6 lath-mills, which turned out 25,072 M. feet deals, 46,607 M. feet pine boards, 36,422 M. feet spruce and hemlock boards. The return of staves for the same year year is 7659 M. timber, 22,592 tons.

SHIPPING.

The number and amount of shipping built between 1853 and 1861 is shown in the following table of statistics:—

Year.	No. of Vessels.	Tonnage.	Value.
1853	203	31,376	1,557,090 dols.
1854	244	52,814	2,546,595 ,,
1855	236	40,469	2,240,710 ,,
1856	208	39,582	1,852,540 ,,
1857			
1858	151	16,336	757,900 ,,
1859			
1860	233	20,684	852,831 ,,
1861	216	23,634	972,448 ,,

In 1846, Nova Scotia owned 141,093 tons of shipping; in 1853, 189,093 tons; in 1861, 248,061 tons. The number of vessels is 3258; value, 6,487,490 dollars. In 1862 the number of registered vessels was 3408, measuring 277,718 tons; the number built was 201, measuring 39,383 tons.

AGRICULTURE.

The agricultural progress of Nova Scotia is most satisfactory. By the census of 1861 it appears there are 37,897 farmers and 9306 farm labourers. The number of acres under cultivation at three successive periods was as follows:—In 1827, 292,009 acres; in 1851, 839,322 acres; in 1861, 1,028,032 acres. Divided into salt marsh, 20,729 acres; dyked marsh, 35,487 acres; cultivated intervale, 77,102 acres; and cultivated upland, 894,714 acres; the total value of which is estimated at 18,801,365 dollars. The average value per acre is—Dyked marsh, 62·06 dollars; salt marsh, 26·04 dollars; cultivated intervale, 27·45 dollars; and cultivated upland, 15·58 dollars. In some counties the cultivated upland sells for 50, 60, and 80 dollars; dyked marsh land brings 80 dollars, and some as high as 300 dollars, or £60 sterling.

The agricultural produce of 1851 shows—Wheat, 297,157 bushels; barley, 196,097 bushels; rye, 61,438; oats, 1,384,437 bushels; buckwheat, 170,301 bushels; Indian corn, 37,475 bushels; potatoes, 1,986,789 bushels; turnips, 467,127 bushels; hay, 287,837 tons; butter, 3,613,890 lbs.; cheese, 652,069 lbs.; horses, 28,786; sheep, 282,180; swine, 51,533; neat cattle, exclusive of cows, 156,857; milch cows, 86,856.

The census of 1861 gives the following as the products of agriculture and the number of live stock:—Wheat, 312,081 bushels; barley, 269,578 bushels; rye, 59,706 bushels; oats, 1,978,137 bushels; buckwheat, 195,340 bushels; Indian corn, 15,529 bushels; peas and beans, 21,333 bushels; potatoes, 3,824,864 bushels; turnips, 554,318 bushels; other roots, 87,727 bushels; apples, 186,484 bushels; plums, 4385 bushels; hay, 354,287 tons; maple sugar, 249,549 lbs.; butter, 4,532,711 lbs.; cheese, 901,296 lbs.; horses, 41,927; sheep, 332,653; swine, 53,217; neat cattle, exclusive of cows, 151,793; milch cows, 110,504.

The value of the agricultural products for the year 1861 is estimated at 8,021,860 dollars. The value of the live stock at 6,802,399 dollars.

THE FISHERIES.

The Fisheries are very productive and exhibit the following results:—

	1851.	1861.
Vessels	812	900
Boats	5,161	8,816
Men employed	10,394	14,322
Quintals of dry fish	196,434	396,425
Barrels of mackerel	100,047	66,108
Barrels of shad	3,536	7,849
Barrels of alewives	5,343	12,565
Barrels of salmon	1,669	2,481
Barrels of herrings		2,738
Boxes of herrings, smoked	53,200	194,170
Barrels of smoked salmon	15,409	35,557

The value of the vessels, boats, and nets, is estimated at 1,780,450 dollars. The value of the fish and oil in 1861 was 2,376,721 dollars.

In 1860 the total value of fish exported was 3,094,499 dollars;

in 1854 it was 2,093,415 dollars. The total value of live stock and agricultural products exported in 1860 was 786,526 dollars; lumber, 767,136 dollars; products of mines and quarries, 658,257 dollars; furs, 72,218 dollars; manufactures, 69,978 dollars; vessels, 168,270 dollars; miscellaneous, 151,132 dollars; imported from other countries and re-exported, 1,019,788 dollars; making the total exports for 1860, 6,787,804 dollars.

COMMERCE.

The value of imports into Halifax from the United States in 1861 was 1,736,879 dollars; from Great Britain to the same port, 2,222,266 dollars; from British North American Provinces, 760,800 dollars; the West Indies, 107,443 dollars; from all other countries, 678,571 dollars. The value of the imports and exports from 1852 to 1861 is shown in the following table:—

	Imports.	Exports.
1852	5,970,877 dollars.	4,853,903 dollars.
1853	7,085,431 ,,	5,393,538 ,,
1854	8,955,410 ,,	3,096,525 ,,
1855	9,413,515 ,,	4,820,654 ,,
1856	9,349,160 ,,	6,864,790 ,,
1857	9,680,880 ,,	6,967,830 ,,
1858	8,075,590 ,,	6,321,490 ,,
1859	8,100,955 ,,	6,889,130 ,,
1860	8,511,549 ,,	6,619,534 ,,
1861	7,613,227 ,,	5,774,334 ,,
1862	8,445,042 ,,	5,646,961 ,,

The number of vessels which entered in 1861 from Great Britain was 194, the tonnage 97,538, manned by 5111 men; from British West Indies, 259 vessels, 31,436 tons, and 1916 men; from British North America, 2681 vessels, 227,596 tons, and 14,451 men; from the United States, 2851 vessels, of 303,638 tons burthen, and 18,225 men; other countries, 338 vessels, 36,555 tons, and 2101 men. Total, 6323 vessels, 696,763 tons, and 41,804 men.

POPULATION.

The following table will show the increase of the population during the last ten years in the different counties:—

	Population 1851.	1861.	Increase.	Rate per Cent. of Increase.
Halifax (city)	19,949	25,026	5,077	25·44
,, (outside city)	19,163	23,995	4,832	25·21
Total in county	39,112	49,021	9,909	25·33

	Population 1851.	1861.	Increase.	Rate per Cent. of Increase.
Brought forward	39,112	49,021	9,909	25·33
Colchester	15,469	20,045	4,576	29·58
Cumberland	14,339	19,533	5,194	36·22
Pictou	25,593	28,785	3,192	12·47
Sydney	13,467	14,871	1,404	10·42
Guysborough	10,838	12,713	1,875	17·30
Inverness	16,917	19,967	3,050	18·02
Richmond	10,381	12,607	2,226	21·44
Victoria } Cape Breton (co.) }	27,580	{ 9,643 } { 20,866 }	2,992	10·62
Hants	14,330	17,460	3,130	21·14
King's	14,138	18,731	4,593	32·48
Annapolis	14,286	16,593	2,467	17·26
Digby	12,252	14,751	2,499	20·39
Yarmouth	13,142	15,446	2,304	17·53
Shelburne	10,622	10,688	46	·43
Queen's	7,256	9,365	2,109	29·06
Lunenburg	16,395	19,632	3,237	19·74
Totals	276,117	330,857	54,740	19·82

QUADRUPEDS, ETC.

The quadrupeds, birds, and fish of Nova Scotia are numerous in variety and of great value. Of quadrupeds there are the moose, cariboo, bear, fox, lynx, weasel, martin, otter, minx, squirrel, fisher, woodchuck, hare, racoon, porcupine, beaver, musquash, rat, and mouse. The birds comprise the bald-eagle, the fish-hawk, the hen-hawk, the sparrow-hawk, the white owl, great-eared owl, speckled owl, horned owl, and barn owl, besides warblers, thrushes, fly-catchers, chatterers, pinches, crossbills, crows, creepers, humming-birds, kingfishers, swallows, night-hawks, grouse, pigeons, herons, snipe, plovers, ducks, and geese. The fish are to be found in every bay, lake, and river in marvellous quantities, and are of the choicest kind—such as mackerel, herring, cod, haddock, halibut, alewives or gaspereau, pollock, salmon, shad, trout, and perch, besides the lobster, mussel, sea-clam, cockle, blue crab, nipple-fish, oyster, periwinkle, quatrog, scallop, razor-fish, shore-clam, sea-spider, soldier-crab, sea-crab, and star-fish.

CROWN LANDS.

The quantity of granted and ungranted lands in the province is as follows:—In Nova Scotia—quantity already granted, 4,935,349½ acres; remaining ungranted, 4,112,384½ acres; estimated as available for settlement, 556,664½ acres; lands open for settlements, 3,412,384½ acres. Cape Breton—granted, 813,543¾, ungranted, 1,207,438¼; available for settlement, 356,676¼; open for settlement, 777,438½. Total—5,748,893 granted; 5,319,822¾ ungranted; 913,340¾ available; 4,189,822¼ open for settlement.

The gross proceeds of lands sold in 1860 was 20,846 dollars 28 cents; in 1861, 16,598 dollars 73 cents.

The revenue for 1860 was 870,055 dollars; the expenditure, 852,133 dollars. The expenditure for 1861 was 870,771 dollars.

In 1860 the debt of the province was 4,901,305 dollars 42 cents—viz., provincial bonds, 4,000,000 dollars; provincial notes, 447,458 dollars; Savings' Bank, 453,847 dollars 42 cents. Total, 4,901,305 dollars 42 cents.

EDUCATION.

There are six colleges in Nova Scotia—viz., King's College, at Windsor, commenced in 1788; Acadia College, in Wolfville County, Baptist denomination; Goreham College, in Liverpool, Queen's County; St. Mary's College, in Halifax; St. Francis Xavier's College, in the town of Atigonish; and Dalhousie College, in Halifax. Six academies: the Windsor Academy, the Horton Academy, the Sackville Academy, the Presbyterian Academy, and the Arichat Academy. There are 44 academies and 1227 school-houses; 128,222 dollars 22 cents were subscribed by the population, and 53,519 dollars 25 cents contributed by the Government, for the common schools; and 9814 dollars 9 cents by the people, and 3274 dollars 95 cents by Government, for the grammar-schools.

GOVERNMENT.

The Government consists of a Lieutenant-Governor; the Legislative Council, consisting of 22 Members, who hold their position for life and are chosen by the Crown; the House of Representatives, consisting of 55 Members, chosen every four years. Every male inhabitant who is either native or a naturalized subject of Great Britain, and is twenty-one years of age, is entitled to a vote.

The principal towns and villages are Annapolis, Royal, Yarmouth, Pictou, New Glasgow, Sydney, and Arichat, in Cape Breton; Windsor, in Hants; Dartmouth, opposite Halifax; Baddeck, in Victoria; Port Hood and Maybon, Truro; Liverpool, Bridgetown, and Digby.

HALIFAX.

Halifax is the principal city. This city occupies a most commanding position, and extends in length over three miles; it is situated on the slope of a hill, and in its rear, far above and overlooking it, rises a bold and frowning fortress, which, in conjunction with other fortifications situated at appropriate points, gives it at once military strength and an imposing aspect.

Halifax is the great British North American seaport, and its future prosperity looks promising indeed; for when the great intercolonial railroad shall have been completed, much of the grain of the West will find its exit through this channel. Steamers and ships will also pour into this port thousands of emigrants, who can find a direct road to the Far West; while the gold-fields promise to prove a source of wealth and temptation that will soon rapidly increase the population of the surrounding country.

GOLD-FIELDS.

That the gold is not a myth we can assert from ocular testimony, having visited the mines within a few months; and certainly the various specimens shown to us prove that the quartz is extremely rich in metal. Some of the specimens quarried while we were present were equal to any we had ever seen, and the opinion of the miners was that, when the proper machinery and organized labour were brought to bear, the product will be such as to astonish those who have not at present a full belief in the material existence of this precious metal. The ascertained extent of the gold-field comprises an area of 6000 or 7000 square miles, being the entire region occupied by the metamorphic lower Silurian rocks of the Atlantic coast. So rich are the quartz veins at "The Ovens," 70 miles west from Halifax, that $1\frac{1}{2}$ ton of quartz has produced 72 oz. of gold, valued at 1296 dollars. One nugget has been discovered valued at 300 dollars, or £60 sterling. At Tangier, 2400 dollars has been realized in a short time; at another, 1300 dollars. The daily yield of gold is about 100 ounces, valued at 18 dollars per ounce. The Provincial Government have surveyed and divided the principal gold-fields into claims of twenty feet by fifty feet, and exact an annual licence-fee, or rent, of 20 dollars for each claim. "In one important respect," says Dr. Gesner, "the Nova Scotian gold-fields possess a very great advantage over those of Australia, California, or British Columbia—namely, that the rocks containing the gold in the greatest abundance are near the Atlantic coast, and intersect a number of the smaller rivers and harbours, whereby facilities are afforded to supply the requirements of mining. It is not at all probable that the richest gold and deposits in Nova Scotia have yet been discovered; but there is enough known to satisfy the most sceptical that the province contains an ample amount of the precious metal to warrant the most extensive operations, and the employment of machinery for its mining and purification."

MINERALS.

Coal.—Dr. Dawson, in his work styled "Acadian Geology," describes the coal-fields of Nova Scotia as vast in extent, and very valuable. The principal mines are the Albion mines, at Pictou.

These mines gave employment to over 2000 persons in 1851, and 60,000 chaldrons were raised. The quantity of coal raised, sold, and exported at Pictou in 1861 was 104,952 tons. The coal-mines of Sydney, at Cape Breton, produce annually about 80,000 tons. There are numerous other mines in Nova Scotia and New Breton, which are capable of supplying the wants of the steam marine to any extent. The total quantity of coal raised in Nova Scotia in 1861 was 200,000 chaldrons.

Iron.—Dr. J. L. Hayes, of Massachusetts, U.S., speaks of iron veins in high terms. He says there are immense fields of iron ore, and that iron ore can be raised for 4 dollars per ton. "I have no doubt that iron of the first quality for purity and strength, and which will command the highest prices in the market, can be made from these ores. If Mr. Mushet's opinion, based on his own experiments—that these ores will furnish steel-iron equal to the best Swedish brands—should prove correct, they possess a rare value; for, of the many charcoal iron establishments in the United States, I know but one which furnishes iron suitable for making the first quality of steel."

Gypsum.—The common gypsum is found in abundance, and is quarried at Windsor, Newport, Walton, and other places. In 1861 there was shipped to the United States 150,000 tons for agricultural purposes, which averaged 2 dollars a ton. Surely, when we review the natural resources and productiveness of Nova Scotia, she presents a picture of present prosperity which her inhabitants may well be proud of; and, with the increased means of development which the union of the provinces promises, she may look forward to a continued and steady increase of her agricultural, manufacturing, and mercantile wealth.

CHAPTER VI.

DESCRIPTION OF NEW BRUNSWICK.

New Brunswick—Rivers and Counties—Capabilities of the Province—Forests—Fisheries—Minerals—Fruit and Vegetables—Manufactures—Counties—Commerce—Finances—Government—Public Schools—Militia—Census of 1861—Agriculture.

NEW BRUNSWICK.

NEW BRUNSWICK lies to the eastward of Canada, and upon the eastward boundary of the State of Maine, U. S. On the east and south it borders the St. Lawrence and the Bay of Fundy; on the west the small river of St. Croix and the meridian of 67° 53' divide it from the territory of the United States; on the north it is terminated by the river Restigouche, which falls into the Bay of Chaleurs on the western side of the Gulf of St. Lawrence. The landscape is of great variety and of most picturesque beauty, being alternations of attractive valleys and hills, which northward assume a bold outline. It is 230 miles in length and 130 in breadth, and is covered with a mantle of magnificent forests that are unrivalled, and constitute a source of industry and wealth which is well nigh inexhaustible. It comprises an area of 27,037 square miles, or about 17,677,360 acres of land, the whole of which abounds in lakes and rivers. Its astronomical position is between latitude 45° 05' and 48° 04' north, and between longitudes 63° 47' and 67° 53' west from Greenwich. Seat of Government, Fredericktown. The surface of New Brunswick is varied along the shores; it is generally flat, but a little inland it rises into hills, some of which are sharp and bold, and serve to protect the interior table-lands and declivities. The quantity of good land sold up to 1861, was 6,000,000 acres, leaving 11,000,000 unsold, 7,500,000 of which are admirable lands for cultivation and farming purposes.

RIVERS AND COUNTIES.

The longest river of New Brunswick is the St. John's; this remarkable and beautiful river rises in the high lands which separate Maine from Canada, and empties into the Bay of Fundy, at St. John's Harbour, after traversing a distance of over 600 miles. The river and its affluents afford navigation for over 1300 miles; it is navigable for sloops up to Fredericktown, a distance of 80 miles, and for flat-bottomed boats up to the Great Falls, a distance of 200 miles from its mouth. The shores of the St. John are mostly covered with primeval forests. In some parts, the banks rise in grand rocky hills, forming in their lines and interlacings pictures of wondrous delight.

The chief tributaries of the St. John, besides the St. Francis and other waters already mentioned, are Aroostook, the Oromocto, and the Eel, on the west; and the Salmon, the Naskwaak, the Tobique, the Kennebecasis, and the Washedemoak, on the east. The St. John affords most valuable fishing, the salmon being as delicious and delicate as the Severn salmon of England. As many as 40,000 salmon, 16,000 barrels of alewives (a species of shad), and 1000 barrels of shad are caught annually, giving employment to 200 boats and 500 men, and producing 100,000 dollars, or £20,000 sterling, annually. The other rivers are the St. Croix, which falls into the Passamaquoddy Bay; the Miramichi, which flows eastward into the Gulf of St. Lawrence, having a course of 120 miles, and being navigable for nearly 40 miles; and the Restigouche, which falls into the Bay of Chaleurs, has a length of about 85 miles.

The climate is healthful, but subject to great extremes of heat and cold; the mercury rising sometimes to 100 in the day-time, and falling to 50 at night. The country is covered with snow for four months in the year.

New Brunswick is divided into ten counties. Frederictown, the political capital of the province, is situated on the south bank of the St. John's River. The other principal towns are—St. Andrew's, situated on the shore of the Passamaquoddy Bay; Liverpool, upon the coast of the Gulf of the St. Lawrence; Newcastle, at the mouth of Miramichi River; and Bathurst, on the south side of the fine Bay of Chaleurs.

CAPABILITIES OF NEW BRUNSWICK.

Professor J. F. W. Johnstone, F.R.S., in a report made to the Government, speaking of its agricultural capabilities, says, "The stranger, if he penetrates beyond the Atlantic shores of the province, and travels through the interior, will be struck by the number and beauty of its rivers, by the fertility of its river islands and intervales, and by the great extent and excellent condition of its roads, and, upon the whole, of its numerous bridges. He will see boundless forests still unreclaimed, but will remark at the same time an amount of actual progress and prosperous advancement, which, considering the recent settlement and small revenue of the province, is really surprising."

Major Robinson, R.E., in his report, thus describes the province:—"Of the climate, soil, and capabilities of New Brunswick it is impossible to speak too highly. There is not a country in the world so beautifully wooded and watered. An inspection of the map will show that there is scarcely a section of it without its streams, from the running brook up to the navigable river. Two-thirds of its boundary are washed by the sea; the remainder is embraced by the large rivers—the St. John and the Restigouche. For beauty and richness of scenery, this latter river and its branches are not surpassed by anything in Great Britain. The lakes of New Brunswick are numerous and most beautiful. Its surface is undulating, hill and dale, varying up to mountain and valley. It is everywhere, except a few peaks of the highest mountains, covered with a dense forest of the finest growth. The country can everywhere be penetrated by its streams. In some parts of the interior, by a portage of three or four miles, a canoe can float away either to the Bay of Chaleurs and the Gulf of St. Lawrence, or down to St. John's in the Bay of Fundy.

THE FORESTS.

As we have before stated, New Brunswick is unusually rich in the amount and variety of her forest-trees, the principal of which are the white pine, the black spruce, the American larch, the black and yellow birch, the white and red beech, the white and red elm, the hemlock spruce, the butternut, the white and black ash, the white cedar, the white maple, and red flowering maple, the white and canoe birch, the balsam poplar, the American aspen, the alder, the willow, the wild cherry, the basswood, the hornbeam, the ironwood, the white spruce, the American silver fir, and last, but most useful of all, the maple sugar-tree. This tree is not only useful for its wood, but furnishes a syrup superior to treacle and molasses, and a sugar which is not only consumed at home, but proves a profitable article of commerce; besides this, it furnishes the best fuel, the best charcoal, and its ashes are rich in alkaline matter. The maple sugar is not only admirably adapted for tea and coffee, but it is delicious as a candy. All that is required to obtain it at the proper season—usually about the 1st of March—is to bore small holes in the trunks of the trees, and the sap is caught in boilers. This is boiled to the consistency of a syrup, kept skimmed to remove impurities, and then poured into moulds. Each tree ordinarily yields about 20 gallons of sap, which will make five or six pounds of sugar. The quantity of sugar obtained in 1861 in New Brunswick was 500,000 lbs.

The amount of timber exported from New Brunswick in 1854 was 127,567 tons; deals (M. feet), 258,004; boards and planks (M. feet), 19,256; masts and spars (No.), 3794; ship knees (No.), 15,248; lathwood (cords), 2223; sawed laths (M.), 19,672; shingles (M.) 24,837; box-shooks (No.), 142,672; besides wood in many other shapes.

In 1850 there were 86 vessels built, the total tonnage of which was 30,356, and the value £242,852 sterling. In 1860 there were 100 vessels, 41,003 tons, value £328,024 sterling.

In 1860 St. John's owned 492 vessels, 123,425 tons, value

£987,400; Miramichi, 132 vessels, 14,910 tons, value £119,380; St. Andrew's, 201 vessels, 8748 tons, value £69,984. Total in 1860 owned in New Brunswick, 825 vessels, 147,083 tons, value £1,176,664 sterling; in 1861, 813 vessels, 158,240 tons; in 1862, 814 vessels, with a tonnage of 157,718.

The produce of the forest in 1860 was 3,180,428 dollars; in 1861, 3,447,910 dollars; in 1862, 2,810,188 dollars.

THE FISHERIES.

In the Bay of Fundy there is the cod, pollock, hake, haddock, herring, mackerel, halibut, and sea-shad, besides numerous tribes of small fish. The Gulf of St. Lawrence, the Bay of Chaleurs, and the mouth of the Miramichi River, swarm with cod, hake, mackerel, salmon, and striped bass, besides oysters, lobsters, clams, crabs, shrimps, and mussels.

In the rivers the fisherman will find fresh-water trout in abundance, with striped bass, white and yellow perch, roach, dace, carp, and white fish.

MINERALS, FRUIT AND VEGETABLES, MANUFACTURES.

Minerals.—Among the most valuable productions are its minerals which may be thus enumerated—bituminous coal, iron ore, manganese, plumbago, lead, copper, granite, gypsum, limestone, marble, red sandstone, grindstone, oilstone, iceland-spar, roofing-slate, sulphuret of iron, bituminous shale (from which *kerosine* or *paraffine* is produced), plastic clay for bricks or pottery, peat, barytes, felspar, quartz, chlorite, jasper, soap-stone, and salt and sulphurous springs.

Fruit and Vegetables.—New Brunswick produces apples, pears, plums, currants, gooseberries, strawberries, raspberries, blackberries, great whortleberries, cherries, besides butter-nuts, hazel-nuts, and beech-nuts. The principal vegetables are potatoes, peas, and beans, turnips, beets, carrots, parsnips, cabbages, cauliflowers, celery, cucumbers, and squashes.

Manufactures.—In 1861 the value of manufactures was as follows:—Boots and shoes, £89,377; leather, £45,162; candles, £19,860; wooden ware (not cabinet-work), £20,505; chairs and cabinet-ware, £13,472; soap, £18,562; hats, £6360; iron castings, £20,205.

COUNTIES.

The various counties are Restigouche County, Gloucester County, Northumberland County, Kent County, Westmoreland County, Albert County, St. John County, Charlotte County, King's County, Queen's County, Sunbury County, York County, Carleton County, Victoria County.

RESTIGOUCHE COUNTY contains 1,426,560 acres, of which 156,979 acres are granted and 1,269,581 acres are vacant; 8895 acres only are cleared. The soil is fertile, and produces fine crops.

GLOUCESTER COUNTY contains 1,037,440 acres—332,902 acres have been granted, and 704,538 acres are yet vacant. The cleared land is 19,812 acres. In 1851, 14,302 grindstones were made and 21,157 lbs. of maple sugar.

NORTHUMBERLAND COUNTY contains 2,980,000 acres, of which 986,168 acres were granted and 1,993,832 are still vacant. The cleared land amounts to 30,221 acres.

KENT COUNTY contains 1,026,000 acres—386,398 granted, 640,002 vacant, 35,496 cleared.

WESTMORELAND COUNTY contains 878,440 acres—577,440 granted, 301,000 vacant, 92,822 cleared.

ALBERT COUNTY contains 433,560 acres—233,700 granted, 199,860 vacant, 32,210 cleared.

ALBERT COUNTY.—This county contains 414,720 acres—309,147 granted, and 105,573 vacant. The population in 1861, with Portland, was close upon 50,000 souls. It occupies a commanding position, and contains 4500 inhabited houses and 4300 stores, barns, and outbuildings. It possesses numerous saw-mills, grist-mills, tanneries, foundries, breweries, factories, and ship-yards. There are three banks—the Bank of New Brunswick, the Commercial Bank of New Brunswick, and a branch of the Bank of British North America. The commerce is large and increasing—about 2000 vessels entering and departing each year.

CHARLOTTE COUNTY contains 783,360 acres—317,245 granted, 466,115 vacant, 45,656 cleared.

KING'S COUNTY contains 849,920 acres—662,752 granted, 187,168 vacant, 120,923 cleared.

QUEEN'S COUNTY contains 961,280 acres—514,204 granted, 444,076 vacant, 63,719 cleared.

SUNBURY COUNTY contains 782,002 acres—377,078 granted, 405,002 vacant, 15,587 cleared.

YORK COUNTY contains 2,201,600 acres—970,914 granted, 1,230,686 vacant, 69,017 cleared.

CARLETON COUNTY contains 700,000 acres—465,802 granted, 234,198 vacant, and 55,537 cleared.

VICTORIA COUNTY contains 2,872,000 acres—345,600 granted, 2,526,400 vacant, 26,834 cleared.

COMMERCE.

In 1860 the imports from the United States were £688,217, the total imports were £1,446,740; the exports to the United States were £248,378, the total exports, £916,372. In 1861 the imports from the United States were £628,070, the total imports were £1,238,133; the exports to the United

States were £175,654, the total exports were £947,091. In 1862, the imports to the United States were £616,814, the total imports were £1,291,604; the exports to the United States were £185,295, the total exports £803,445. The value of exports and imports in 1862 was—exports, 3,856,528 dollars; imports, 6,199,701 dollars. Of the imports, 2,960,703 dollars were from the United States, and of the exports, 889,416 dollars were to the United States.

The produce of mines and minerals for 1860, was 395,540 dollars; in 1861, 332,970 dollars; in 1862, 303,477 dollars. The produce of fisheries was, in 1860, 374,408 dollars; in 1861, 269,249 dollars; in 1862, 303,477 dollars.

FINANCES (1862).

The receipts for the year were 668,197 dollars, and the expenditure was 675,189 dollars; or, in sterling, the revenue was, 1862, £148,960. In 1863 the revenue was £176,000. The expenditure in 1862 was £166,766 sterling; that of 1863 considerably within the income.

Principal Sources of Revenue.—Railway impost, 93,000 dollars; import duties, 515,000 dollars; export duties, 55,000 dollars; casual revenue, &c., 20,000 dollars; court fees, 4300 dollars; proceeds of seizures, 1000 dollars; auction duty, 200 dollars.

Principal Items of Expenditure.—Civil list, 58,000 dollars; legislature, 47,343 dollars; judiciary, 12,130 dollars; collection of revenue, 40,346 dollars; post-office, 26,400 dollars; public works, 124,290 dollars; education, 116,275 dollars; interest on railway debt, 146,170 dollars; interest on debentures, &c., 45,364 dollars; lunatic asylum, 16,000 dollars; agriculture, 9734 dollars; penitentiary, 7200 dollars.

Public Debt.—The public debt of the province appears to be divisible into three classes, as follows:—Funded debt, 398,733 dollars; floating debt, 649,553 dollars—total of debt proper, 1,048,286 dollars. Railway debt, 4,739,880 dollars. Aggregate, 5,788,166 dollars. The railway obligations were incurred on account of aid extended to the European and North American Railway and the St. Andrew's and Quebec Railway.

GOVERNMENT (JANUARY, 1864).

Lieut.-Governor Commander-in-Chief, &c., since Oct. 26, 1861, His Excellency the Honourable Arthur Hamilton Gordon, C.M.G.

Executive Council, or Ministry.—Provincial Secretary, Hon. S. L. Tilley—salary, 2400 dollars; Attorney-General, Hon. J. M. Johnson, jun.—salary, 2400 dollars; Surveyor-General, Hon. J. M'Millan—salary, 2400 dollars; Postmaster-General, Hon. J. Steadman—salary, 2400 dollars; Chief Commander of Board of

Works, Hon. G. L. Hathway—salary, 2400 dollars; Solicitor-General, Hon. C. Watters—salary, 1000 dollars. Without office: Hon. E. Perley, Hon. W. H. Steeves, Hon. P. Mitchell.

Other Executive Officers.—Provincial Treasurer, B. Robinson, Esq.; Auditor-General, J. R. Partelow, Esq.; Comptroller of Customs, &c., Wm. Smith, Esq.; Emigration Agent, R. Shives.

The Lieutenant-Governor is appointed by the Crown, and is the representative of royalty in the province. He selects the Executive Council from the majority side of the Provincial Legislature, and they are responsible for the government. Of the members of the Ministry above named, all are from the House of Assembly excepting Messrs. Steeves and Mitchell, who are from the Legislative Council.

Provincial Legislature.—This body consists of a Legislative Council of 21 Members, appointed for life by the Crown (with the concurrence of the Executive Council), and a House of Assembly of 41 Members, chosen by the qualified electors of the province for a term of four years. The qualification for membership of the Assembly is the ownership of a freehold of the clear value of £300 —about 1500 dollars. All elections are by ballot; and every male British subject is a voter who is not legally incapacitated, and who is assessed on the registry for real estate to the value of £25, or personal estate to the value of £100, or having an annual income of £100.

Judiciary : Supreme Court.—Chief Justice, Sir James Carter, Kt.; Master of the Rolls, Hon. Neville Parker; Judges, Hon. R. Parker, Hon. S. Ritchie, Hon. L. A. Wilmot.

PUBLIC SCHOOLS, MILITIA OF THE PROVINCE, CENSUS OF 1861, AGRICULTURE IN 1860.

Public Schools.—From the report of John Bennett, Esq., Chief Superintendent of Schools, we compile the following statistics, exhibiting the condition of the public schools of the province for the year 1862:—Whole number of children between the ages of six and sixteen, 64,000; attendance during the year, 29,500; number of teachers, 810. Provincial expenditure on account of schools, 94,437 dollars; amount of local contributions, 106,524 dollars—total expenditure for schools, 200,961 dollars. Expended for superior schools, 5288 dollars; superior schools in operation, 23; number of pupils in superior schools, 1164; average annual salary of teachers in superior schools, 566 dollars. Number of school-houses built, 1862, 68. In the superior schools Greek was taught in 2, Latin in 15, French in 9, and the mathematics in all. Besides the foregoing, there is a training-school for educating teachers, into which 167 applicants were admitted after passing an examination, at which 27 applicants were rejected. There are also 12 grammar schools, in which there were, in 1862, 397 pupils.

Latin and the mathematics were taught in all these schools, Greek in 7, and French in 8.

Militia of the Province.—The return of the enrolled militia for 1862 is as follows :—Volunteers, 1738 ; 1st class—single men, and widowers without children, 18,859 ; 2nd class—married men, and widowers with children, 6131 ; sedentary militia (over 45), 3714. Total, 30,442.

Census of 1861.—Inhabitants: males, 129,948 ; females, 122,099—total, 252,047. Native born, 199,445 ; foreign born, 52,602. Indians, 1112 ; coloured, 1591. Religions : Catholics, 85,238 ; Baptists, 57,730 ; Episcopalians, 42,776 ; Presbyterians, 36,072 ; Methodists, 25,637 ; Congregationalists, 1290 ; Christians, 1326 ; Universalists, 646 ; Covenanters, 559 ; all others, 773. Deaf and dumb, 166 ; blind, 172 ; insane or idiotic, 518. Births in 1860, 8722 ; marriages in 1860, 905 ; deaths in 1860, 2390. Dwellings inhabited, 33,700 ; dwellings uninhabited, 1537 ; houses building, 1695 ; stores, barns, &c., 46,464. The increase of population in the province in the ten years, from 1851 to 1861, was 30·05 per cent. Of the whole population 49·76 per cent. are agricultural, or very nearly one-half ; 21·71 per cent. are labourers ; 15·90 per cent. are mechanics and handicraftsmen ; 4·48 are engaged in commerce ; 3·93 in the fisheries and at sea ; 1·85 are professional ; and the remainder miscellaneous.

Agriculture (1860).—Wheat, 279,775 bushels ; barley, 5227 acres ; barley, 94,679 bushels ; oats, 96,268 acres ; oats, 2,656,883 bushels ; buckwheat, 41,936 acres ; buckwheat, 904,321 bushels ; Indian corn, 635 acres ; Indian corn, 17,420 bushels ; rye, 3944 acres ; rye, 57,504 bushels ; potatoes, 37,667 acres ; potatoes, 4,041,339 bushels ; flax (scutched), 4,501,477 lbs. ; butter, 218,067 lbs. ; wool, 633,757 lbs. ; pork (slaughtered), 9,692,169 ; maple sugar, 230,066 ; hay, 324,169 tons.

The Lieutenant-Governor, in his report to the Colonial Secretary, says :—" The year 1862 has, on the whole, been one of progress ; and, although the effects of the war on this continent are undoubtedly still severely felt, prosperity has revived more rapidly than could have been anticipated. Agricultural occupations were attended with abundant success, and I may safely conclude with the expression of my belief that the province at large is thriving and contented."

CHAPTER VII.

THE CANADAS.

The Lakes, Rivers, and Canals—The Pictured Rocks—The Great Lakes—Mineral Wealth—Commerce, Shipping, Trade, and Statistics—Rivers—The Rapids—Canadian Song—Emigration—Montreal, Toronto, Quebec, Kingstown, Hamilton, Cobourg, &c.—The Farming Interest of Canada—Agricultural Statistics and Tables.

GENERAL DESCRIPTION.

CANADA is bounded on the south by the United States; upon the north side it has no defined limit, but is regarded as including all the country watered by streams which flow into the St. Lawrence—that is, all the land which lies within the watershed between the St. Lawrence and the rivers falling into Hudson's Bay. It extends in an irregular line for 1300 miles, while its breadth varies from 100 to 300 miles.

Its astronomical position is between latitudes 41° 47' and 52° 40' north, and between longitudes 61° 54' and 90° 20' west.

The whole area covered by the Canadas is 340,000 square miles (or 240,000,000 acres), 140,000 of which belong to Upper Canada and 200,000 to Lower Canada. The frontier between Canada and the United States is formed by the great lakes and the course of the river St. Lawrence, as far as the point where that stream is intersected by the parallel of 45°, thence by the line of that parallel as far east as the meridian of 71° and to the south-east of the river, and terminates at the head of the Bay of Chaleurs, on the west side of the St. Lawrence. To the north of the 49th parallel, therefore, both banks of the St. Lawrence are included within British territory.

The general topography is as follows :—The province is divided into Upper or Western Canada and Lower or Eastern Canada. Lower Canada contains five districts—Gaspé, Quebec, Three Rivers, St. Francis, and Montreal, which are subdivided into thirty-six counties. The two important cities of Montreal and Quebec are in this portion of the province.

Upper Canada is divided into twenty districts, which are again subdivided into counties. Toronto, Ottawa, Kingston, Cobourg, London, Oxford, Guelph, Stratford, Chatham, Goderich, and Amherstburg, are all cities and towns which will contrast favourably with the best of the interior cities and towns of England, while in a progressive sense they are far in advance.

Upper Canada is generally level, with but few variations, excepting some table heights, and is considered the most fertile.

Lower Canada is extremely varied and beautiful in its physical aspect, presenting to the delighted eye a magnificent gallery of charming pictures of forest wilds, prairies, hill and rock bound rivers, rushing waters, bold mountain heights, and all everywhere intermingled, and their attractions embellished by intervening stretches of cultivated fields, and rural villages and villa homes.

The mountains are confined to Canada East. The principal mountains are the Laurentides, which stretch from Lake Superior to Labrador and separate the valley of the St. Lawrence from the region tributary to Hudson's Bay; the Green Mountains, which lie along the St. Lawrence; the Mealy Mountains, which in some places attain an altitude of 1500 feet; and the Wotchish Mountains.

THE LAKES AND RIVERS.

The grand lakes of the world wash a greater portion of the shores of Canada. Lakes Superior, Huron, St. Clair, Erie, Ontario, and the River St. Lawrence, with the assistance of the St. Lawrence and Welland Canals, afford internal navigation for vessels a distance of over 2000 miles from the ocean. According to the last Government survey, the following is the exact measurement of these lakes:— Lake Superior: greatest length, 855 miles; greatest breadth, 160 miles; mean depth, 988 feet; height above the sea, 627 feet; area, 31,000 square miles. It is united by means of the St. Mary's River, and a system of splendid locks, with Lake Huron, into which it pours its waters. Lake Huron: greatest length, 200 miles; greatest breadth, 160; mean depth, 300 feet; height above the sea, 574 feet; area, 20,000 square miles. It is divided by the great Manitonbrin Island into two parts, the northern one of which is called Georgian Bay. French River, which is situated on its northern portion, connects Lake Nipissing with Lake Huron. A canal of 29 miles would open navigation with the Ottawa River, which would save traversing Lake Erie and Lake Ontario, and shorten the distance from Montreal to either Chicago or Fond du Lac, on Lake Superior, 344 miles. The distance between the French River and Montreal is 430 miles. The distance between Chicago and Montreal, *viâ* Lake Erie, Ontario, and the St. Lawrence River, is 1348 miles; by the Ottawa and Huron Canal route, 1005 miles.

Lake Michigan, another of the grand fresh-water seas, is connected with Lake Huron by the Straits of Mackinaw. It contains an area of 20,000 square miles: greatest length, 360 miles; greatest breadth, 108 miles; mean depth, 900; height above the sea, 587 feet. Green Bay, a portion of Lake Michigan, and situated on its western aspect, has an area of 2000 square miles. Lake St. Clair unites Lake Erie and Lake Huron. It is 265 miles long and 50 broad, and covers an area of 360 miles. Its mean depth is 120 feet. Lake Erie possesses an area of 6000 square miles: greatest length, 250 miles; greatest breadth, 80 miles; mean depth, 200 feet; height above the sea, 555 feet. The whole of these waters discharge twenty millions of cubic feet, or 600,000 tons per minute, over an abrupt precipice which forms the Falls of Niagara; and then pass along Niagara River, till they enter Lake Ontario. In order to connect navigation, the Welland Canal was constructed between Lake Erie and Lake Ontario. It consists of the Feeder branch from Grand River to Junction, and is 21 miles in length. The Broad Creek branch, from Lake Erie to the Feeder, is a mile in length; and the Main Trunk, from Lake Erie to Lake Ontario, 28 miles, the total cost of which was 6,269,000 dollars, or little more than £1,250,000.

Lake Ontario: length, 180 miles; mean breadth, 65 miles; mean depth, 500 feet; height above the sea, 262 feet; area, 6000 square miles. Total length of five lakes, 1345 miles; total area, 84,000 square miles. The scenery of the lakes excites the wonder of all travellers. There is nothing similar to it in Europe, as far as our observation and reading will permit us to judge.

Lake Superior is situated between latitudes 46° and 49°, with an altitude of over 200 yards above the level of the ocean, and a depth reaching far below that level; a coast of surpassing beauty and grandeur, more than 1200 miles in extent, and abounding in geological phenomena, varied mineral wealth, agates, cornelian, jasper, opal, and other precious stones; with its rivers, bays, estuaries, islands, presque isles, peninsulas, capes, pictured rocks, transparent lakes, leaping cascades, and bold highlands, limned with pure veins of quartz, spar, and amethystine crystals, full to repletion with mineral riches; reflecting in gorgeous majesty the sun's bright rays, and the moon's mellow blush; o'ertopped with ever-verdant groves of fir, cedar, and the mountain ash; while the background is filled up with mountain upon mountain, until rising in majesty to the clouds, distance loses their inequality, resting against the clear vault of heaven.

THE PICTURED ROCKS.

Lake Superior is surrounded by a cordon of flourishing cities and villages, which is only broken by the Pictured Rocks and iron and copper mines. The Pictured Rocks have been so minutely and graphically described, and in construction and appearance are so entirely novel and beautiful, that we have transferred an extract from Messrs. Foster and Whitney's " Report of the Geology of the Lake Superior District."

" Beyond the sand-beach at Miners' River the cliffs attain an altitude of 173 feet, and maintain a nearly uniform height for a considerable distance. Here one of those cascades of which we have before spoken is seen foaming down the rock.

" The cliffs do not form straight lines, but rather arcs of circles, the space between the projecting rocks having been worn out in symmetrical curves, some of which are of large dimensions. To one of the grandest and most regularly formed we gave the name of 'The Amphitheatre.' Looking to the west, another projecting point—its base worn into cave-like forms—and a portion of the concave surface of the intervening space are seen.

"It is in this portion of the series that the phenomena of colours are most beautifully and conspicuously displayed. These cannot be illustrated by a mere crayon sketch, but would require, to reproduce the natural effect, an elaborate drawing on a large scale, in which the various combinations of colour should be carefully represented. These colours do not by any means cover the whole surface of the cliff, even where they are most conspicuously displayed, but are confined to certain portions of the cliffs in the vicinity of the Amphitheatre; the great mass of the surface presenting the natural, light-yellow, or raw-sienna colour of the rock. The colours are also limited in their vertical range, rarely extending more than thirty or forty feet above the water, or a quarter or a third of the vertical height of the cliff. The prevailing tints consist of deep brown, yellow, and grey —burnt sienna and French grey predominating.

"There are also bright blues and greens, though less frequent. All of the tints are fresh, brilliant, and distinct, and harmonize admirably with one another, which, taken in connexion with the grandeur of the arched and caverned surfaces on which they are laid, and the deep and pure green of the water which heaves and swells at the base, and the rich foliage which waves above, produce an effect truly wonderful.

"They are not scattered indiscriminately over the surface of the rock, but are arranged in vertical and parallel bands, extending to the water's edge. The mode of their production is undoubtedly as follows:—Between the bands or strata of thick-bedded sandstone there are thin seams of shaly materials, which are more or less charged with the metallic oxides, iron largely predominating, with here and there a trace of copper. As the surface-water permeates through the porous strata, it comes in contact with these shaly bands, and, oozing out from the exposed edges, trickles down the face of the cliffs, and leaves behind a sediment, coloured according to the oxide which is contained in the band in which it originated. It cannot, however, be denied that there are some peculiarities which it is difficult to explain by any hypothesis.

"On first examining the Pictured Rocks we were forcibly struck with the brilliancy and beauty of the colours, and wondered why some of our predecessors, in their descriptions, had hardly adverted to what we regarded as their most characteristic feature. At a subsequent visit we were surprised to find that the effect of the colours was much less striking than before: they seemed faded out, leaving only traces of their former brilliancy, so that the traveller might regard this as an unimportant feature in the scenery. It is difficult to account for this change, but it may be due to the dryness or humidity of the season. If the colours are produced by the percolation of the water through the strata, taking up and depositing the coloured sediments, as before suggested, it is evident that a long period of drought would cut off the supply of moisture, and the colours, being no longer renewed, would fade, and finally disappear. This explanation seems reasonable, for, at the time of our second visit, the beds of the streams on the summit of the table-land were dry.

"It is a curious fact that the colours are so firmly attached to the surface that they are very little affected by rains or the dashing of the surf, since they were, in numerous instances, observed extending in all their freshness to the very water's edge.

"Proceeding to the eastward of the Amphitheatre, we find the cliffs scooped out into caverns and grotesque openings, of the most striking and beautiful variety of forms. In some places huge blocks of sandstone have become dislodged, and accumulated at the base of the cliff, where they are ground up, and the fragments borne away by the ceaseless action of the surge.

"To a striking group of detached blocks the name of 'Sail Rock' has been given, from its striking resemblance to the jib and mainsail of a sloop when spread—so much so that, when viewed from a distance, with a full glare of light upon it, while the cliff in the rear is left in the shade, the illusion is perfect. The height of the block is about forty feet.

"Masses of rock are frequently dislodged from the cliff, if we may judge from the freshness of the fracture and the appearance of the trees involved in the descent. The rapidity with which this undermining process is carried on, at many points, will be readily appreciated when we consider that the cliffs do not form a single unbroken line of wall; but, on the contrary, they present numerous salient angles to the full force of the waves. A projecting corner is undermined until the superincumbent weight becomes too great, the overhanging mass cracks, and aided, perhaps, by the power of frost, gradually becomes loosened, and finally topples with a crash into the lake."

It is impossible, by any arrangement of words, or by any combination of colours, to convey any idea of this wonderful scene.

We remember once entering a cave, by the side of whose grand proportions the portal, the nave, and the dome of St. Paul's sink into insignificance. Two hundred feet in height, 400 feet in width, and for a distance of 600 feet, this structure projected into the lake. The grand portal, which opens out on the lake, is of magnificent dimensions, being about 100 feet in height, and 168 feet broad at the water-level. The distance from the verge of the cliff over the arch to the water is 133 feet, leaving 33 feet for the thickness of the rock above the arch itself. The extreme height of the cliff is about 50 feet more, making in all 180 feet. The vast dimensions of the cavern; the vaulted passages; the varied effects of the light, as it streams through the great arch and falls on the different objects; the deep emerald green of the water; the unvarying swell of the lake, keeping up a succession of musical echoes; the reverberations of one's own voice coming back with startling effect: all these must be seen, and heard, and felt, to be fully appreciated. *Iron* mines and mountains are plentiful; and since their discovery, in 1846, and the completion of the Saut Ste. Marie canal, in 1855, they have been rapidly developed. The Jackson Mountains rise to a height of 600 or 700 feet, and are a solid mass of ore, yielding from 50 to 60 per cent., and at present yield 1000 tons a week. There is also the New England Iron Mountain, the Burt Iron Mountain, and the Cleveland Iron Mountain. The beds of ore are inexhaustible, and analysis and practical demonstration have proved them to be the richest and best in the world.

REPORT OF THE HON. S. P. CHASE.

In the Report of the Hon. S. P. Chase, Secretary of Treasury of the United States for 1864, he states as follows:—

In 1862, the number of vessels engaged in the trade of Lake Superior was, schooners, 543; tons, 175,595. Propellers, 121; tons, 65,124. Steamers, 174; tons, 124,833. Total, 365,552 tons. These vessels carried outward 150,000 tons of iron and iron ore, and 9300 tons of pure or native copper, valued together at 12,000,000 dollars. The inward or westward shipment of merchandise, machinery for working works, is estimated at 10,000,000 dollars.

Shipments of copper from Lake Superior from 1858 to 1862:—

	Tons.	Value.
1858	5,896	1,610,000 dollars.
1859	6,041	1,932,000 ,,
1860	8,614	2,520,000 ,,
1861	10,347	3,180,000 ,,
1862	10,000	4,000,000 ,,

Products of iron and iron ore in Lake Superior region:—

	Tons, Ore.	Tons, Pig.	Value.
1855	1,445		14,470 dollars.
1860	116,998	5,660	736,490 ,,
1861	45,430	7,970	410,460 ,,
1862	115,721	8,590	984,976 ,,

The Mineral Wealth of Lake Superior.—The whole basin of Lake Superior indicates the presence of iron and copper. The mountains which divide the waters of Lake Michigan to the south-east, of the Mississippi River and its tributaries to the south-west and west, of the Rainy Lake River to the north-west, and of Hudson's Bay to the north and north-east—the outer rim of the Superior basin —are found, wherever explored, to contain iron ore. The mines at Marquette, Michigan, have been successfully worked, in consequence of the construction of a railroad from the harbour of Marquette to the Iron Mountain, 18 miles distant; but iron deposits in the same mineral range are situated at no greater distance south of Bayfield and Superior, in Wisconsin, and thence have been traced around the north shore of the lake, in Minnesota and in Canada.

Nearer the lake coast, and apparently a lower formation, are the copper districts. The only locality on the southern shore which has attracted attention, is a district extending from Keweenaw Point to the Montreal River, 100 miles in length by 4 to 20 miles in width. On the north shore of the lake, in Minnesota, near the western extremity of the lake, and in Canada for a distance of 200 miles northwest from the Saut Ste. Marie, are well-defined copper regions which are now attracting the attention of capitalists, and will probably prove as productive as the Keweenaw, Portage Lake, Ontonagon, and Carp Lake districts, as the subdivisions of the Michigan copper-bearing territory are termed.

During the year 1863, discoveries were made in the vicinity of Marquette, which suggest that Michigan is destined to become, at an early day, a great silver-yielding State.* The newly-discovered district is known as the granite range, lying between the schistose or iron range and Lake Superior, and is from 10 to 20 miles in breadth, and about 50 miles in length. Lodes of argentiferous galena have been found in this region, yielding from 10 to 30 pounds of silver to the ton of metal. Assays made on some of the ores have discovered gold in them to the value of 60 to 240 dollars. If these statements are confirmed, the silver district of Lake Superior will exceed in value either of the ranges now yielding copper and iron.

Under the impulse of the present demand for iron and copper, the Minnesota district, extending from Fond du Lac to the Grand Portage at the mouth of Pigeon River, has been thoroughly explored with satisfactory results; while Canada has taken effective measures for the encouragement of mining enterprises on the remainder of the northern shore. Title to mineral lands on Lake Superior can now be acquired from Canada at one dollar per acre, subject to a tax of one dollar per ton of ore. This order will have the effect to transfer English capital to the Nepigon, Pic and Michipicoton districts of Lake Superior, as it is now admitted that the copper-mines of Great Britain have lately failed of their former productiveness. A correspondent of the London *Mining Journal* states that "the very rich mines of Cornwall and Devon are limited in the present day, and that some thirty or forty of the greatest and richest mines in those counties are exhausted, at least for copper." There were, in March, 1864, more than fifty bills before the Canadian Parliament to incorporate companies for mining gold, silver, lead, antimony, iron, and copper.

Similar and greater activity prevails in all the American districts of Lake Superior. The total amount of capital invested in the fee-simple and development of the copper-mines now worked in Michigan, not including the value of the metal produced, is estimated at 6,000,000 dollars, while their stocks are worth over 15,000,000 dollars. The aggregate amount of copper produced in 1863 was not less than 9000 tons of stamp work, barrel and mass, or about 7500 tons of ingot, worth at its present value over 6,000,000 dollars; but as the largest portion was probably sold at an average of 35 cents per pound, the aggregate receipt of sales will not be much over 5,000,000 dollars. The products of the Marquette iron-mines for 1863 are reported as 185,000 gross tons of ore, and 13,732 gross tons of pig iron. In 1855 the product of the same mines was only 1447 tons of iron ore, with no production of pig iron; in 1858, 31,035 tons of iron ore, and 1627 tons of pig iron.

The exports, of all values, for 1863, from Lake Superior, will amount to 10,000,000 dollars; imports, 12,000,000; consisting, in addition to provisions and merchandise for the mining villages, of

---

* In the same vicinity, the Huron mountains are reported to be gold-bearing, and at the latest date (June 13, 1864) there is a probability that the discoveries and production of gold in this district of the Lake Superior basin will fully equal the facts in regard to silver.

shipments of machinery and other materials for permanent improvements.

SHIPPING.

A review of the progress and increase of the shipping employed upon the lakes for the last few years will give an idea of the magnitude of the trade which is carried on, and also prove that it has been steadily progressive and remunerative.

Table showing the Number, Class, Tonnage, and Valuation of Vessels, American and Canadian, engaged in the Commerce of the Lakes, 1858 to 1864.

CLASS OF VESSELS.	AMERICAN.			CANADIAN.		
	No.	Tonnage.	Valuation.	No.	Tonnage.	Valuation.
1858—Steamers	72	48,031	....	67	24,784	....
Propellers	113	56,994	....	14	4,197	....
Tugs	69	6,366	....	5	415	....
Barques and Brigs	129	42,592	....	37	10,793	....
Schooners	830	177,170	....	212	32,959	....
Totals	1,213	331,153	....	335	73,148	....
			Dollars.			Dollars.
1859—Steamers	68	46,240	1,779,900	54	21,402	989,200
Propellers	118	55,657	2,217,100	16	4,127	140,500
Tugs	72	7,779	456,500	17	2,921	184,800
Barques	32	9,666	482,800	15	5,720	134,000
Brigs	64	30,452	456,000	14	3,295	78,400
Schooners	833	173,362	4,378,900	197	32,198	778,300
Totals	1,198	323,156	9,811,200	313	69,663	2,305,200
1860—Steamers	75	47,333	2,439,840	77	25,939	1,499,680
Propellers	190	57,210	3,250,390	27	7,289	407,290
Barques	44	17,929	584,540	23	7,882	246,460
Brigs	76	21,505	484,250	16	3,815	94,380
Schooners	831	172,526	5,233,085	217	31,792	898,560
Totals	1,216	316,503	11,992,105	360	76,717	3,146,390
1861—Steamers	65	42,683	1,489,800	63	21,107	1,019,200
Propellers	107	50,018	2,123,000	15	4,562	176,000
Tugs	91	9,155	565,700	22	4,842	202,300
Barques	48	19,616	469,000	19	7,153	188,500
Brigs	75	22,124	435,900	15	4,223	101,000
Schooners	843	180,357	4,525,000	222	33,771	822,300
Totals	1,229	323,953	9,608,400	356	75,658	2,509,300
1862—Steamers	66	43,683	1,403,800	64	28,104	1,020,200
Propellers	122	52,932	2,344,800	16	5,154	181,000
Tugs	132	17,280	922,200	22	8,482	202,300
Barques	60	26,555	786,800	22	7,871	224,500
Brigs	75	22,124	466,700	14	4,223	107,000
Schooners	908	199,423	5,439,800	229	35,062	872,500
Totals	1,363	361,997	11,364,100	367	88,896	2,607,500

Comparative Statement of the Tonnage of the North-Western Lakes and the River St. Lawrence on the 1st day of January, 1862 and 1863.

CLASS OF VESSELS.	1862.			1863.		
	No.	Tonnage.	Value.	No.	Tonnage.	Value.
			Dollars.			Dollars.
Steamers	147	64,669	2,668,900	143	53,622	2,190,300
Propellers	203	60,951	2,814,900	254	70,253	3,573,300
Barques	62	25,118	621,800	74	23,203	982,900
Brigs	86	25,871	501,100	85	24,831	526,200
Schooners	989	204,900	5,248,900	1,068	227,831	5,955,550
Sloops	15	2,800	11,850	16	667	12,770
Barges				3	3,719	17,000
Totals	1,502	383,309	11,862,450	1,643	413,026	13,257,020

The following is the increase of the lake marine in 1862, distinguishing American and Canadian vessels, as reported by the same authority:—

CLASS OF VESSELS.	United States Vessels Building.			Canadian Vessels Building.		
	No.	Tonnage.	Value.	No.	Tonnage.	Value.
			Dollars.			Dollars.
Steamers	3	1,114	83,550	2	970	72,750
Propellers	5	3,815	276,125	6	1,960	147,000
Propeller Tugs	8	1,194	89,550			
Barques	2	1,037	46,665	6	2,690	121,050
Schooners	38	15,546	654,570	10	3,100	139,500
Barges				19	6,600	198,000
Totals	56	21,706	1,150,455	43	15,320	678,800

Summary.

		Aggregate Tonnage.
5	steam-boats	2,084
11	propellers	3,775
8	steam tugs	1,194
8	barques	3,727
48	schooners	17,646
19	barges	6,600
99	vessels building. Total tonnage	37,026

The Chicago statement shows that 1730 vessels, with an aggregate capacity of 450,893 tons, were engaged in lake commerce of a general character, east and west, in 1862, of which one-fifth was Canadian.

Chicago shipped eastward, in 1862, 1,739,849 barrels of flour; 13,808,898 bushels of wheat; 29,452,610 bushels of corn; 3,112,366 bushels of oats; 871,796 bushels of rye; 532,195 bushels of barley; of which Canada, Collingwood, Goderich, Sarnia, Kingston, Port Colborne, Montreal, and Toronto received, in 1862—flour, 420,544 barrels; wheat, 3,098,424 bushels; corn, 6,005,661 bushels; oats, 157,252 bushels; rye, 200,659 bushels; barley, 71,919 bushels; being nearly one-fourth of the whole quantity.

RIVERS.

Canada is as rich in the beauty and extent of her rivers as she is proud of her share in the noble lakes that adorn the interior of America.

The St. Lawrence.—This is her grandest river, and drains the vast inland seas of America that extend from Lake Ontario, 750 miles, to the Gulf of St. Lawrence, and thence to the sea. The entire length, including the great lakes, by which it is fed, is 2200 miles. Its principal tributaries are the Ottawa and the Saguenay; and the lesser ones are the Richelieu or Sorel, the St. Francis, the Chaudière, and other streams.

The *Ottawa* is 780 miles in length, and 300 miles from its source it passes through Lake Temiscamin; 67 miles lower, at the head of the lake, Blanche River falls in. Thirty-four miles further down it receives the waters of the Montreal River, coming 120 miles from the north-west; next it receives the Keepawasippi, which has its origin in Lake Keepawa. Then, 197 miles below Ottawa City, it receives the Matawhan; next, the Petawawa River, 140 miles long, draining 2200 square miles; the Black River, draining 1120 square miles; the Madawoska River, 200 miles long, draining 4100 square miles; the Gastineau River, 420 miles long, draining 12,000 square miles; the Rivière du Lièvre, draining an area of 4100 square miles. One hundred and thirty miles below the city of Ottawa (the capital of the future British North American Confederacy) the waters of the Ottawa River, after draining 80,000 square miles of rich and fertile country, mingle with the noble St. Lawrence.

The *Saguenay* is another of the great tributaries to the St. Lawrence. It is almost straight in its direction, and crowned on either side by grand precipices. It has neither windings, nor projecting bluffs, nor sloping banks, nor sandy shores like other rivers, nor is its stern, strange aspect varied by either village or villa. "It is," says a voyager thither, "as if the mountain range had been cleft asunder, leaving a horrid gulf, of 60 miles in length and 4000 feet in depth, through the grey mica schist, and still looking fresh and new. One thousand five hundred feet of this is perpendicular cliff, often too steep and solid for the hemlock or dwarf oak to find root; in which case, being covered with coloured lichens and moss, their fresh-looking fractures often appear in shape and colour like painted fans, and are called the 'Pictured Rocks.' But those parts more slanting are thickly studded with stunted trees—spruce, maple, and birch growing wherever they can find crevices to extract nourishment; and the bare roots of the oak, grasping the rock, have a resemblance to gigantic claws. The bases of these cliffs lie far under water, to an unknown depth. For many miles from its mouth no soundings have been obtained with 2000 feet of line; and, for the entire distance of 60 miles, until you reach Ha-Ha Bay, the largest ships can sail, without obstruction from banks or shoals, and, on reaching the extremity of the bay, can drop their anchor in 30 fathoms. The view up this river is singular in many respects. Hour after hour, as we sail along, precipice after precipice unfolds itself to view, as in a moving panorama; and we sometimes forget the size or height of the objects we are contemplating, until reminded by seeing a ship of 1000 tons lying, like a small pinnace, under the towering cliff to which she is moored—for even in these remote and desolate regions industry is at work, and, although we cannot much discern it, saw-mills have been built on some of the tributary streams which fall into the Saguenay. But what strikes one most is the absence of beach or strand; for, except in a few places where mountain torrents, rushing through gloomy ravines, have washed down the *detritus* of the hills, and formed some alluvial land at the mouth, no coves, nor creeks, nor projecting rocks are seen in which a boat could find shelter, or any footing be obtained. The characteristic is a steep wall of rock rising abruptly from the water; a dark and desolate region where all is cold and gloomy; the mountains hidden with driving mist; the water black as ink and cold as ice. No ducks nor sea-gulls sitting on the water or screaming for their prey; no hawks nor eagles soaring overhead, although there is abundance of what might be called 'Eagle Cliffs;' no deer coming down to drink at the streams; no squirrels nor birds to be seen among the trees; no fly on the water nor swallows skimming over the surface. It reminds us of—

'That lake whose gloomy shore
Skylark never warbled o'er.'

Now we reach Cape Eternity, Cape Trinity, and many other overhanging cliffs, remarkable for having such clean fractures, seldom equalled for boldness and effect, which create constant apprehension of danger, even in calm; but if we happen to be caught in a thunder-storm, the roar and darkness and flashes of lightning are perfectly frightful. At last we terminate our voyage at Ha-Ha Bay, that is, smiling or laughing bay, in the Indian tongue, for we are perfectly charmed and relieved to arrive at a beautiful spot, where we have sloping banks, a pebbly shore, boats, and wherries, and vessels riding at anchor, birds and animals, a village church, French Canadians, and Scottish Highlanders." The course of the Saguenay is 126 miles from Lake St. John to the St. Lawrence, which it enters 140 miles below Quebec.

All the streams falling into the great lakes or the St. Lawrence River are mostly rapid, and are navigable only for a short distance from their mouths.

The following are the principal rivers that are navigable for any considerable length.

AMERICAN SIDE.

River	Route	Miles
St. Louis River, Min.	Superior to Fond du Lac	20
Fox, or Neenah, Wis.	Green Bay to L. Winnebago	36
St. Joseph, Mich.	St. Joseph to Niles	26
Grand River	Grand Haven to Grand Rapids	40
Muskegon	Muskegon to Newaygo	40
Saginaw	Saginaw Bay to Upper Saginaw	26
Maumee, Ohio	Maumee Bay to Perrysburgh	18
Genesse, N. T.	Charlotte to Rochester	6

CANADIAN SIDE.

River	Route	Miles
Thames	Lake St. Clair to Chatham	24
Ottawa	La Chine to Carillon	40
Ditto	By means of locks to Ottawa City	70
Richelieu or Sorel	Sorel to Lake Champlain by means of locks	75
Saguenay	Tadusac to Chicoutimi	70
	Thence to Lake St. John	50

It is said that the St. Lawrence River carries by Montreal 50,000,000 cubic feet of water per minute, and in the course of one year bears 143,000,000 tons of solid materials, held in solution, to the sea.

"The main stream of the St. Lawrence," says Buckingham, speaking of the Thousand Islands, "is so thickly studded with islands that it is like passing through a vast archipelago, rather than navigating a mighty river. They are for the most part rocky islets, sometimes rising in abrupt cliffs from the water, and so bold and steep that you may run the boat near enough to touch the cliffs from the vessel. A few only are low and flat, but being nearly all wooded they form a perpetual succession of the most romantically beautiful and picturesque groups that can be conceived. Among the Thousand Islands are usually found immense quantities of waterfowl and other kinds of wild game, which, during the spring and summer months, afford great pleasure to the sportsman. The fishing is also excellent for the most part of the year. During the months of July and August pleasure-parties from the surrounding country, and strangers from a distance, resort here for their amusement, enjoying themselves to their hearts' content by hunting, fishing, and bathing, being surrounded by wild and interesting scenery and invigorating air, not exceeded by any section of the United States or Canada."

The St. Lawrence River, in fact, for its entire length of several hundred miles, presents a magnificent appearance, well worthy the attention of the tourist.

THE RAPIDS.

The *Rapids*, now successfully navigated on their downward trip by steamboats of a large class, returning through the canals, afford a deeply interesting excursion. The cultivated fields and settlements interchanging with bolder features impart a grandeur as well as variety and beauty to the river and its shores, which no other stream on the continent possesses in an equal degree. Read the following description by a tourist describing his impressions of a trip down the St. Lawrence:—

"The St. Lawrence is, perhaps, the only river in the world possessing so great a variety of scenery and character in the short distance of 180 miles—from Kingston to Montreal. The voyage down this portion of the St. Lawrence in a steamer is one of the most exciting and interesting that our country affords to the pleasure-seeking traveller. Starting at daylight from the good old city of Kingston, we are at first enraptured by the lovely and fairy-like scenery of the 'Lake of the Thousand Isles,' and oft we wonder how it is that our helmsman can guide us through the intricate path that lies before him. Surely he will make some mistake, and we shall lose our way, and our steamer wander for ages ere the trackless path be once more discovered. However, we are wrong, and long before the sun has set we have shot the 'Long Saut,' and are passing through the calm and peaceful Lake St. Francis. Gently we glide along, and are lost in pleasing reveries, which grace the scenes of our forenoon's travel. Suddenly we are awakened from our dreams by a pitch, and then a quick jerk of our vessel, and rising to see the cause, we find ourselves receiving warning in the Coteau Rapids of what we may expect when we reach the Cedars, a few miles farther on. Now the bell is rung for the engine *to slow* its speed, and, glancing toward the beam, we find it merely moving sufficient to keep headway on the vessel; now looking toward the wheelman's house, we see four men standing by the wheel; backward we turn our gaze, and four more stand by the *tiller*, to assist those at the wheel in guiding our craft down the fearful leaps she is about to take. These preparations striking us with dread, we, who are now making our first trip, involuntarily clutch the nearest object for support, and, checking our breath, await the first plunge. "Tis over." We are reeling to and fro, and dancing hither and thither among billows of enormous size, caused solely by the swiftness of the current. With difficulty we keep our feet while rushing down the tortuous channel, through which only we can be preserved from total wreck or certain death. Now turning to the right, to avoid a half-sunken rock, about whose summit the waves are ever dashing, we are apparently running on an island situated immediately before us. On! on we rush! we must ground! But no; her head is easing off, and, as we fly past the island, a daring leap might land us on its shores; and now again we are tossed and whirled about in a sea of foam. We look back to scan the dangers past, and see a raft far behind, struggling in the waves. While contemplating its dangers we forget our own, and the lines of Horace appear peculiarly applicable to the Indian who first entrusted his frail canoe to these terrific rapids—

'Illi robur et æs triplex
Circa pectus erat, qui fragilem truci

Commisit pelago ratem
Primus.——'"

Tom Moore has immortalized the Ottawa River and the little village of St. Anne's, situated at the south-west end of the island of Montreal, in verse :—

"CANADIAN SONG.

"By Thos. Moore.

" Faintly as tolls the evening chime,
Our voices keep tune and our oars keep time :
Soon as the woods on shore look dim,
We'll sing at St. Anne's our parting hymn.
  Row, brothers, row, the stream runs fast,
The Rapids are near, and the daylight's past.

" Why should we yet our sail unfurl?
There is not a breath the blue wave to curl ;
But when the wind blows off the shore,
Oh ! sweetly we'll rest our weary oar.
  Blow, breezes, blow, the stream runs fast
The Rapids are near, and the daylight's past

" Ottawa's tide ! this trembling moon
Shall see us float over thy surges soon.
Saint of this green isle, hear our prayers!
Oh! grant us cool heavens and fav'ring airs.
  Blow, breezes, blow, the stream runs fast,
The Rapids are near, and the daylight's past."

EMIGRATION.

The Canadian Almanac for 1864 contains such a concise and excellent chapter on the reasons for emigrating to Canada, and describes so graphically the peculiar features of the land, its capabilities, its physical characteristics, and the character of the people, together with such carefully-arranged statistics, showing their educational and religious status, that we have transferred much of it to these pages, believing that we cannot better serve the emigrant than by publishing a portion at least :—

"Ten Reasons for Emigrating to Canada.

" The aim of the man who contemplates changing the land of his birth for another being, generally speaking, the improvement of his condition, the question where the circumstances may be looked for most favourable to the realization of his desire, claims his best thought. Such thought he owes to himself, to his family if he has one, and to those among whom he may decide on taking up his abode ; because mistake in his choice may involve him and those he loves in disappointment and distress, and entail weakness on those to whom he should bring strength.

" In favour of the selection of Canada as his future home, the attention of the intending emigrant is respectfully invited to the considerations which follow:—

"1. *Its accessibility.*

" Compared with other regions open to him, it may be reached in a very short time (eleven days by steam), at a trifling expense, and with a small amount of inconvenience.

" In sailing-vessels, the rates of steerage passage vary, according to accommodation, from £3 to £4 or £5 sterling. The charge between Liverpool, Londonderry, or Glasgow, and Toronto, by the Montreal Steamship Line, is 34 dollars, including provisions; between Glasgow and Quebec or Montreal, 29 dollars. By the Anchor Line, the charge between Glasgow and Quebec is 25 dollars. The Great Eastern charges 30 dollars between Liverpool and New York. Its cabin rates are—1st cabin, 95-135 dollars; 2nd cabin, 70 dollars; 3rd cabin, 50 dollars. By the Montreal Line, the cabin passage varies, with accommodation, from 72-88 dollars. The cabin fare between Glasgow and Quebec, by the Ocean Line, is 68 dollars; intermediate, 44 dollars. By the Anchor Line, 60 dollars; intermediate 30 dollars. Children are carried by them all at lower rates, generally half-price.

" Once landed at Quebec or Montreal, the emigrant may pass on to Toronto, or Hamilton, or any intermediate locality, by steamboat or railway; and thence by railway to the western extremity of the province. The Northern Railway will take him to any place he pleases on the route between Toronto and Collingwood, Lake Huron, whence he can pass on to Owen Sound and intermediate places by steamer. The cost of the passage by deck of steamer and second-class cars is, from Quebec to Toronto, a distance of 500 miles, about 5 dollars, with corresponding rates for places intermediate; to Windsor, the western extremity of the province, 631 miles from Quebec, 7 dols. 12½ cents.; to Barrie, 565 miles, 6 dols. 50 cents.; to Collingwood, 593 miles, 7 dollars. The time between Quebec and Toronto is, by railway, about 36 hours; by steamboat, a day or two longer. Toronto may be reached by railway from Portland, the ocean terminus of the Grand Trunk, in from 25 to 26 hours.

" As, moreover, he may return to his old home so much more easily, should he for any reason wish to do so, he is less irretrievably committed by coming here than by going elsewhere. A visit to it is also at any time much more practicable, other things being equal. His friends may likewise, if so disposed, follow him with much less of difficulty; thus renewing associations of which necessity had compelled the temporary interruption.

" 2. *The scope afforded by its extent, both for the successful employment of his capabilities, and the gratification of his tastes in the choice of a home.*

" Leaving out the territory to the north-west, the opening of which may be looked for ere long, Canada occupies a space, stretching in a south-westerly direction from the Island of Anticosti in the Gulf of St. Lawrence, to the south-western extremity of Lake Erie, of about 1400 miles in length; with a breadth varying from 200 to 400 miles. Including water-surface, it is computed to contain an area of 349,821 square miles— 242,482 exclusive of water. The number of acres comprised within it is estimated at 160,405,219—128,659,684 of which are reckoned to Canada East; to Canada West, 31,745,533.

" 3. *The physical characteristics of the country, its natural resources, and its healthfulness.*

" In its mines, in its forests, and in its fisheries, Canada has stores of untold, of almost inconceivable wealth, which its numerous lakes and rivers supply facilities for conveying to market.

" Of metallic minerals, the following are enumerated in a catalogue contained in ' Canada at the Universal Exhibition, in 1855,' to wit, Magnetic Iron Ore, Specular Iron Ore, Limonite (Bog Ore), Titaniferous Iron, Sulphate of Zinc (Blende), Sulphate of Lead (Galena), Copper, Nickel, Silver, Gold. Non-metallic:—Teranium, Chromium, Cobalt, Manganese, Iron Pyrites, Graphite, Dolomite, Carbonate of Magnesia, Sulphate of Baryta, Iron Ochres, Steatite, Lithographic Stone, Agates, Jasper, Labradore, Felspar, Aventurine, Hyacinth, Corumdum, Amethyst, Jet, Quartzose Sandstone, Retinite and Basalt, Gypsum, Shell Marl, Phosphate of Lime, Millstones, Grindstones, Whetstones, and Tripoli. Under the head of ' Building Materials,' are specified Granites, Sandstone, Calcareous Sandstone, Limestones, Hydraulic Limestones, Roofing Slates, Flagging Stones; clays suitable for the formation of red and white bricks, tiles, and coarse pottery; Moulding Sand, Fuller's Earth; and Marbles, white, black, red, brown, yellow and black, grey and variegated, and green. Of combustibles—Peat, Petroleum, and Asphaltum are named. Some of these are confined to a single locality, others to a few places; but the more useful of them are widely distributed, and their quantities very great.

" Though our fisheries are as yet in their infancy, they employ from 1200 to 1500 boats, with nearly 100 vessels. The annual value of their products is, for Lower Canada, 942,528 dollars; for Upper Canada, 380,000 dollars; total, 1,322,528 dollars.

" Exclusive of furs, the products of the forest amounted, in 1860, to 11,012,253 dollars.

" Our climate, notwithstanding the extremes of cold and heat to which it is liable, which, however, are often greatly exaggerated, is eminently favourable, as the tables of longevity and the habits of the people prove, both to life and enjoyment.

" According to Professor Guy, the proportion of deaths to the population is, in

Austria	1 in 40	Belgium	1 in 43
Denmark	1 in 45	England	1 in 46
France	1 in 42	Norway and Sweden	1 in 41
Portugal	1 in 40	Prussia	1 in 39
Russia in Europe	1 in 44	Spain	1 in 40
Switzerland	1 in 40	Turkey	1 in 50
United States	1 in 74	Upper Canada	1 in 102
Lower Canada	1 in 92	All Canada	1 in 98

" ' The salubrity of the province,' remarks Mr. Hogan, from whom we have taken the above table, ' is sufficiently proved by its cloudless skies, its elastic air, and almost entire absence of fogs. The lightness of the atmosphere has a most invigorating effect upon the spirits. The winter frosts are severe and steady, and the summer suns are hot, and bring on vegetation with wonderful rapidity. It is true that the spring of Canada differs much from the spring of many parts of Europe; but after her long winter, the crops start up as if by magic, and reconcile her inhabitants to the loss of that which, elsewhere, is often the sweetest season of the year. If, however, Canada has but a short spring, she can boast of an autumn deliciously mild, and often lingering on, with its Indian summer and golden sunsets, until the month of December.

"' A Canadian winter, the mention of which some years ago, in Europe, conveyed almost a sensation of misery, is hailed rather as a season of increased enjoyment than of privation and discomfort by the people. Instead of alternate rain, snow, sleet, and fog, with broken-up and impassable roads, the Canadian has clear skies, a fine bracing atmosphere, with the rivers and many of the smaller lakes frozen, and the inequalities in the rough tracks through the woods made smooth by snow, the whole face of the country being literally macadamized by nature for a people as yet unable to macadamize for themselves.'

" 4. *The constituents and character of its population.*

" As a matter of course, its inhabitants share in the common characteristics of the races whence they have sprung—which include the leading peoples of Europe, those especially of the British Islands, and France and Germany—and natives of the United States. The circumstances in which they are placed—the constant demand on them for exertion during the earlier period of their residence in the country, the self-dependence they are called on to exercise, connected with the measure in which they are thrown on one another's sympathy, and the hope amidst which they work —have a direct tendency to develop not a few of their better qualities. Even the variety of their previous modes of thought and action, though occasioning perhaps for a time some inconvenience, is a gain to them in the end by the contributions which it enables them to make severally to the common stock of ideas, and the habit which it produces of tolerance for unessential differences, consideration for one another's feelings, and appreciation of each other's virtues.

" An incidental advantage of no small value, resulting from the variety of origin to which allusion has been made, is the sympathy which the new comer may look for from his countrymen, with the measure in which the privilege of association with them helps to make him feel himself at home. This is a source of comfort specially open to emigrants from Britain, France, and the neighbouring States.

" Among the larger portion of our people there exists, alongside of the variety of origin alluded to, a homogeneousness which greatly facilitates their welding into one community, imparting to them, while the process is going on, a coincidence of feeling which makes living among them easy and pleasant, and secures their acting together in all matters of special moment.

" The beneficial influence mutually exerted by the new comer and the older resident on one another, is well brought out in the following passage of Mr. Hogan:—

"' It is a remarkable fact that the farmers of Upper Canada have opportunities of improvement, and of enlarging and correcting their views, beyond what are enjoyed by many of their class even in England. And this arises from the circumstance of the population being made up of so many varieties. The same neighbourhood has frequently a representative of the best farming skill of Yorkshire, of the judicious management and agricultural experiences of the Lothians, and of the patient industry and perseverance of Flanders. In a country so peopled, the benefits of travel are gained without the necessity of going away from home. Other countries, in fact, send their people to teach Canadians, instead of Canadians having to go to other countries to learn; a thousand experiences are brought to their doors, instead of their having to visit a thousand doors to acquire them. Nor is the advantage of this happy admixture of population altogether on the side of the Canadian; for whilst he gleans from the old countryman his skill and his science, he teaches him, in return, how to rely upon himself in emergencies and difficulties inseparable from a new country, how to be a carpenter when a storm blows down a door and there is no carpenter to be had, and how to be an undismayed wheelwright when a waggon breaks down in the midst of a forest and there is no one either to instruct or assist him. The one, in short, imparts to a comparatively rude people the knowledge and skill of an old and civilized country; the other teaches skilled labour how to live in a new land. The consequence is, the old countryman of tact becomes, in all that relates to self-reliance and enterprise, a capital Canadian in a few years; whilst the Canadian, in all that pertains to skilful industry, becomes an Englishman.'

"The operation of the same fact—the mixed character of our population—on the culture of taste is shown in continuance of the above, but our space compels us to leave it unquoted. The principle may be applied more widely than it is by Mr. Hogan. Its power is, in fact, coextensive with our whole thinking and working.

"5. *Its institutions.*

"Nowhere is a more perfect freedom enjoyed than here. Of a state of liberty more complete it would indeed be difficult to form even a conception. We live under laws of our own making or voluntary adoption, administered in courts established by ourselves, and by judges of our own appointing. The men by whom our general affairs are managed are chosen by ourselves and responsible to us for their conduct. Our municipal system gives the people a power in local matters which is supreme, and affords to the more ambitious and intelligent among them an opportunity of preparing themselves for the performance of higher duties, as well as of attracting the notice and securing the respect of the community. Of influence or station, there is nothing among us to which the poorest may not aspire.

"The general features of the municipal law of Upper Canada, and which, with some modifications suited to the different state of society in Lower Canada, may be stated as the system in force throughout the province, are—

"The inhabitants of each county, city, town, and township, are constituted corporations, their organization proceeding wholly upon the elective principle; and provision is made for the erection of new municipalities, as the circumstances of the country require, by their separation from those already existing. A complete system is created for regulating the elections, and for defining the duties of the municipalities and their officers. Their powers may be generally stated to embrace everything of a local nature, including the opening and maintenance of highways, the erection of school-houses, and the support of common and grammar schools; the provision of accommodation for the administration of justice, gaols, &c., and the collection of rates for their support, as well as for the payment of petty jurymen; granting shop and tavern licences; regulating and prohibiting the sale of spirituous liquors; providing for the support of the poor; preventing the obstruction of streams; effecting drainage, both in the cities and county; inspection of weights and measures; enforcing the due observance of the Sabbath, and protection of public morals; establishing and regulating ferries, harbours, markets, &c.; abating nuisances; making regulations for and taking precautions against fires; establishing gas and water works; making police regulations; levying rates upon all real and personal property, including incomes, for all purposes; and, for certain objects, borrowing money; together with a great number of minor matters, essential for the good government of a community.

"In educational advantages we know of no country so young that exceeds us. By few of that class are we even equalled. Our common schools, established on the best principles, and taught by well-qualified and honourably-conducted teachers, offer to our youth at large the means of qualifying themselves for the intelligent and efficient performance of the duties awaiting them in their present social positions, or aiding them, if such be their wish, to raise themselves to such as are higher, either without cost or at a charge little more than nominal. For the obtaining of a still better culture our grammar-schools, which are rapidly improving in character, offer all reasonable facilities; while our colleges and universities place professional training and instruction in the higher departments of learning and science within the reach of the possessors of moderate means, or such as, in the absence of these, may be disposed to maintain for a time a manly struggle for their own advancement.

"From a valuable table (T) given in Dr. Ryerson's Report for 1861 we extract the following particulars, illustrative of the educational progress of Upper Canada, between 1842 and 1861.

"The number of common schools was, in 1842, 1271; 1847, 2727; 1852, 2992; 1857, 3631; 1861, 3910. The pupils attending these numbered in 1842, 65,978; 1847, 124,829; 1852, 179,587; 1857, 262,673; 1861, 316,287. Of Roman Catholic separate schools there are reported, for 1851, in which year they first appear in the returns, 16; 1857, 100; 1861, 109. There were, in 1845, 2860 common school teachers employed; in 1850, 3476; in 1855, 3565; and in 1861, 4336. There was paid for salaries of teachers of common and separate schools, erection and repair of school-houses, libraries, and apparatus, in 1850, 410,472 dollars; in 1855, 899,272 dollars; in 1861, 1,191,413. Of the schools thus reported there were 252 free in 1850; 1211 in 1855; and in 1861, 2903.

"In 1842, there are supposed to have been in existence 25 county grammar-schools. They numbered 32, in 1847; in 1852, 60; in 1857, 72; in 1861, 86. On these schools there were in attendance, in 1847, 1000 pupils; in 1852, 2643; in 1857, 4073; in 1861, 4766. The salaries paid the masters were, in 1855, the first year in which they are given separately, 46,255 dollars; in 1861, 71,034 dollars.

"In 1842, we have reported, in addition to the above, 44 separate schools and academies (a supposed approximation); in 1847, 96; in 1852,

181; in 1857, 276; in 1861, 337. The number of pupils in these institutions was, in 1847, 1831; in 1852, 5684; in 1857, 4073; in 1861, 4766:
"We had in operation, in 1847, 6 colleges, with an attendance of 700 students; in 1852, 8, with 751 students; in 1857, 12, with, 1335 (approx.); 1861, 13, with 1373 (approx.).

"The amounts reported as paid for educational purposes, in Upper Canada were, in 1851, 599,980 dollars; in 1856, 1,326,992 dollars; in 1861, 1,476,107 dollars.

"The following table, by J. G. Hodgins, LL.B., F.R.G.S., taken from 'Eighty Years' Progress,' &c. (p. 524), will give an idea of the educational advance of Lower Canada between 1852 and 1861:—

Year.	Educational Institutions of all kinds.	Pupils.	Assessments and Fees.
1853	2,352	108,284	165,848 dollars
1854	2,795	119,733	238,032 ,,
1855	2,868	127,058	249,136 ,,
1856	2,919	143,141	406,764 ,,
1857	2,986	148,798	424,208 ,,
1858	2,985	156,872	459,366 ,,
1859	3,199	168,148	498,436 ,,
1860	3,264	172,155	503,859 ,,
1861	3,345	180,845	526,219 ,,

"As to religious privileges, we are also on the whole favourably situated. The right of judging for ourselves in these matters is universally recognized; and in the eye of the law we stand on an equality. The common denominations have all a place among us, so that we may each, if such be our desire, have the opportunity of connexion, in the older portions of the country, at any rate, with those among whom we may have been brought up, or who may be preferred by us. Fair allowance being made for difference in circumstances, the means of instruction will compare favourably, as to character, in the greater part of these bodies, with those enjoyed by them elsewhere. Speaking generally, the usual forms of Christian exertion—the Sabbath school, Bible class, Bible, Tract, and Missionary Societies, and kindred organizations—are found in healthful and vigorous operation among them. Notwithstanding their differing views, these denominations, moreover, dwell side by side in peace, treat each other with the courtesies common in other parts of the Christian world, and co-operate with one another for common objects, as much at least as is common in the lands whence they have come. The institutions for the relief of want and distress in its various forms, which usually follow in the wake of Christianity, have place, and are carrying on their good work in our midst.

"6. *The union which it offers of the advantages characteristic both of the older and the newer states of society.*

"By selecting as their home the older parts of the country, those whose tastes would lead them to give the preference to the former may secure them in fair measure, provided they bring with them the necessary requisites in character, habits, and means; while such as are willing to share the usual fortunes of the latter, may calculate on the chances open to them in ordinary circumstances. Growth, with its attendant advantages, is in these chiefly a question of time and patience. At a much earlier age, and with much less of struggle than is requisite in older countries, the diligent and economical may hope to place themselves in a position of independence. As a general thing, the means of comfortable support is within the reach of the industrious, on conditions much less onerous than in these.

"7. *Its relations and status.*

"The emigrant to Canada has, in the fact of its forming part of the British Empire, the guarantee of one of the most powerful nations of the earth for his protection against injury from without. In this respect, as in every other, the mother country has of course a right to expect that we shall make every reasonable effort to help ourselves. Should the necessity arise, this will be done; and being done, there need be feared on her part no failure.

"Against the risk of any movement from within, which would interfere injuriously with him, he has equal assurance in the hearty loyalty and affectionate attachment of our people to the parent state, which would make them contemplate the prospect of separation with dislike, rather than pleasure.

"The connexion of Canada with Britain gives her also a standing which, in addition to its agreeableness, is fitted to render important aid in her development. It tends to operate thus by the feeling of self-respect which it inspires and fosters, by the honours which it holds out to the ambitious the hope of sharing, and by the examples that are felt to be constantly inviting imitation.

"Retaining, as he does, his connexion with the land of his birth, the native of the British Islands who chooses Canada as his home, is saved from much of the feeling of expatriation which he would experience elsewhere. He finds himself but half a stranger, if even that. He looks with a pride of which he was perhaps never previously conscious, on the old flag, as it floats over him; exults in his country's glories as his own; and finds a hymn in the National Anthem.

"8. *The steadiness and satisfactoriness of its growth.*

"A few particulars are all our space will admit in illustration of this.
"The population of United Canada numbered in the year 1800, 240,000. It was in 1825, 581,920; by 1851 it had reached 1,842,265. In 1861 it amounted to 2,506,755. The advance in Upper Canada between 1825 and 1861 has been from 581,027 to 1,396,091—not much less than 800 per cent. in 36 years.

"In 1831, the number of cultivated acres in the whole of Canada, Upper and Lower, was 2,884,345. It came up, in 1844, to 4,968,408; and in 1851, to 7,300,837. The returns for Lower Canada for 1861 have not yet been published. In Upper Canada alone, 6,051,619 are reported for that year.

"Upper Canada had in 1851, 99,906 occupiers of land. They numbered in 1861, 131,983. It produced in 1851, 12,682,550 bushels of wheat; 11,391,867 of oats; 9,982,186 of potatoes; 3,110,118 of turnips; 59,680 lbs. of flax or hemp; 3,669,874 lbs. of maple sugar. Its produce of these articles was, in 1861—wheat, 24,260,425 bushels; oats,

21,220,874; potatoes, 15,325,920; turnips, 18,206,959; flax or hemp, 1,225,934 lbs.; maple sugar, 6,370,605 lbs. The value of the live stock in Upper Canada was, in 1861, as much as 53,227,486 dollars; its agricultural implements, 11,280,347 dollars; its farms, 295,162,315 dollars. A similar progress will, we doubt not, be shown in Lower Canada, when its agricultural statistics for the year in question appear.

"In 1808, the value of the entire trade of Canada was about 8,400,000 dollars. The value reached in 1852—exports, 14,055,973 dollars; imports, 20,286,493 dollars; total, 34,342,466 dollars. In 1861, its imports amounted to 36,614,195 dollars; exports, 43,046,823 dollars; total, 79,661,018 dollars. The value of the trade with the United States alone was, in the last of these years, 35,455,815 dollars; the imports from that country reaching 21,069,388, and the imports to it 14,386,427 dollars.

"In 1851, the net revenue yielded by the customs was 2,808,831 dollars; in 1861, 4,411,160 dollars. The value of books imported was, in 1850, 243,580 dollars; in 1861, 5,056,943 dollars.

"On roads, navigation, and railroads, the province has expended as much as 60,000,000 dollars, over and above the interest in the latter of parties out of the country. There are in use at this moment between 1800 and 1900 miles of railway; besides 3422 of electric telegraph, belonging to the Montreal Telegraph Company, which had, in 1861, a capital stock of 400,000 dollars (to which it had advanced from 60,000 dollars in 1847), employed 400 persons (35 in 1847), and conveyed 300,000 messages; the number conveyed in 1847 having been 33,000.

"Our post-offices have multiplied from 3, in 1766, to 69 in 1824; 601 in 1850, and 1698 in 1860. The number of miles of established post roads was, in the first of these years, 170; in the second, 1992; in the third, 7595; and in the last, 14,202. The miles travelled were, in 1824, 369; in 1766, 616; in 1851, 2,287,000; in 1860, 5,712,000. In 1852, 3,700,000 letters were transmitted; in 1860, 9,000,000. The expenditure of the Post-Office was, in the former of these years, 276,191 dollars, and its revenue 230,629 dollars; in the latter, its expenditure was 534,681 dollars, and its revenue 658,451 dollars. One hundred and ten thousand dollars additional is paid per annum, by way of subsidy, to railroads, and 416,000 to steamships.

"From the above it will be seen that our growth has been rapid, steady, and general—not coming by fits and starts, or confined in its sphere.

"9. *Its prospects.*

"It cannot fail, without fault on the part of its people, to continue growing, and to become strong, and prosperous, and influential; for it has in itself, in its geographical position and in its relations, all the elements of greatness. But such failure is not to be anticipated, as self-respect, interest, and duty unite in urging us to make the best of our position. The worst part of the struggle is over. To carry us to the height of any reasonable ambition, all that is necessary is perseverance for a moderate time in the self-denial and exertion of the past, with the careful avoidance of its errors, as far as they may be discovered.

"The motive to throw in their lot with us, held out by such a state of things to those who may be contemplating change, is manifest. To witness progress is pleasant; how much more to share in it, and to be made partakers of the advantages it yields.

" 10. *The common feeling of such as have made trial of the country.*

"Few who have lived in it for any length of time, possessing the characteristics and pursuing the course necessary to success, would willingly exchange it for the lands whence they came. Nothing is more common than for those who visit their old homes, after a few years' residence in it, to feel impatient till they get back. Numbers who have left it with the intention of remaining at home, have returned to it, unable to enjoy themselves there. The freedom realized here from the burthensome restraints of older societies, and the social consideration which the deserving seldom fail to receive, help to explain the above state of feeling. In the fact of its existence the new comer, or the man contemplating coming, has fair promise and assurance that he will, in due time, feel himself one of us and at home among us.

" The classes to which Canada will be found specially adapted are—

" 1. Farmers, and parties accustomed to agricultural pursuits.

" These may, if they bring moderate means with them, find cleared or uncleared farms, according to their taste, in most parts of the country, at prices moderate, though of course varying with quality of land, value of improvements, and location. Such as may be without the advantage of means may generally, if prepared to accept of reasonable wages, find employment and comfortable homes among our farmers. By satisfying themselves for a time with these, they gain an acquaintance with the country, the modes of working best suited to it, the most desirable locations, prices of land, &c., which will save them much to which they would be in danger otherwise of being subjected, and help them to work at advantage to themselves.

" Though not in an equal degree, parties previously unaccustomed to agriculture, if disposed to devote themselves to it, may secure these advantages by the pursuance of the same course. Numbers are found all through the country, with good farms and in comfortable circumstances, who had their knowledge to acquire after their arrival. If possessed of the physical requisites and the power of adapting themselves to new circumstances, none who make up their minds to persevere need despair, though, compared with the others, they must labour for a time under disadvantage.

" 2. Mechanics, those especially of the more common descriptions.

"'These may generally find employment in one part or another, indeed in almost any part of the province, at fair wages and within a reasonable time. If well-behaved, industrious, and economical, they may hope to attain ultimately a good position both as to comfort and standing. Many of this class are to be met with in our cities, and even smaller towns and villages, living on their savings while yet comparatively young. Those of trades less common run, of course, more risk, though numbers even of these succeed in making themselves positions in the cities.

" 3. The possessors of spare means.

" What they may be able and disposed to invest will afford this class much better returns here, without the adoption of any course involving wrong, than at home. They may also, if desirous of making themselves useful, obtain (provided they possess the necessary requisites) abundant means of doing so in harmony with their habits and tastes.

" The things needful to success in Canada, without which none can hope for it, and with which none need despair of it, are—
" 1. Fair health, intelligence, and capacity for useful action.
" 2. Good principles and correct honourable habits.
" 3. Steady and patient perseverance.
" 4. A cheerful and hopeful spirit.
" 5. The blessing of God."

MONTREAL.

The principal cities of Canada are Montreal, Quebec, Toronto, Kingston, Hamilton, and Ottawa.

Montreal is situated at the foot of Royal Mountain, and contains the largest population of any city in British North America, amounting at the last census to over 75,000 inhabitants. She possesses numerous admirable hotels—such as the "St. Lawrence Hall" in Great St. James's Street, the "Donegana" in Notre Dame Street, the "Ottawa," Great St. James's Street; and the "Montreal House," Custom House Square. The churches are generally beautiful specimens of architecture, and are numerous. The French cathedral is the grandest cathedral in America; it is 255¼ feet in length, and 134½ feet in breadth; it has two towers, each of which has a noble elevation of 225 feet; it is capable of accommodating between 8000 and 9000 people. There is also a university, several seminaries, schools, and convents. The quays and the market are the finest on the continent, being built of solid limestone.

The trade of Montreal shows the following results:—The total exports for 1862 were 8,765,594 dollars. The imports for the same period, 20,183,836 dollars.

The amount of duties collected in 1862 was 2,490,557 dollars.

Exports of Flour, Grain, and Produce from Montreal.

ARTICLES.	SHIPMENTS IN 1861.			SHIPMENTS IN 1862.		
	By River St. Lawrence.	By Lachine Canal.	Total.	By River St. Lawrence.	By Lachine Canal.	Total.
Flour .... barrels	605,492	10,341	615,833	597,477	28,593	626,070
Wheat ...... bushels	5,584,727	17,044	5,601,771	6,500,796	37,257	6,538,053
Peas .... do...	1,529,136	2,029	1,531,165	711,192	1,626	712,818
Barley .... do...	2,472	105	2,577	373	84	457
Oats .... do...	276,375	2,800	279,175	8,072	16,716	24,788
Oatmeal ..... barrels	25,158	......	25,158	4,040	963	5,003
Corn .... bushels	1,477,114	......	1,477,114	1,774,546	......	1,774,546
Ashes ...... barrels	22,147	244	22,391	23,135	700	23,835
Butter .... kegs	49,546	176	49,722	59,804	......	59,804
Pork .... barrels	626	2,677	3,303	3,225	4,581	7,806
Lard .... do...	178	......	178	455	17	472
Beef....tcs. and bbls.	1,618	......	1,618	222	......	222
Tallow ..... barrels	112	28	140	154	35	189

Flour and Grain Trade of Montreal compared for the Three Years,
1861 to 1863.

ARTICLES.	1861.		1862.		1863.	
	Receipts.	Shipments.	Receipts.	Shipments.	Receipts.	Shipments.
Wheat .... bushels	7,829,684	5,900,100	8,529,622	6,945,815	5,506,324	3,806,306
Corn ....do...	1,565,477	1,477,114	1,661,611	1,774,347	855,328	635,387
Oats ....do...	122,399	287,877	96,792	8,072	373,463	3,001,766
Peas ....do...	1,409,859	1,409,859	534,679	727,277	....	....
Barley ......do...	132,749	2,457	236,930	373	294,524	640,380
Rye ....do...	24,812	....	82,665	200	32,278	170
Flour .....barrels.	1,081,160	654,966	168,174	632,052	1,173,096	692,868
Meal, Oat and Corn ... barrels	21,221	32,015	2,426	4,039	1,789	9,353

TORONTO.

Toronto is situated on Lake Ontario. It is 333 miles from Montreal; from Quebec, 501 miles; from Hamilton, 38 miles; and from Niagara Falls, 81 miles. The population is 50,000. It possesses a Parliament House, market, two or three colleges, some splendid churches, an exchange, a lovely park, and is a large, thriving, and beautiful city, which is advancing in wealth, extent, and in the number of fine rows of shops and dwellings. Its lake and railway commerce is large, as the following table of exports for 1862-61-60 will show:—

Detailed Statement for 1862.

DESTINATION.	FLOUR.	WHEAT.	BARLEY.	PEAS.
	Barrels.	Bushels.	Bushels.	Bushels.
Oswego	10,672	273,383	219,147	7,385
Cape Vincent	2,824	106,232	....	12,024
Rochester.................	450	8,025	....	....
Ogdensburg...............	8,385	7,586	....	4,847
Montreal	70,839	483,977	....	21,570
Quebec...................	645	17,743	....	1,090
Other Ports...............	12,404	36,329	....	466
Total................	106,219	933,275	219,147	47,382
Total, 1861...........	163,737	1,268,629	280,806	119,810
Decrease	57,518	335,354	61,659	72,428
Total, 1860...........	178,510	1,192,417	234,144	148,836

QUEBEC.

Quebec is one of the most famous fortified cities in the world, and has been called the Gibraltar of America. It is situated upon the left bank of the St. Lawrence, and contains a population of over 50,000. The city is divided into two sections, called the Upper and Lower Towns; the Upper Town occupying the highest part of the promontory, which is surrounded by strong walls and other fortifications; and the Lower Town being built around the base of Cape Diamond. The latter is the business quarter.

Quebec is 317 miles from Boston *via* the Grand Trunk Railway, 650 miles from New York, 168 miles from Montreal, and 340 miles from the ocean.

Quebec has numerous excellent hotels (the principal of which are "Russell's" and the "Clarendon"), a Roman Catholic cathedral, an English Protestant cathedral, artillery barracks, exchange, post-office, several banks, &c.

It possesses many attractions for the tourist, besides the citadel and the plains of Abraham, where Wolfe and Montcalm fought their great battle for the possession of Quebec, which resulted in a victory for the arms of England, though Wolfe fell in the moment of triumph.

Some of the most romantic falls in America are near Quebec. The Falls of St. Orme, only 24 miles below the city, are of great picturesque beauty. The Falls of the Chaudière are 130 feet high.

The Falls of Montmorenci, eight miles below Quebec, are 60 feet wide and 250 feet high.

The effect of the view of these falls upon the beholder is most delightful. The river at some distance seems suspended in the air, in a sheet of billowy foam, and, contrasted as it is with the black, frowning abyss into which it falls, it is an object of the highest interest. The sheet of foam which first breaks over the ridge, is more and more divided as it plunges, and is dashed against the successive layers of rock, which it almost completely veils from view; the spray becomes very delicate and abundant, from top to bottom, hanging over and revolving around the torrent, till it becomes lighter and more evanescent than the whitest fleecy clouds of summer; than the finest attenuated web; than the lightest gossamer; constituting the most airy and sumptuous drapery that can be imagined. Yet, like the drapery of some of the Grecian statues, which, while it veils, exhibits more forcibly the form beneath, this does not hide, but exalts the effect produced by this noble cataract.

Those who witness the falls in the winter, see one fine feature added to the scene, although they may lose some others. The spray freezes, and forms a regular cone of 100 feet and upwards in height, standing immediately at the bottom of the cataract, like some huge giant of fabulous notoriety.

Quebec is noted as the great lumber-port of Canada, and also as possessing fine ship-building yards. In 1861 there were built 53 ships, with a total tonnage of 26,737 tons, and two steamers. In 1861, 1277 ships, of 703,908 tons burthen. In 1861 there arrived at Quebec from sea, vessels: 1277; tonnage, 703,908; men, 19,339. Steamers: 67; tons, 71,894; men, 4335. The amount of timber shipped from Canada in 1861, was 30,000,000 cubic feet in the rough state; and about 400,000,000 feet, board measure, of sawed lumber, the value of which was 9,572,645 dollars.

The shipments of timber from Quebec, for the year ending December 1, 1862, as compared with those of 1860 and 1861, were as follows :—

	1860	1861	1862
Oak	1,485,400 ft.	1,725,160 ft.	1,463,680 ft.
Elm	1,021,560 ,,	1,269,329 ,,	1,099 200 ,,
Ash	88,440 ,,	96,560 ,,	99,840 ,,
Birch	462,160 ,,	255,320 ,,	165,480 ,,
Tamarac	58,240 ,,	50,240 ,,	57,120 ,,
White Pine, sq. and wavy	18,252,600 ,,	19,447,920 ,,	15,493,080 ,,
Red Pine	2,502,880 ,,	2,855,240 ,,	2,491,120 ,,

The stock on hand in 1862 exceeded by 9,000,000 that of the four previous years, being 19,000,000 instead of 10,000,000 feet.

KINGSTON, HAMILTON, COBOURG, ETC.

Kingston is a thriving city on the St. Lawrence River, and on the line of the Grand Trunk Railway. It is 341 miles from Quebec, 173 miles from Montreal, and 180 miles from Toronto. It was founded in 1783, and possesses at the present time several very strong fortifications. The population is about 18,000; the principal hotels are Kent's British American and Irons' Hotel.

Hamilton is situated at the head of Lake Ontario. It is 539 miles from Quebec; from Montreal, 371 miles; from Toronto, 38 miles; from Niagara, 43 miles. The population is 20,000.

Cobourg has a population of 5000. It is 70 miles from Toronto, and 90 miles from Kingston.

Prescott, St. Catherine, and Peterboro', are all thriving towns.

THE FARMING INTEREST OF CANADA.

The official census taken in January, 1861, furnishes reliable *data* for arriving at the agricultural condition of the country, and an official report from the Bureau of Agriculture, issued in 1863, provides estimates of two years later date. From these returns it appears that the number of persons in actual occupation of land in Upper Canada, in the year 1860, was not less than 131,983, and in Lower Canada 105,671. The quantity of land held was as follows:—

Persons holding in

	U. Canada.	L. Canada.
10 acres and under	4,424	6,822
10 acres to 20	2,675	3,186
20 acres to 50	26,630	20,074
50 acres to 100	64,891	44,041
100 acres to 200	28,336	24,739
Above 200 acres	5,027	6,809
Total occupiers	131,983	105,671

It thus appears that there were, three years ago, not fewer than 237,654 persons in Canada who cultivate their own land; and if the army of farm-servants, choppers, carpenters, blacksmiths, waggon-makers, harness-makers, &c., directly employed on farm-work, be added, it will be seen at once how vast a proportion of the half million of male adults in Canada are directly employed in the cultivation of the soil.

AGRICULTURAL STATISTICS AND TABLES.

Then as to the capital employed. The estimated cash value of the farms and farming implements was, in January, 1861, as follows:—

In Upper Canada . . . . . 306,442,662 dollars.
In Lower Canada . . . . . 178,870,271 ,,

Total value . . . . . . 485,312,933 dollars.

And this enormous sum does not include the live stock and crops on hand. The last census showed the live stock to have been then as follows:—

	U. Canada.	L. Canada.
Milch cows, No. of head	451,640	328,370
Oxen and steers	99,605	200,991
Young cattle	464,083	287,611
Horses, of all kinds	377,681	248,515
Sheep	1,170,225	682,829
Pigs	776,001	286,400

At present prices, these cannot be valued at much under 100,000,000 dollars; and the amazing rapidity with which the live stock of the country is increasing in number and value can readily be seen by a comparison of the census returns of 1851 and 1861.

But perhaps a more satisfactory idea of the agricultural industry of the province can be gained from a statement of the annual product of our farms. In the year 1860 the crop was as follows:—

		U. Canada.	L. Canada.	Total.
Wheat	bushels,	24,620,425	2,654,354	27,274,779
Barley	,,	2,821,962	2,281,674	5,103,636
Rye	,,	973,181	844,192	1,817,373
Peas	,,	9,601,396	2,648,777	12,250,173
Oats	,,	21,220,874	17,551,296	38,772,170
Buckwheat	,,	1,248,637	1,250,025	2,498,662
Indian corn	,,	2,256,290	334,861	2,591,151
Potatoes	,,	15,325,920	12,770,471	28,096,391
Turnips	,,	18,206,959	892,434	19,099,393
Man. wurzel	,,	546,971	207,256	754,227
Carrots	,,	1,905,598	293,067	2,198,665
Beans	,,	49,143	21,384	70,527

Clover and Timothy		U. Canada.	L. Canada.	Total.
seeds	bushels,	61,818	33,954	95,772
Hay	tons,	861,844	689,977	1,551,821
Hops	,,	247,052	53,387	300,439
Maple sugar	lbs.,	6,970,605	9,325,147	16,295,752
Cider	gallons,	1,567,831	21,011	1,588,842
Wool	lbs.,	3,659,766	1,967,388	5,627,154
Butter	,,	26,828,264	15,906,949	42,735,213
Cheese	,,	2,687,172	686,297	3,373,469
Flax and Hemp	,,	1,225,934	975,827	2,201,761
Tobacco	,,	777,426	...	...

The total value of these products of the farm in 1860 was close upon 100,000,000 dollars! And if we add the increase of that same year on the live stock, the improvements made on old farms, and the new lands brought into cultivation, a pretty good estimate may be formed of the highly satisfactory condition of the farming interest in Canada.

And then the work is but begun. The total number of acres that have passed from the Government into private hands is—

In Upper Canada 13,354,907
In Lower Canada 10,375,418

Total acres sold 23,730,325

Of this there are in cultivation, acres:—
In Upper Canada 6,051,619
In Lower Canada 4,804,235
——— 10,855,854

Leaving yet wild 12,874,471

Imports.—The total value of all the imports into Canada for 1862 was 48,600,633 dollars:—From Great Britain, 21,179,312 dollars; British Colonies, North America, 535,469 dollars; West Indies, 38,851 dollars; United States, 25,173,157 dollars; other countries, 1,673,844 dols. Amount of duty, 4,652,748 dols. 73 cents.

Exports.—Produce of the mine, 702,906 dollars; fisheries, 703,896 dollars; forest, 9,482,897 dollars; animals and their products, 3,923,590 dollars; agricultural products, 15,041,002 dollars; manufactures, 415,327 dollars; coin and bullion, 178,997 dollars; other articles, 242,002 dollars; ships built at Quebec, 988,428 dollars. Total value, 31,679,045 dollars; of which 15,224,417 dollars went to Great Britain, and 826,871 dollars to British North America; to the West Indies, 13,775 dollars; United States, 15,063,730 dollars; to foreign countries, 550,252 dollars.

Canals.—The canals of Canada have been built at an expense of 20,000,000 dollars. They consist of the Welland Canal, a little over 50 miles in length, running around the Falls of Niagara, and connecting Lake Erie with Lake Ontario. On the river St. Lawrence there are the Williamsburg, the Cornwall, the Beauharnais, and the Lachine Canals, 40—50 miles in length; and costing, with lock-gates and improvements, 8,550,518 dollars 35 cents. On the Richelieu River are the Chambly Canal, and St. Ours Lock and Dam, 11—50 miles in length; and costing 543,212 dollars 69 cents. On the Ottawa River, the St. Ann's Lock and Dam, and Chats Canal, cost 484,988 dollars 55 cents. The Carillon, Chute à Blondeau, and Granville Canal, passing the Long Saut of the Ottawa River, 8—84 miles; 1,011,904 dollars. The Rideau Canal, connecting Ottawa with Kingston, 126—25 miles; 4,380,000 dollars. These canals enable vessels to enter to and from the lakes.

CARRYING TRADE AND NAVIGATION OF THE PROVINCIAL CANALS OF CANADA.

No. 1.—*Summary Statement of the Business of the Welland, St. Lawrence, Chambly, Burlington, Ottawa and Rideau Canals, St. Ours and St. Ann's Locks, shewing the Total Quantity of each description of Property passed through and on the same, and the Amount of Tolls collected, during the year* 1862.

ARTICLES.	Welland Canal.		St. Lawrence Canal.		Chambly Canal & St. Ours Lock		Burlington Bay Canal.		St. Ann's Lock.		Ottawa and Rideau Canals.	
	Tons.	Tolls.	Tons.	Tolls.	Tons.	Tolls.	Tons.	Tolls.	Tons.	Tolls.	Tons.	Tolls.
		$		$		$		$		$		$
Vessels, all kinds.	1476,842	32,823	1049,230	13,427	154,532	1,764	286,718	1,751	241,729	3,021	373,32?	5,815
Passengers (No).	5,087	401	28,214	1,468	1,535	25	...	...	17,365	173	1,018	28
Produce of Forest.	238,213	26,385	381,305	13,172	87,296	5,731	47,467	3,314	212,268	3,009	316,500	9,593
Farm Stock......	134	33	1,268	174	232	8	103	9	246	12	2	...
Animal Produce..	9,116	2,367	7,526	1,470	438	55	3,142	1,633	728	36	905	93
Vegetable Food ..	721,149	163,918	421,265	62,957	29,770	2,813	91,798	15,874	4,186	209	4,800	490
Agricult. Prodts..	6,732	1,662	17,452	2,937	2,662	172	5,419	842	228	11	297	32
Manufactures....	171,977	34,746	75,022	12,052	4,876	504	20,528	5,337	5,605	251	8,665	842
Merchandise	96,453	21,501	60,556	10,528	23,017	1,984	23,320	8,663	4,835	212	6,204	918

No. 2.—*Statement showing the Number, National Character, and Tonnage (computed from aggregate number of Trips made during the Season of Navigation) of Vessels which passed on and through the Welland, St. Lawrence, Chambly, Burlington Bay, Rideau and Ottawa Canals, St. Ours and St. Ann's Locks, during the year* 1862, *and amount of Tolls collected thereon.*

VESSELS.	From Canadian to Canad. Ports		From Canad. to Am. Ports.		From Amer. to Can. Ports		From Amer. to Am. Ports.		Total.		Amount of Tolls on Vessels
	No.	Tons.	No.	Tons.	No.	Tons.	No.	Tons.	No.	Tons.	
Canadian Vessels and Steamers.											$ ct.
Welland...............	1,537	216,915	853	138,340	932	151,297	33	5,703	3,355	511,355	7,363 25
St. Lawrence	10,364	994,077	237	20,968	103	13,588	...	...	10,704	1028,663	13,271 87
Chambly and St. Ours Lock	550	24,167	654	46,840	657	44,032	...	...	1,861	115,039	1,277 52
Burlington Bay.........	1,164	180,798	385	53,198	286	40,157	...	...	1,835	274,153	1,677 30
St. Ann's Lock	3,707	220,675	207	15,668	...	...	...	...	3,914	236,343	2,954 30
Rideau and Ottawa	6,086	370,953	...	...	2	110	...	...	6,088	371,063	5,781 68
Total Canadian Vessels....	23,408	2006,685	2,336	275,014	1,980	249,184	33	5,703	27,737	2536,586	$32,326 12
American Vessels and Steamers.											
Welland...............	34	5,477	558	83,440	614	99,660	2,718	776,901	3,924	965,487	25,459 78
St. Lawrence	...	...	122	8,227	147	10,297	31	2,073	300	20,597	155 06
Chambly and St. Ours Lock	7	358	312	18,398	330	20,211	8	546	657	39,513	486 74
Burlington Bay.........	10	963	44	6,575	29	5,027	...	...	83	12,565	74 30
St. Ann's Lock	...	...	...	...	43	2,693	43	2,693	86	5,386	67 43
Rideau and Ottawa	29	1,859	...	...	6	403	...	...	35	2,262	33 93
Total American Vessels ...	80	8,657	1,036	116,649	1,169	138,291	2,800	782,213	5,085	1045,810	$26,277 74
Grand Tot.: Canad. & Amer.	23,488	2015,342	3,372	391,663	3,149	387,475	2,833	787,916	32,842	3582,396	$58,603 86

No. 3.—*An Account of the Gross and Net Revenue from all sources of the Provincial Canals of Canada, for the year 1862.*

	Dols.
Gross Amount of—	
Tolls, as per Tariff	497,302 96
Welland Canal, Damages and Fines, 593 dollars; Rents, 7,363 dollars, 90 cents	7,956 90
St. Lawrence Canal, Damages and Fines, 1,895 dollars, 17 cents; Rents, 12,493 dollars, 55 cents	14,388 72
Storage and Winterage, 4,836 dollars, 91 cents; Wharfage, 3,075 dollars, 49 cents	7,912 40
Chambly Canal Rents	· 20 00
Ottawa and Rideau Canal, Winterage	25 90
Gross Revenue from all sources	527,606 88
Less—Charges for—	
Collectors' Salaries, Lock Tenders, &c. . . . 125,017 35	
Repairs and other Incidental Expenses . . . 73,980 63	
Tolls refunded and not collected as per Order in Council, May, 1860 . . . . 288,815 55	
	482,813 53
Net Revenue, all Incidental Expenses deducted . .	44,793 35

CHAPTER VIII.

HUDSON'S BAY TERRITORY.

The Hudson's Bay Company: its Charter, its Profits, its Furs—The Fur Trade: its Extent and Value—The Territory: its Government, its Physical Features, its Plains, Lakes, and Rivers—The Saskatchewan Valley—Testimony of Captain Blakiston, Captain Palisser, Sir George Simpson, Monsieur Bourgeau, Father De Smet, Professor Hind, and others in reference to its Agricultural Resources—The Railway Route—Its Minerals, Grass, Fish, Animals, Birds, Roots, Berries, &c.—The Red River Settlement—American Trade—Homes for the Emigrant—The Company's Lands in the Market—Crossing the Rocky Mountains—Progress of the West—The Future Policy of the Hudson's Bay Company.

THE CHARTER.

THE Hudson's Bay Company was originally established in the year 1670, by a royal charter in the reign of Charles II., and was defined to include all territories within the limits watered by rivers falling into Hudson's Bay; "together with all the lands and territories upon the countries, coasts, and confines of the seas, bays, lakes, rivers, creeks, and sounds aforesaid, that are not already actually possessed by the subjects of any other Christian prince or state, with the fishing of all sorts of fish, whales, sturgeons, and all other royal fishes in the seas, bays, inlets, and rivers within the premises, and the fish therein taken, together with the royalty of the sea upon the coasts within the limits aforesaid, and all mines royal, as well discovered as not discovered, of gold, silver, gems, and precious stones. to be found or discovered within the territories, limits, and places aforesaid; and that the same land be from henceforth reckoned and reputed as one of our plantations or colonies in America called Rupert's Land."

The great object in view was not, however, the fisheries, but the fur-bearing animals which swarmed through all the plains to the Rocky Mountains.

The grant, however, of King Charles gave the Company a complete and arbitrary control over a country described in the 3rd clause as follows:—"And furthermore, we do grant unto the said Governor and Company, and their successors, that they and their successors, and their factors, servants, and agents, for them and on their behalf, and not otherwise, shall for ever hereafter have, use, and enjoy, not only the whole, entire, and only trade and traffic, and the whole entire, and only liberty, use, and privilege of trading and trafficking to and from the territory, limits, and places aforesaid, but also the whole and entire trade and traffic to and from all havens, bays, creeks, rivers, lakes, and seas, into which they shall find entrance or passage by water or land out of the territories, limits, or places aforesaid; and to and with all the nations and people inhabiting, or which shall inhabit, within the territories, limits, and places aforesaid; and to and with all other nations inhabiting any of the coasts adjacent to the said territories, limits, and places aforesaid; and to and with all other nations inhabiting any of the coasts adjacent to the said territories, limits, and places which are not already possessed as aforesaid, or whereof the sole liberty, or privilege, or traffic is not yet granted to any other of our subjects."

Armed with such complete power, it is not to be supposed that any body of men who had obtained fairly the right to govern such a territory would easily forego that right. For nearly two centuries their agents have continued to extend their influence: and, though it is claimed they have misrepresented its natural advantages as a basis for future colonies, that they have governed arbitrarily and selfishly, and that they have assumed a despotic sway from the coast of Labrador to the Pacific, we must certainly do them the credit to say that, were it not for the judicious manner in which they have conducted their affairs, we should not now hold such a claim on this extensive territory. During all that period of time between 1670 to the present, we perceive that, while the United States has been at continual war with the Indians as their pioneers advanced westward, the few inhabitants which have occupied the trading posts, scattered hundreds of miles apart, have conducted their fur operations with the Indians with hardly a cessation of peaceful relationship. Year after year the products have increased in value, and though, during the time of long-continued warfare between the French and the English, they lost in the attacks upon their establishments over £100,000, yet they were enabled to pay a dividend in 1684 of 50 per cent.; in 1688, another dividend of 50 per cent.; in 1689, 25 per cent.; between 1690 and 1800, a period of 110 years, they paid between 60 and 70 per cent. per annum.

For some years after this they had a serious difficulty, and found a dangerous opponent and formidable rival in the North-West Company; but after several years' warfare they absorbed that company by consolidation. In 1837 they paid a dividend of 5 per cent., with a bonus of 6 per cent. In 1849, 10 per cent. In 1850, 20 per cent. In 1856 the dividend was 10 per cent.; but 268 proprietors had paid 220 to 240 per cent. for their stock.

VARIETY, NUMBER, AND VALUE OF FURS.

The value of the furs alone which are purchased, and their number, can only be properly conveyed by a statistical table.

From September, 1856, to September, 1857 (considered a bad year), the total number of furs, excluding buffalo robes, was as follows:—

	Hudson's Bay Company.	United States.
Muskrat	302,131	862,330
Beaver	90,604	8,594
Otter	11,573	4,368
Fisher	5,561	4,025
Silver fox	7,071	477
Cross fox	3,143	1,608
Red fox	10,498	44,558
White fox	4,940	1,657
Kitt fox	5,776	5,366
Marten	170,956	15,399
Mink	45,091	78,510
Sea otter	188	167
Lynx	23,341	824
Black bear	7,483	3,313
Brown bear	942	116
Grey white bear	769	476,022
Racoon	1,894	41
Wolf	9,831	25
Wolverin	916	209
Skunk	7,740	6,973
Wild cat	184	6,673

It will be perceived that the majority of all the valuable furs came from Hudson's Bay Territory, by the following table of valuation:—Price of beaver, 9s. 3d. each; badger, 1s. 8d.; bear, 34s.; fisher, 28s. 8d.; silver fox, 153s. 5d.; cross fox, 46s. 2d.; red fox, 11s.; lynx and cat, 10s. 8d.; marten, 13s. 11d.; mink, 4s. 3d.; musquash, 11¾d.; otter, 7s. 9d.; sea otter, 373s. 7d.; racoon, 2s. 7d.; seal hair, 3s. 11d.; wolf, 5s. 8d.; wolverin, 12s. 6d.

Furs have increased greatly in their value since that time, the silver fox being worth £50 per skin at the present period.

Captain Blakiston, R.E., who accompanied the Palisser Expedition, says, in respect to buffalo, " Having taken some trouble to obtain the most reliable *data* in respect of the numbers annually killed, in which I have been aided by gentlemen in the fur trade, I consider, since, 1842, when the Hudson's Bay Company first commenced to trade to any great extent in robes, there have been no less than 145,000 buffalo annually killed in British Territory; while on the great prairies on the American side, where the trade has been carried on to a far greater extent, the amount annually slaughtered at the early part of the period mentioned, was upwards of 1,000,000. In 1855, on the British side alone, there were 20,000 robes and skins received at York Factory on Hudson's Bay, which, making all allowances, would give about 230,000 slaughtered the previous year. This, in a civilized country, allowing 2 lbs. per head per diem—a very liberal allowance—would have served to sustain a population of 250,000, while probably 30,000 only profited by the slaughter."

The Commissioner of Statistics for the United States for 1860, says, "The entire imports of the Company for the supply of the trading posts east of the Rocky Mountains, and mainly tributary to Minnesota, was stated by Sir George Simpson, in 1857, at 200,000 dollars, 100,000 dollars going to the supply of the Indians west of the Rocky Mountains." According to an English authority, the gross value of the furs and skins exported to England, in return for the annual outfit, varies from 1,000,000 to 2,500,000 dollars. At the half-yearly sale in April, 1857, held in London, the proceeds of the trade were stated to be 1,150,000 dollars. In March, 1853, the trade sales amounted to nearly 2,500,000 dollars. They sold then 80,000 buffalo robes at 12 dollars each. The average annual export may be fairly stated, then, at 1,500,000 dollars, showing a return of 500 per cent. on the imports. One million dollars of this is the product of Rupert's Land having its outlet through Minnesota.

In 1864, the sales of Hudson Bay furs amounted to over £200,000, and for 1865 it was computed they would reach £240,000.

GOVERNMENT OF HUDSON'S BAY.

Since the new change of government, the Hudson's Bay Company's power is restricted to Rupert's Land, or east of the Rocky Mountains; but previous to the new organization, the extent of territory controlled by them exceeded 4,500,000 square miles, and extended into the United States and Russian America. The whole territory was divided into five departments, in each of which were established certain trading posts:—

Departments.	Dépôts.	No. of Posts.
1. Northern	York Factory, Hudson's Bay	69
2. Southern	Moose Factory	42
3. Montreal	Lachine	22
4. Oregon	Fort Vancouver, W.T.	16
5. Western	Victoria, V.I.	15

The northern department is under the command of a chief pastor, and he is responsible for the districts into which his department is divided. The trading posts are separated hundreds of miles apart, and the furs collected here are transported for thousands of miles in barges and canoes, through the lakes and rivers of the Arctic water system, and down the Saskatchewan to Lake Winnipeg, whence, till recently, they have been carried through the precipitous rivers which debouch into Hudson's Bay at Fort York.

At Norway House, at the north end of Lake Winnipeg, early in the summer, a meeting takes place between the chief commissioners and the governor of the territories; the number and value of the furs are considered; the several proportions of earnings are allotted; various promotions are made; the various supplies are given out, such as blankets, materials for and articles of wearing apparel of woollen and cotton manufacture; hardware and earthenware, beads, ribbons, pipes, fire-steels, and other miscellaneous articles; also tea, coffee, sugar, rice, raisins, wine, tobacco, salt, flour, gunpowder, shot, ball, fire-arms, &c.

Having perfected their business, and spent a few days in the mutual enjoyment of relating their experiences, they set out upon their return vogages to their homes. Of course, their arrival is looked for with much anxiety; for they bring a whole year's news from the Old World. Then the various presents are carefully examined and mutually prized; and in the evening, the valley or the plain echoes with merriment, as the men and maidens dance, sing, and regale on the festive occasion.

Then come the preparations for winter. Fisheries are established, the various parties scatter to their posts, the Indians receive advances of supplies for the coming furs, boats are mended, tools and guns put in order, pemmican from buffalo meat is made, and fish are dried and salted. In the spring the hunting commences—furs are pressed and packed; and when the "up river" boat arrives, they are prepared to start for the annual meeting again.

The total number in the employ of the Hudson's Bay Company is 3000, including agents, voyageurs, traders, and servants, and about 100,000 Indian hunters.

PHYSICAL FEATURES.

Captain Blakiston, R.E., in speaking of the physical features of the interior of British North America, divides them as follows:— "1, The northern or Arctic basin. 2, Hudson's Bay. 3, The Central Plains. 4, The Rocky Mountains. 5, The Pacific slope and (if Canada were included it would be a sixth) the St. Lawrence basin."

The northern or Arctic basin "extends from the northern part of Canada East, skirting the upper great lakes, curving round to Lake Winnipeg, and thence taking a north-easterly direction, reaching the Arctic Sea in the region between the Coppermine and Back's Great Fish River. This great belt extends for 150 to 200 miles in width, and is extremely rocky—in fact, the whole region is most inhospitable except for the hunter and the fur trapper."

Hudson's Bay.—The region around Hudson's Bay is generally of much the same character as the wooded portion of the Arctic regions, and the extent to which the country is annually submerged is described as almost incredible. The Arctic regions and central plains are alike cheerless, unfit for pasturage, and worthless for agriculture.

Between the Rocky Mountains, Lake Winnipeg, the Lake of the Woods, and the 49th parallel, we have a country entirely distinct from the rest of Rupert's Land. It is variously denominated the "Valley of the Saskatchewan," the "Basin of Winnipeg," and the "High Central Plains." This district contains about 380,000 square miles, with a width of 750 miles.

A prominent feature in the commercial physics of this northwestern country is the extent of its navigable water-line, which may be taken as the natural exponent of the commercial value of its resources.

In the following table we give what is known of the continuous distances capable of steamboat navigation on the rivers which interlock in Lake Winnipeg.

Navigable Water-Line and Shore-Line of the Basin of the Winnipeg.

	Water-Line. Miles.	Shore-Line. Miles.
Red River from Breckinridge— Mouth of Sioux Wood to Lake Winnipeg	531	1062
Tributaries of Red River— Red Lake River, Minnesota	100	200
Assiniboine, British Territory— Navigation uncertain	200	400
Lake Winnipeg	264	782
Lakes Manitoba and Winnipegoos	220	660
Saskatchewan River— From Lake Winnipeg to junction.	422	844
North Branch to Edmonton	540	1080
South Branch to Chesterfield House	480	960
Total	2757	5988

Captain Blakiston says—"Taking either branch of the Saskatchewan River, it is navigable for boats from Lake Winnipeg to near the base of the Rocky Mountains, a distance of 1200 miles. I am glad to say I was fortunate enough to travel on it from its mouth to Fort Edmonton, 1000 miles up, at a time of year when I saw the water at its lowest."

THE FERTILE BELT.

The valley of the Saskatchewan contains an extended belt of land, called the "Fertile Belt," which is unsurpassed for the richness of its soil and its adaptability for agricultural purposes. The explorations of Simpson, Hind, Palisser, Hector, Sullivan, and Blakiston, all serve to prove that within British Territory the most fertile soil west of the Mississippi exists—and that so vast, so rich is this great valley that it is capable of subsisting 20,000,000 people.

TESTIMONY OF PALISSER.

Captain Palisser describes the region drained by the Saskatchewan in the following words:—"The extent of surface drained by the Saskatchewan, and other tributaries to Lake Winnipeg, which we had an opportunity of examining, amounts in round numbers to 150,000 square miles. This region is bounded to the north by what is known as the 'strong woods,' or the southern limit of the great circum-Arctic zone of forest which occupies these latitudes in the northern hemisphere. This line, which is indicated in the map, sweeps to the northwest from the shore of Lake Winnipeg, and reaches its most northerly limit about 54° 30′ N. and longitude 119° W., from whence it again passes to south-west, meeting the Rocky Mountains in latitude 51° N., longitude 115° W. Between this line of the 'strong woods' and the northern limit of the true prairie country, there is a belt of land varying in width, which at one period must have been covered by an extension of the northern forests, but which has been gradually cleared by successive fires.

"It is now a partially wooded country, abounding in lakes and rich natural pasturage, in some parts rivalling the finest park scenery of our own country. Throughout this region of country the climate seems to preserve the same character, although it passes through very different latitudes, its form being doubtless determined by the curves of the isothermal line. Its superficial extent embraces about 65,000 square miles, or 40,000,000 acres, of which more than one-third may be considered as at once available for the purposes of the agriculturist. Its elevation increases from 700 to 4000 feet as we approach the Rocky Mountains; consequently, it is not equally adapted throughout to the cultivation of any one crop; nevertheless, at Fort Edmonton, which has an altitude of 3000 feet, even wheat is sometimes cultivated with success."

TESTIMONY OF M. BOURGEAU.

Mons. E. Bourgeau, who accompanied Palisser in his explorations, addressed the following remarks to Sir William Hooker, in reference to Hudson's Bay Territory:—"But it remains for me to call the attention of the English Government to the advantage there would be in establishing agricultural districts in the vast plains of Rupert's Land, and particularly in the Saskatchewan, in the neighbourhood of Fort Carlton. This district is much more adapted to the culture of staple crops of temperate climates, wheat, rye, barley, oats, &c., than one would have been inclined to believe from this high latitude. In effect, the few attempts at cereal culture already made in the vicinity of the Hudson's Bay Company's posts demonstrate by their success how easy it would be to obtain products sufficiently abundant largely to remunerate the efforts of the agriculturist. *There,* in order to put the land under cultivation, it would be necessary only to till the better portions of the soil. The prairies offer natural pasturage as favourable for the maintenance of numerous herds as if they had been artificially created. The construction of houses for habitation and for pioneer development would involve but little expense, because in many parts of the country, independent of wood, one would find fitting stones for building purposes, and in others clay to make bricks. In the latter district extend rich and vast prairies, interspersed with wood and forests, where thickwood plants furnish excellent pasturage for domestic animals. The vetches found here are as fitting for the nourishment of cattle as the clover of European pasturage. The abundance of buffaloes, and the facility with which the herds of horses and oxen increase, demonstrate that it would be enough to shelter animals in winter, and to feed them in the shelters with hay collected in advance. The harvest could in general be commenced by the end of August or the first week in September, which is a season in which the temperature is sufficiently high and rain is rare.

"In the gardens of the Hudson's Bay Company's posts—but more particularly in those of the different missions, succulent vegetables of the leguminous family, such as beans, peans, and French beans, have been successfully cultivated; also cabbages, turnips, carrots, rhubarb, and currants. Different species of gooseberries, with edible fruits, as well as raspberries, grow wild here."

REPORT OF THE NEW YORK CHAMBER OF COMMERCE.

It was supposed that the valleys of the Mississippi and the St. Lawrence Rivers exhausted the northern and central areas which are available for agriculture. A report to the New York Chamber of Commerce very soon corrected the erroneous impression. " There is in the heart of North America," said the report, " a distinct subdivision, of which Lake Winnipeg may be regarded as the centre. This subdivision, like the valley of the Mississippi, is distinguished for the fertility of its soil, and for the extent and gentle slope of its great plains, watered by rivers of great length, and admirably adapted for steam navigation. It has a climate not exceeding in severity that of many portions of Canada and the Eastern States. It will, in all respects, compare favourably with some of the most densely peopled portions of the continent of Europe. In other words, it is admirably adapted to become the seat of a numerous, hardy, and prosperous community. It has an area equal to eight or ten first-class American States. Its great river, the Saskatchewan, carries a navigable water-line to the very base of the Rocky Mountains. It is not at all improbable that the valley of this river may yet offer the best route for a railroad to the Pacific. The navigable waters of this great subdivision interlock with those of the Mississippi."

The Red River of the North, in connexion with Lake Winnipeg, into which it falls, forms a navigable water-line, extending directly north and south 800 miles. The Red River is one of the best adapted to the use of steam in the world, and waters one of the finest regions on the continent. Between the highest point at which it is navigable, and St. Paul, on the Mississippi, a railroad is in process of construction; and when this road is completed, another grand division of the continent, comprising 500,000 square miles, will be open to settlement.

TESTIMONY OF SIR GEORGE SIMPSON.

Sir George Simpson, speaking of the land which is drained by the Red Deer and Swan Rivers, which drain a country of rare beauty and fertility, and which lies west of Lake Winnipeg, draws the following glowing picture:—

" In this part of the country we saw many sorts of birds, geese, loons, pelicans, ducks, cranes, two kinds of snipe, hawks, owls, and gulls; but they were all so remarkably shy, that we were constrained to admire them from a distance. In the afternoon we traversed a beautiful country with lofty hills and long valleys, full of sylvan lakes; while the bright green of the surface, as far as the eye could reach, assumed a foreign tinge, under an uninterrupted profusion of roses and blue-bells. On the summit of one of these hills we commanded one of the few extensive prospects we had of late enjoyed. One range of heights rose behind another, each becoming fainter as it receded from the eye, till the farthest was blended in almost undistinguishable confusion with the clouds; while the softest vales spread a panorama of hanging copses and glittering lakes at our feet."

A writer in the *New York Knickerbocker Magazine* for October, 1858, thus expresses himself:—

"Here is the great fact of the north-western area of this continent—an area not inferior in size to the whole United States east of the Mississippi—which is perfectly adapted to the fullest occupation by cultivated nations, yet is almost wholly unoccupied, lies west of the 98th meridian, and above the 43rd parallel—that is, north of the latitude of Milwaukee, and west of the longitude of Red River, Fort Kearney, and Corpus Christi; or, to state the fact in another way, east of the Rocky Mountains, and west of the 98th meridian, and between the 43rd and 60th parallels, there is a productive cultivable area of 500,000 square miles. West of the Rocky Mountains, and between the same parallels, there is an area of 300,000 square miles."

TESTIMONY OF FATHER DE SMET.

Father De Smet, a devoted Jesuit missionary to the Indians of Oregon (mentioned by Governor Stevens, in an address before the New York Geographical Society, as "a man whose name is a tower of strength and faith"), thus describes what he calls "the vast plain —the ocean of prairies":—

"The entire region in the vicinity of the eastern chain of the Rocky Mountains, serving as their base for thirty or sixty miles, is extremely fertile, abounding in forests, plains, prairies, lakes, streams, and mineral springs. The rivers and streams are innumerable, and on every side offer situations favourable for the construction of mills. The northern and southern branches of the Saskatchewan water the district I have traversed for a distance of about 300 miles. Forests of pine, cypress, thorn, poplar, and aspen trees, as well as others of different kinds, occupy a large portion of it, covering the declivities of the mountains and banks of the rivers.

"These originally take their rise in the highest chains, whence they issue in every direction, like so many veins. The beds and sides of these rivers are pebbly, and their course rapid, but as they recede from the mountains they widen, and the currents lose something of their impetuosity. Their waters are usually very clear. The country would be capable of supporting a large population, and the soil is favourable for the production of barley, corn, potatoes, and beans, which grow here as well as in the more southern countries.

"Are these vast and innumerable fields of hay for ever destined to be consumed by fire or perish in the autumnal snows? How long shall these superb forests be the haunts of wild beasts? And these inexhaustible quarries—these abundant mines of coal, lead, sulphur, iron, copper, and saltpetre—can it be that they are doomed to remain for ever inactive? Not so. The day will come when some labouring hand will give them value; a strong, active, and enterprising people are destined to fill this spacious void. The wild beasts will, ere long, give place to our domestic animals; flocks and herds will graze in the beautiful meadows that border the numberless mountains, hills, valleys, and plains of this extensive region."

LIFE AT EDMONTON.

Life at Edmonton during the winter season is thus sketched:—
"The number of servants, including children, is about eighty. Besides a large garden, a field of potatoes and wheat belonging to the establishment, the lakes, forests, and plains of the neighbourhood furnish provisions in abundance. On my arrival at the Fort, the ice-house contained 30,000 white fish, each weighing four pounds, and 500 buffaloes, the ordinary amount of the winter provisions. Such is the quantity of aquatic birds in the season, that sportsmen often send to the Fort carts full of fowls. Eggs are picked up by thousands in the straw and weeds of the marshes. I visited Lake St. Anne (a missionary station fifty miles north-west from Edmonton). The surface of this region is flat for the most part, undulating in some places—diversified with forests and meadows, and lakes teeming with fish. In Lake St. Anne alone were

caught, last autumn, more than 70,000 white fish, the most delicious of the kind. They are taken with a line at every season of the year.

"Notwithstanding the rigour and duration of the winter in this northern region, the earth in general appears fertile. Vegetation is so forward in the spring and summer that potatoes, wheat, and barley, together with other vegetables of Canada, come to maturity."

On the 12th of March, Father De Smet started on his return trip, proceeding with sledges drawn by dogs over the snow, to Fort Jasper, situated north-west from Edmonton on the Athabasca River, half a degree north of latitude 54°. Here occurred the following hunting adventure:—

"Provisions becoming scarce at the Fort, at the moment when we had with us a considerable number of Iroquois from the surrounding country, who were resolved to remain until my departure in order to assist at the instructions, we should have found ourselves in an embarrassing situation had not Mr. Frazer come to our relief, by proposing that we should leave the Fort and accompany himself and family to the Lake of Islands, where we could subsist partly on fish. As the distance was not great we accepted the invitation, and set out to the number of fifty-four persons and twenty dogs. I count the latter because we were as much obliged to provide for them as for ourselves. A little note of the game killed by our hunters during the twenty-six days of our abode at this place will afford you some interest—at least it will make you acquainted with the animals of the country, and prove that the mountaineers of the Athabasca are blessed with good appetites. Animals killed—12 moose deer, 2 reindeer, 30 large mountain sheep or big-horn, 2 porcupines, 210 hares, 1 beaver, 10 muskrats, 24 bustards, 115 ducks, 21 pheasants, 1 snipe, 1 eagle, 1 owl; add to this from 30 to 55 white fish and 20 trout every day."

THE RAILWAY ROUTE.

Professor Henry Youle Hind, in speaking of the natural advantages of the basin of Lake Winnipeg for a route across the continent, says: "It is impossible to examine a correct map of the North American Continent without being impressed with the remarkable influence which the Great American Desert must exercise upon the future of the United States and British North America. The general character of this desert south of the 49th parallel is described elsewhere, and the important fact has been noticed *that any railroad constructed within the limits of the United States must pass for a distance of twelve hundred miles west of the Mississippi through uncultivable land, or, in other words, a comparative desert.* Along the 32nd parallel the breadth of this desert is least, and the detached areas of fertile soil greatest in quantity; but the aggregate number of square miles of cultivable land amounts only to 2300 in a distance of 1210 miles. The northern limit of the Great American Desert is an imaginary line drawn from the Touchwood Hills to the Moose Woods on the south branch, then South of Battle River as far as longitude 112°, when, turning south, it sweeps along the flanks of the Rocky Mountains in longitude 115°. North of this limit of the Great American Desert there is a broad strip of fertile country, rich in water, woods, and pasturage, drained by the North Saskatchewan and some of its affluents, and being a continuation of the fertile prairies of Red River, the eastern watershed of the Assiniboine and Red Deer River, with the outlying patches called the Touchwood Hills, File Hill, &c.

"*It is a physical reality of the highest importance to the interests of British North America, that this continuous belt can be settled and cultivated from a few miles west of the Lake of the Woods to the passes of the Rocky Mountains, and any line of communication, whether by waggon road or railroad, passing through it will eventually enjoy the great advantage of being fed by an agricultural population from one extremity to the other.*"

We have been particular to quote the descriptions of this "Fertile Belt," because when we come to the consideration of a railroad from the Atlantic to the Pacific Oceans, the importance of this testimony in relation to this magnificent country will then be perceived.

MINERALS, VEGETABLE PRODUCTIONS, ANIMALS, FISH, ETC.

Minerals.—Gold has of late been discovered in the banks of the river Saskatchewan, near the foot of the Rocky Mountains. News received as late as December, 1864, states men are gathering as much as £4 per day. Copper and malachite exist in the region of Coppermine River; plumbago, iron, and mineral pitch, have been found on Lake Athabasca; salt has been found in a very pure state near Great Slave Lake, as well as salt springs, on the borders of Lake Manitoba and Winnipegosis; Limestone occurs at Red River and Lake Winnipeg; granite is found in inexhaustible quantities between Lake Winnipeg, Lake Superior, and Hudson's Bay; coal has been discovered on the Assouri River, near Fort Edmonton, and also on Red Deer River.

Vegetable Productions.—The principal trees which abound are the balsam, the poplar, and the aspen, and are the common trees of the plain country; there is also, in limited quantities, the white spruce, the American larch, the fir, bank pine, white or bass wood, the sugar maple, spruce tree, the ash, the oak, as far as Red River and Lake Manitobas. But the Rocky Mountains are covered with a luxury and splendour of timber growth sufficient to supply the wants of the valleys at her feet for centuries. If the vast tracts of prairie land teem with verdant grasses which preclude the forest's growth, the watercourses can carry into all its river ramifications timber of every variety.

Grass.—Grass is everywhere, spreading in fields of natural verdure that would gladden the eye of any agriculturist. When we think of the millions of buffaloes that year after year find pasture sufficient for their wants, we may imagine what herds of cattle and horses could subsist upon the nutritious grasses and vetches that abound on the plains and the numerous swamps.

Berries and Roots.—These are abundant and various, and include the cranberry, sasketoom, pembina, currant (black and red), gooseberry, raspberry, and strawberry. Wild rice is plentiful, the prairie turnip peculiar to Hudson's Bay, besides numerous roots used for medicinal and dyeing purposes.

Animals.—The various fur-bearing animals we have previously specified, and will therefore add those which are used for purposes of food and usefulness.

The bear, reindeer, moose, muskrat, porcupine, beaver, hare, musk ox, buffalo, antelope, big-horn, and mountain goat, and the wapeti.

Fish.—The principal fish are the white fish (a delicious fish, and found in all the lakes), the sturgeon, pike, gold-eyes, trout, catfish, suckers, &c.

Aquatic Animals.—The seal, the waburs, the white bear, and the white tortoise, called the "white whale," frequent Hudson's Bay and Straits.

RED RIVER SETTLEMENT

was originally projected by Lord Selkirk, a Scottish nobleman largely interested in the Hudson's Bay Company, who held a vast extent of land by charter from the British Crown. Of the Company, he made an extensive purchase, and brought over his first colonists in 1813, and remained with them twelve months. Another accession was made in 1817, and another in 1823; and they now number, in Europeans, French Canadians, and half-breeds, about 10,000 souls. One half the population are hunters, and the other half farmers. The main settlement, known as "Red River," is about 60 miles north of Pembina, or down the river, and is on an extensive plain, which extends, somewhat broken and interspersed with timber, east to Lake Winnipeg. The hunters, mostly half-breeds, do nothing but hunt buffalo. They make two grand excursions each year; one commencing on the 20th of June, and lasting two months, and the other on the 10th of September, and lasting till the 10th of November. The hunters lead a free, happy, wild, romantic life, and are, when in the settlement, temperate and well-behaved.

The farmers raise wheat, oats, barley, potatoes, cattle and sheep. Turnips, onions, peas, cabbage, rhubarb, radishes, mangel, hops, pumpkins, and melons grow in abundance. In 1856, there were 922 houses, 1232 stables, 399 barns, 1503 horses, 1296 mares, 2796 oxen, 290 bulls, 3593 cows, 2644 calves, 4674 pigs, 2429 sheep, 585 ploughs, 730 harrows, 2045 carts, 522 canoes, 55 boats, 8347 acres of cultivated land; number of acres in 1864, 22,000.

Oxen are worth from 60 to 100 dollars a yoke; cows from 15 to 20 dollars; a good cart-horse, 80 dollars; and a horse trained to hunt buffalo will bring 150 to 200 dollars.

Their wheat is equal to any in the world, weighing from 65 lbs. to 70 lbs. to the bushel; barley and oats are also heavy, and potatoes and all kinds of garden vegetables grow luxuriantly. *The land is never manured.* From $3\frac{1}{2}$ to 4 feet of snow falls in winter, and rain is unknown from November to April.

They originally received their supplies of merchandise from York Factory, a store of the Hudson's Bay Company, 700 miles from Red River. It required two months to make the journey, and there were thirty-six portages (carrying-places) to be made in going that distance. The title of the settlement is "The Red River Colony," and it is ruled by a governor appointed by the Queen. The magistrates, councillors, and officers, receive their commissions from the committee of the Hudson's Bay Company. The jurisdiction of the governor extends 100 miles in all directions from Fort Garry, except over the American line.

American Trade.—The census of 1856 shows the fruit of its recent intercourse with the new American settlements in Minnesota, in the introduction of new agricultural machinery:—8 thrashing machines, 3 steam saw-mills, 2 reaping machines, 1 carding machine, 800 harrows, 2000 carts, 500 ploughs, 2 steam-ploughs, and 56 merchant shops. Its rapidly increasing intercourse with an American market has developed a spirit of enterprise among the people, new forms of industry, and a growing demand for American commodities.

HOMES FOR THE EMIGRANT.

Trade must find its natural outlet, and agriculture demands its most advantageous markets. We cannot well force commerce through unnatural currents, and we cannot for ever shut out the solid cohorts of advancing emigrants when they are thundering at our gates for a passage to lands inviting them by their extent, their accessibility, and their richness. It is better to open the gates willingly—better to guide than to be jostled by the throng. The splendid landscapes of the Assiniboine that adorn the great picture gallery of nature, cannot be closed for ever. The measureless prairies that stretch in vast waves of beauty from the Lake of the Woods to the base of the Rocky Mountains, redolent and gorgeous with the richest profusion of rose-bushes, blue-bells, woodbine, convolvulus, helianthii, and thousands of nameless and delicate flowers, tell the beholder the wealth of soil that supports them in their entangled and untrained luxuriance of variety and numbers. The thousands of small lakes

—sweet eyes of earth—that dot the valleys, invite him with their clear waters and fisheries; the rivers that spread, interlace, and ramify for thousands of miles, tell of a well-watered soil. The yellow sand of the Saskatchewan, made brilliant by the noonday sun, flashes and sparkles with auriferous wealth; the dark black seams that crumble beneath his tread, are signs of coal, that tell him his hearth shall glow with a genial warmth that shall bid defiance to the external frost. The stately elms, the graceful ash and bending willow, the grand spreading oak and the ever-verdant pine, that fringe the prairies, gather in assemblies, and crowd so close upon the mountains that their leaves, limbs, and trunks shoulder and jostle each other in progressive development, tell him there is labour for the forester, the lumberer, and the builder. Granite, as compact and strong as that on which the Pyramids of Egypt rest, is scattered in numerous quarries throughout this great province. Game, such as the buffalo, swarm over the plains, while the stately cariboo, the prowling bear, the wily fox, the pretty mink, the busy otter, the nimble squirrel, and the scented rat are swarming through the forest, and by lake and river. Of birds, there is the majestic eagle and the blue-winged jay, the murderous hawk and the little jewelled humming-bird; together with duck and pigeon, sandpiper and cherry-bird, loom and partridge, magpie and blackcap, nightingale and swallow, grouse and snipe, kingfisher and plover. Here experiments have been carried on for fifty years, and here we find corn, and wheat, and fruit, and vegetable thrive in a remarkable manner, and where wheat can be grown " for twenty years in succession." But all this land has been shut out from the knowledge of the world. A new era is at hand. The people of the Atlantic are wooing the people of the Pacific; they would be united by an iron band. The great North-East invites British Columbia to share her future with her, and to march forward hand in hand with her; to send her the tributes of the Pacific—the gold of Vancouver, Australia, California, and Columbia—and the spices, silks, and teas of India, China, and Japan; while from across the Atlantic will come an endless variety of exchanges.

THE HIGHWAY IS ACROSS THE HUDSON'S BAY TERRITORY.

Gentlemen of the Hudson's Bay Company, you have possessed for two centuries a splendid monopoly. We are not of those who wholly condemn the manner in which you have administered the power delegated to you; on the contrary, a careful knowledge of the history and results of your rule, prove that your affairs have been administered with much ability, discretion, and judgment. Your labours have been prosperous to an unparalleled degree, and the amicable manner in which you, and those under your authority, have conducted your relations with the Indians, and to which they bear testimony, for so lengthened a period, certainly is in the highest degree creditable to you when contrasted with the exterminating warfare which has characterized the relations of the United States' Government with them. It cannot be expected that a monopoly so entire should be carried on without producing many animosities, and that acts have not been committed which appear unwise, impolitic, and arbitrary. It would be unreasonable to suppose that you are so devoid of self-interest as to be willing to give up a power so long possessed, and providing such a splendid interest on the capital employed, or that you are willing to forego any right you may possess for the general good. When merchants place their surplus profits in a joint-stock company, they do so for the purpose of securing continued and safe interest. Now, the cry against the Hudson's Bay Company is, that locked in the valleys of the Assiniboine and Saskatchewan, there is 65,000 square miles of cultivable land, of which 27,000 square miles, or 17,000,000 acres, is at once available for the agriculturist; and this land is black with richness. The whole of your land is 150,000 square miles. The principal means from which you derive your income at present is the fur trade. In the year 1864, the sales of furs in London amounted to £262,869; but the public believe that there are many other sources of supply to swell the dividends. As the operations of the Company have not been published as widely as those of many joint-stock companies of London, we have taken the latest statement which we have received previous to the abridgment of the Company's power over Vancouver's Island and British Columbia. On June 1, 1856, the capital of the Hudson's Bay Company was as follows:—

Amount of assets	£1,468,301 16 3
Amount of liabilities	203,233 16 11
Capital	£1,265,067 19 4

Consisting of—

Stock standing in the names of the proprietors	£500,000 0 0
Valuation of the Company's lands and buildings, exclusive of Vancouver's Island and Oregon	318,884 12 8
Amount expended up to 16th September, 1856, in sending miners and labourers to Vancouver's Island, in the coal-mines, and other objects of colonization, exclusive of the trading establishments of the Company, and which amount will be repayable by Government, if possession of the island is resumed	87,071 8 3
Amount invested in Fort Victoria, and other establishments and posts in Vancouver's Island, estimated at	75,000 0 0
Carry forward	£980,956 0 11

Brought forward	£980,956	0	11
Amount paid to the Earl of Selkirk for Red River Settlement	84,111	18	5
Property and investments in the Territory of Oregon, ceded to the United States by the treaty of 1846, and which are secured to the Company as possessory rights under that treaty, 1,000,000 dollars	200,000	0	0
Total	£1,265,067	19	4

Now we must deduct all interests in Vancouver's Island which are in direct possession of the British Government.

THE COMPANY'S LANDS IN THE MARKET.

Let us take away the whole of the 17,000,000 acres of available land; the fur trade would suffer but very little. Suppose that, instead of allowing the whole of the Indians to subsist by trapping and hunting, one-half were taught the first elements of agriculture and located at various points on a given line, which leads from Pembina to the Rocky Mountains. It is all nonsense to say we cannot civilize the savage. Give him the implements and the seeds, set over him or them an overseer to guide, direct, and teach them, and keep away the curse of rum, and there will be no difficulty in civilizing them. They farm well enough at Red River, and, be assured, when they are convinced that by proper attention and a certain amount of labour they may provide comforts for the long winter, the revolution will be complete. For the other half there is employment beyond the prairies. The fur-bearing animals are not found in great numbers or variety here; therefore we maintain that the cultivation of this district would not materially affect the fur trade. There are regions adapted for fur-bearing animals and not adaptable for purposes of agriculture; the land of the Ojibways east and north of Lake Winnipeg, Winnipeg River, and Rainy River, and away to Labrador and Hudson's Bay; all the land north of 55°; the land of the Black Foot Indians, a portion of the Assiniboine Indians' land, and the Rocky Mountains. "Give us a market for our cattle and we can raise incalculable numbers,"—so say the people of the Red River Settlement.

The *Nor'-Wester*, a newspaper published for the first time at the Red River Settlement on the 28th December, 1859, mentions Mr. Gowler's success as an agriculturist in the following terms:—
" He sowed 63 bushels of wheat, 36 of barley, 24 of oats, and 101 of potatoes, and from these he realized 700 of wheat, 350 of barley, 480 of oats, and 2100 of potatoes. The cost of the seed was £50; in preparing and tilling the soil about £25 more were expended; and the cost of gathering in and threshing the crops is set down at £100—making a total expenditure of £175. Place against that the

sums representing the sale of wheat at 6s., and the barley at 5s. 9d., the oats at 2s. 6d., and the potatoes at 1s. 3d. per bushel (average price which the produce will easily command), and an argument more strong and convincing than could be wrought out by any other process of reasoning, stands stubbornly forth in favour of the claims of the settlement as being one of the best agricultural countries on the face of the globe. It should be added that Mr. Gowler's profits have already enabled him to enlarge the bounds of his estate to 600 acres, to stock it with a noble herd of cattle and horses, and to make the necessary preparations for erecting thereon, next summer, a snug and comfortable mansion."

Imagine the value of 20,000,000 acres of rich land ready for cultivation thrown into the market. When the lands in Connecticut and New York reached £10 in value, the people moved westward to Michigan and Ohio; when, in a few years, lands which had cost 10s. an acre increased to £10, they moved to Wisconsin and Illinois, and bought lands as low as 5s. sterling an acre. Then lands increased here to 2000 per cent. over their original price. Then Iowa and Minnesota soon came into the market, and these lands are being rapidly taken up, and their value has increased in a marvellous ratio.

Westward is the movement towards the Pacific beyond the Mississippi; the arid districts of the Upper Missouri are barren tracts, wholly uncultivatable; the coming exodus of people will soon overrun Minnesota, and seek the rich lands of the "Fertile Belt." Who shall stop them? The splendid and complicated system of the Hudson's Bay Company is admirably adapted to map out this vast tract; the army of servants who obey their behests could soon survey every part. Before long, the rumbling of wheels, and the whistle of the advancing locomotive, will be heard at Pembina; the great bodies of emigrants who seek the gold-fields of the Pacific and the Saskatchewan are coming with their long trains. Surely it is time for the Company to awake; the great modern revolutionizer is near them—the iron bands are waiting to span the prairies. But it is said the Rocky Mountains are an insuperable obstacle to a railroad.

CROSSING THE ROCKY MOUNTAINS.

Can it be supposed that a people who have tunnelled the Alps and the Thames; who have arched the Loire and the Seine a hundred times; who have united the shores of the St. Lawrence, and crossed its mighty current with two miles of iron tubing; who have leaped yawning chasms at a bound; who have, amidst discouragement, difficulty, doubt, and fatigue, but with iron will, constructed in this age *one hundred thousand miles of railroads* across prairies—by the side of yawning precipices—overlooking miles upon miles of cities and towns—ascending peak after peak—and descending awful slopes—now sweeping in graceful curves by the side of rushing rivers—then rumbling over the tops of houses whose dwellers lived in security—off again into the daisied and cowslipped fields—. speeding through umbrageous forests that formed an avenue o'ertopped and arched with foliage—leaping rivers innumerable, on its iron supports—pushed beneath the hills, which towered above hundreds of feet—till once again the shrill whistle announced a stoppage to its progress: the people who have erected palaces of glass and iron; who have built ships as large as the ark; who can build ships impervious to cannon balls, and lay a cable beneath the ocean three thousand miles wide: are not going to stop or halt at the foot of the Rocky Mountains because those mountains are tall. They are going over them, up them, or down them—around their sides, across their passes, or through them or under them; but iron rails must be wedded to iron rails from one side of the slope to the other—and once wedded, there will be no divorce. Every nerve should be strained, every influence used, and every desire of the Company should be, to open a track for the emigrant. The ultimate value of their possessions, once under the sway of agriculture, no figures could calculate.

PROGRESS OF THE WEST.

Say that the capital was £2,000,000; why, this land will yet sell for £3,500,000 at only 4s. an acre. Think of the marvellous increase which all the West shows. Only a few years since, Texas, Iowa, Wisconsin, Minnesota, and Missouri, were an untracked wilderness, and land hardly worth a song. In Texas, in 1850, there was under cultivation 643,976 acres; in 1860, 2,649,207. Iowa, in 1850, 824,682 acres; in 1860, 3,780,253. Wisconsin, in 1850, 1,045,499 acres; in 1860, 3,746,036. Minnesota, in 1850, 5035 acres; in 1860, 554,397. Missouri, in 1850, 2,938,425 acres; in 1860, 6,246,871. Minnesota, 1st January, 1865, had 1,000,000 acres of land under cultivation, and the value of her farms was estimated at 34,000,000 dollars. Thus, in 1850, this new-born state possessed a less number of acres under cultivation than the Red River Settlement, which was 6392 acres in 1849; in 1860, 10,000 acres; and only 20,000 in 1864.

When Professor Hind was about to bid adieu to Mr. Gowler, one of the best farmers at Red River Settlement, the latter said, as he closed the wicket-gate, "Look at that prairie; 10,000 head of cattle might feed and fatten for nothing. If I found it worth my while, I could enclose 50, 100, or 500 acres, and from every acre get 30 to 40 bushels of wheat, year after year. I could grow Indian corn, barley, oats, flax, hemp, hops, turnips, tobacco—anything you wish, and to any amount; but what would be the use? There are no markets—it's a chance if my wheat is taken, and my potatoes I may have to give to the pigs. If we had only a market, you'd have to travel long before you would see the like of these prairies about the Assiniboine."

Professor Hind says that he saw wheat that had grown 56 bushels to the acre. Swedish turnips were magnificent; four of them weighed 70 lbs.—two weighing 39 lbs., and two others 31 lbs. I counted thirteen, fourteen, and sixteen potatoes averaging $3\frac{1}{2}$ inches in diameter at each root respectively. They were a round, white-skinned variety, like those known in Canada as the "English White."

We believe the directors of the Company are far-seeing enough to know what is the best policy for themselves and those they represent, and that we shall see them ready and willing to assist in advancing the interests of the stockholders, promoting the good of the settler, developing the resources of the country, opening up the highways of travel, and extending the influence and power of a Government, strong, protective, and beneficent.

CHAPTER IX.

BRITISH COLUMBIA AND VANCOUVER'S ISLAND.

The Rocky Mountains: their Extent, their Altitude, their Passes—British Columbia: Early Discovery, Boundary-line, Lakes, Rivers, &c.; Gold and the Gold-mines; Discovery of the Gold; Testimony of Governor Douglas, G. Forbes Macdonald, Esq., and the *Times* Correspondent—Gold on Fraser River—Richness of the Mines—Mines on Thompson River—Lillooett Gold-mines—Cariboo Gold River—Steele's Company—Labour in British Columbia—Export of Gold in 1863—Fertility of Soil in the Gold Neighbourhood—Progress of the Colony—Vancouver's Island: its Agricultural Resources, Coal-beds, Importance as a Naval Station, Imports and Exports; Prospecting, Panning, and Washing Gold.

THE ROCKY MOUNTAINS.

THE ROCKY MOUNTAINS stretch from north to south of the North American Continent for a distance of 3000 miles. They are a succession of centres of disturbance, rather than a continuous range of backbone dividing the continent. Their greatest altitude is attained at Mount Brown, which is 15,000 feet above the sea. At their arctic termination they are about 1000 or 2000 feet in height; they then increase in altitude as they go southward, averaging 7000 to 8000 feet; while Mount Brown, Mount Hooker, Fremont's Peak, and Long's Peak attain a much greater height.

The general width of the Rocky Mountains is from 40 to 100 miles. South of 42° there is no route across the mountains capable of being traversed; but north of this there are two passes, called the North and South Passes, within the boundaries of the United States, and averaging 7000 feet in height. In British America the passes are numerous. Those at present discovered are—

		Lat.
1. Cow-Dung Lake Portage, or Leather Pass		54° 0'
2. Boat Encampment, or Original Athabasca Portage		53° 45'
3. Howe's Pass		51° 45'
4. Kicking Horse Pass		51° 25'
5. Vermilion Pass		51° 10'
6. Kananaski, or Emigrant Pass		50° 40'
7. Crow-Nest Pass		49° 40'
8. Kootanay Pass		49° 25'

These passes will be more particularly referred to when we consider the subject of a railway across the continent.

BRITISH COLUMBIA.

British Columbia occupies an area of 225,250 square miles. It is about 420 miles long, and 300 miles broad. It comprises " all such territories within the dominions of Her Majesty as are bounded to the south by the frontier of the United States of America, to the east by the main chain of the Rocky Mountains, to the north by Simpson's River and the Finlay branch of the Peace River, and to the west by the Pacific Ocean," and all the islands adjacent to these territories.

EARLY DISCOVERY.

Early in the sixteenth century, the Spaniards, who had explored a great deal of the shores of the Pacific, and planted several small colonies, extended their adventures gradually northward, and discovered the coasts of British Columbia. The Straits of Juan de Fuca were discovered by a Spanish pilot, who had visited its shores. In 1578, Drake touched at Vancouver on his voyage round the world. In 1792, Captain Vancouver, an officer in the English Navy, who had been sent to settle some difficulties with the Spaniards in reference to the seizure of some English ships, arrived at Nootka; but not finding the Spanish admiral there, he sailed through the Straits of Fuca, entered the Gulf of Georgia, and, forcing his way through, passed at length into the Pacific by Queen Charlotte Sound, giving his name to the island he had thus circumnavigated.

Sir A. Mackenzie, in 1792, explored the shores of the Peace River for a distance of 200 miles.

In the year 1806, Mr. Fraser, a gentleman in the employ of the North-West Company, crossed the Rocky Mountains at Leather Pass, from Canada; descended the river which bears his name, until he arrived at a lake, which he also christened after himself; and here he erected a fort, and established a trading post, at the 54th parallel of latitude. In 1810, an American company, called the Pacific Fur Company, under the superintendence of John Jacob Astor (who afterwards became the wealthiest merchant in America), a German merchant of New York, formed other trading communities.

BOUNDARY-LINE.

At a later period, difficulties arose as to the right of possession between various governments. Russia claimed certain territory west of the Rocky Mountains and north of 54° 40′, including Sitka and its neighbourhood. In 1823, President Monroe announced his celebrated Monroe doctrine, that further colonization by European Powers would be opposed. From this time forward, up to 1844, matters between England and the United States wore a threatening aspect. "Fifty-four, forty, or fight," was the rallying cry of the American Democratic party. Fortunately, negotiations and diplomatic arrangements were not controlled by the rabble. The line of the 49th parallel, from the Rocky Mountains to the sea, was the basis of settlement for this vexed question; but, alas! no human foresight can prevent contingencies. The line was to continue through the centre of the Gulf of Georgia, and thence southward, through the channel which separates the continent from Vancouver Island, to the Straits of Juan de Fuca. Now, subsequent exploration proved there were three channels instead of one. Of course the Americans claimed the furthest north as the boundary-line, the British the furthest south. Thanks to nature, there is a centre one; and it is to be hoped both parties will amicably arrange this matter, at the earliest possible moment.

LAKES AND RIVERS.

The surface of the whole country is intersected with mountains, hills, lakes, rivers, and plains. There is a range of mountains called the Cascade Mountains, between the coast and the Rocky Mountains: further south they are called the Sierra Nevada.

The principal lakes are Stuart's Lake, in lat. 54° 50', long. 124° W. This lake is fifty miles in length, and from three to four miles in breadth. Fraser's Lake is fifty miles west of this, and about eighty-five miles in circumference. M'Leod's Lake, in latitude 55°, is in circumference about fifty-five miles. Further south we have Lakes Quesnelle, Chilcotin, and Axe, all connected with Fraser's River. Green Lake, Shoushwap Lake, Kamloop's Lake, and Harrison's Lake are all connected with Thompson River.

The Okanagan Lake, Upper and Lower Arrow Lake, and Flat Bow Lake are all connected with the waters of Columbia River, which crosses the boundary-line at 49° lat., and extends its branches northward and westward as far as 52° 40', and along the western base of the Rocky Mountains.

Mr. Hazlitt, in a useful little volume, entitled "The Great Gold-Fields of Cariboo," speaking of the rivers, says:—" The principal rivers of British Columbia are Fraser's River, Salmon River, Thompson's River, Quesnelle's River, Chilcotin River. The head waters of the chief of these, Fraser's River—called by the natives Tatoutche Tesse—rise near those of Canoe River, the most northern branch of the Columbia. After a western course of about 150 miles, it receives the Salmon River from the north, and somewhat lower the waters of Stuart's River are added from the north-west. The stream is then swollen by the Quesnelle River, rising from a ridge of the Rocky Mountains, and running west into the main river of the district. Next comes the Chilcotin River, so called from a cognominal lake, in which it has its source. This stream, which is shallow and full of rapids, runs in a S.S.E. direction from Fort Alexandria; its course is serpentine, and its whole length 180 miles, the breadth varying from forty to sixty yards.

" Further on, this main stream is joined, on the left shore, by Thompson's River, which, rising near the source of Quesnelle's River, flows at the base of the mountains which bound the Columbia to the west: this receives the waters of several lakes in a course of above 300 miles. The principal of these is Thompson's, above which it is joined by the Shoushwap, which has its rise between the Okanagan lakes and main streams of the Columbia.

"The place at which Thompson's River joins Fraser's River is called 'The Forks.' In parallel 49° this now important river breaks through the Cascade range of mountains, in a succession of falls and rapids, and then running westward about ninety miles, falls into the Gulf of Georgia, six miles north of 49° N., that parallel being the boundary-line between the British territories and those of the United States. The whole length is stated at about 400 miles. The country along its lower section is hilly and thickly wooded, and the soil is for the most part suitable both for arable and pasture land. Further north the country is equally well wooded, but it is less genial and fertile, and is intersected by mountains, torrents, gullies, and ravines.

"At its mouth, Fraser's River is about a mile wide, with a serpentine channel leading through a mud flat. Fort Langley is situated on the left bank, thirty-five miles from the mouth. Thus far the stream is navigable for vessels of considerable burden. The next post is Fort Hope, at the mouth of Que-Queallon River, sixty-five miles above Fort Langley. Between Fort Hope and Fort Yale, sixteen miles, the river presents no difficulties whatever to a canoe ascending, excepting in one place, where there is a rapid, which, however, is no great obstacle, as close to the shore, in the eddy, a canoe is easily towed past it. But, about one half mile above Fort Yale, the river finds its passage between huge rocks—the sides almost perpendicular—and a canoe cannot be taken any farther. From thence, all goods have to be packed. Now and then a stretch of a mile or so is found, where the canoe can be of service.

"From Fort Yale to the forks of Thompson and Fraser Rivers is ninety miles; and from these to the Grand Falls, thirty."

GOLD AND THE GOLD-MINES.

Before we proceed to a consideration of the agricultural resources of British Columbia, or attempt a description of its forests, or any other of its elements of wealth, we know that the emigrant has linked the name of gold with all connected with this territory, and that that subject is the one he feels most interest in.

"Why this
Will buy your priests and servants from your sides;
Pluck stout men's pillows from below their heads.
 This yellow slave
Will knit and break religions; bless the accursed;
Make the hoar leprosy adored; place thieves,
And give them title, knee, and approbation,
With senators on the bench!"

It is indeed a wondrous talisman, and an all-powerful agent for good or evil. It tempted a Judas to betray his master, and an Arnold his country; it gave Cæsar the means of purchasing the allegiance of his enemies, and it made James, King of England, the tool of Louis of France. It melted the heart of Diana with its glittering hue, and has gifted old age with the fascinations of Mars. Princes and merchants, youth, beauty, and innocence, are alike its willing worshipper.

> "Gold is the strength, the sinews of the world;
> The health, the soul, the beauty most divine.
> A mask of gold hides all deformities;
> Gold is Heaven's physic, life's restorative."

The luxuries, comforts, and quietude of a happy home, with the dear family links that should bind us there—the warm appeals from those who have a right to counsel and advise; the warnings given with prophetic utterance of privations and hardships in store; the love of country, her institutions and her protective influence; the long and weary voyage across the stormy ocean, with its attendant discomforts and dangers; the slow and laborious travel over cheerless plains, up and down rugged mountains, and over numberless streams; the solitude of night on the vast and wide-spread prairies; the disappointments that continually cross our path—are alike incapable of stopping our onward progress. Gold has burnt its name into our brain—every marvellous story of sudden accumulated or discovered wealth is treasured up in our memory. In visions and in dreams we gild and silver the rafters and walls of our quiet and comfortable cottage with the products of the mines of Mexico and Peru, Australia and California. The solid pyramid at Sydenham Palace, that raises its gilded column as a symbol of the wealth of one of England's colonies, is but another incentive to our already disquieted brain, and tempts us to seek the source from whence it came. All that produces gold, or is a symbol of wealth, alike fascinates us. Has the sight of the Koh-i-noor—that "mountain of light," that "monarch of diamonds," that a Queen alone is thought worthy to wear—ever ceased to be forgotten? Rather has the beholder travelled in imagination to Golconda, and pondered over its wealth of diamonds, rubies, chrysolites, garnets, amethysts, cornelians, jaspers, agates, and opals. We never reflect upon the labour or the means by which they are obtained. The proud duchess only thinks of the effect of the diamonds that flash from her coronet—the thousands of wedded brides, when the golden symbol is slipping surely on the finger that links them heart and altar bound, in the moment of their royal joy, have no thought of the miner who washed it from the sands, or picked it from the crushed quartz thousands of miles across the ever-moving sea, and who is, perhaps, now laid quietly in

> "Death's northern sea of frozen waves."

Neither does the coy maiden, who, with downcast gaze, is idly toying with a string of pearls, yet is listening with eager attention to her lover's words, think of the agony which swelled the veins to bursting of the poor diver who groped the sands beneath the waves to gather gems for her adornment. No; we never ask how many fingers grew weary over the embroidered dress that is now a wonder of taste; we never think, when gazing on some statue that seems to us a miracle of beauty, of the study, thought, and patient labour by which it was brought from its unshapen state to its perfect form. We never ask what labour was bestowed on this or that. The Pyramids are towering in their height on Egypt's sands; the Vatican proudly lifts her classic columns above the capitoline hills of imperious Rome; the gloomy architectural pile of St. Paul's rises in stately grandeur in the midst of a city who is to-day Queen of the commercial world. We look, we see, and are satisfied. The busy hand, the combined herculean strength, the architectural conceivers, and the mechanical employers have all gone: marble, stone, and brick remain.

Gold is embedded in the quartz and sand of the Pacific to an unlimited extent, and in sufficient quantities to supply the demands of the world for centuries to come.

Australia, California, and British Columbia, between the years 1849-63, have produced £350,000,000, or equal to 58 per cent. upon the total computed stock of £600,000,000 sterling of gold existing in various forms in Europe and America.

With such evidence as this in existence, is it to be wondered at that the brain becomes dazzled with figures, and that there is a longing in the mind of the dissatisfied to try the chances in this great lottery of gold?

All the glittering stories of Pizarro have been realized; the rainbow bubble of the South Sea has burst into showers of auriferous wealth. The gifts of the Queen of Sheba, the wealth of Indian rajas, and the hidden stores of the misers of Egypt, are atoms in the scale where the splendours of the Pacific weigh in the balance.

" God made mankind;
See what mankind have made their god."

So says Alfred Evelyn, in Bulwer's play of " Money."

The colonies of Victoria, New South Wales, and New Zealand—the slopes of the Sierra Nevada in California; the vast interior district of Cariboo, which parts the waters of the Columbia, Fraser, Saskatchewan, Athabasca, and Peace Rivers, to every point of the compass; the slopes of Gold Hill and Snowy Mountain in Colorado—possess rivers like that of Pison, " encompassing the whole land of Havilah, where there is gold, and the gold of the land is good."

DISCOVERY OF THE GOLD.

As early as June, 1856, Governor Douglas reported to the

Secretary of State the discovery of gold in British Columbia. D. G. Forbes Macdonald, C.E., F.R.G.S., in his work on British Columbia, thus expatiates on the effects which the discovery of gold produced:—" The announcement was received, however, with comparative disbelief until June 1858, when the reported wealth of the Fraser River mines produced an excitement which resulted in an unparalleled exodus. The fever all over the State of California was intense, and few, if any, escaped its contagion. Multitudes pressed on to the new Eldorado by steamers, sailing-vessels, barques, brigs, and schooners, until upwards of 40,000 souls had landed on Vancouver's Island. The poor, the rich, the old, the young, and even the decrepit, had gone; merchants, doctors, lawyers, loafers, all had gone. Brethren of the creeds of Calvin, Luther, and Penn, the admirers of Voltaire, and the fellow-thinkers of Tom Paine, had gone also to add their quota to the motley crowd. The price of revolvers and bowie-knives advanced; and everything indicated that the State of California would lose nearly all her male population. Business men of all classes abandoned their occupations. Many went without money, many with; some to invest in real estate, others to swindle, many to gamble; some out of curiosity, some to steal, and many to die. In this remarkable throng were blended all ranks, all professions, and all parties. An eager strife of tongues prevailed in this second Babel; and even the voice of women rose loud and incessant in the throng. People of all nations went; and many borrowed sums at ruinous interest, advanced on goods and property, which soon passed away into the ruthless hands of the usurer."

The comprehensive and carefully written letter of the special correspondent of the London *Times* conveys so correct an idea of the country, and treats in detail the whole subject so minutely, and its facts have been since so clearly established, that we have transferred much of the letter to these pages.

" *Victoria, Vancouver's Island, Jan.* 20, 1862.

" Beginning with Fraser River, the main artery of the auriferous region, I may state that gold is known to exist and has been worked at a great many places in the river and on its banks from a point about 45 miles from the mouth of the river up to near its source in the Rocky Mountains; in other words, from the 49th up to the 53rd parallel of north latitude, a distance (taking in the windings) of some 800 miles. The south branch of the Fraser has its sources near Mount Brown in the Rocky Mountains, in about 53° north latitude, 118° 40' west longitude. Thence this branch flows for 290 miles to Fort George, a post of the Hudson's Bay Company. The north branch rises in an opposite direction. It receives its supply from a series of lakes lying between 54° and 55° of north latitude, longitude about 124° 50' west, and runs a course of 260 miles to its junction with the south branch, some miles below the 54th parallel of north latitude. Here the union of the two branches forms the Fraser River proper. Adding the north branch, which is also a gold-bearing stream, and which was 'worked' last season, to the other arm, the two will give us a continuous stretch of auriferous riverain territory upwards of 1000 miles in length, extending for many miles back into the country on both sides, but not including the tributary rivers which fall into the Fraser. In short, the river itself is now known to be auriferous, and to pass through a gold-bearing country throughout its whole course. Gold is also found in most of the tributaries of the Fraser, of which no less than fifty-nine are known. The great length of the main river and the number of its tributaries will give some idea of the auriferous resources of the country.

GOLD ON FRASER RIVER.

" Besides the gold found in the beds and on the shores of these streams, the Fraser itself and many of its tributaries are skirted or bordered by terraces, all of which yield gold also. These terraces, or 'benches,' as the miners call them, run at intervals, along both sides of the rivers for miles in length; and they recede where the mountains retire, for distances back into the valleys, varying from a few acres to a few miles in breadth. They are objects of curiosity and speculation, and add much to the beauty of the rude scenes in which they occur, from the regularity and evenness of their structure. They generally occur on both sides of the river (opposite to each other), at the same place, sometimes at the same elevations on both sides, sometimes at different elevations, high on this and low on the other side of the river; and in some places they are multiplied into several successive level parallel plateaux, rising one above the other as they recede from the bank. These terraces are composed of the ordinary alluvial deposits—loam, gravel, stones, sand and boulders; and they are thick masses rising generally to a height of 150 to 200 feet.

" This geological formation occurs more frequently on the Fraser than on the other rivers. The terraces are also larger on the main river, in some cases assuming the proportions of hills, all with regular and perpendicular faces. Their formation is perhaps due to the fact that the valleys between the mountains were at one period filled up, or perhaps formed lakes. Each 'bench' may mark successive periods of drainage or subsidence of the water; and their present elevation above the rivers may be due to their having been cut away by the rapid-flowing streams. The tumultuous and swift-flowing Fraser would soon cut a bed for itself (as it has done) down to the rock.

" The terraces contain vast deposits of gold; and to be worked to advantage, the 'bench diggings' must command a stream of water supplied from a source higher than their own surfaces, so as to give a fall, to enable the miner to apply the water to the face of the 'bench' by a hose. The force of the stream is due to the height of the fall. A good strong stream playing upon the face of the hill will disintegrate a great quantity of 'pay dirt' in a short time. The floating rubbish, or 'dirt,' is caught in a long sluice at the base, provided with 'riffles' on the bottom, and spread with quicksilver to catch the gold. This mode of mining is called by the miners 'hydraulic mining.' Such is the wealth of Cariboo, that no quicksilver was used, for the miner could afford to lose all the 'fine dust,' and to be satisfied with the 'lumps.'

"It happens, fortunately, that Fraser River and most of its tributaries supply water in abundance at an elevation which affords the necessary fall, from the elevated and broken character of the country; while there are inexhaustible supplies in the numerous lakes dispersed all over the upper district. Timber for the erection of 'flumes' is also abundant everywhere.

"The canal system of British Columbia will be comparatively inexpensive, from the abundance of water and its eligibility—encouraging facts to the miner, because the small outlay of capital required will keep his 'water dues' low.

"A good deal of capital has been already invested profitably in 'water ditches,' or canals, for the supply of the miners on the Fraser, by old miners who had saved money, and by persons unconnected with mining. This interest will, in time, become a good subject for the investment of English capital, as the mining population increases.

"In British Columbia, property is fully protected by law, and its legitimate profits are secured to the capitalist who has invested his money in canals, not more by the operation of the Gold-Fields Act than by the existence of a healthy public sentiment. On the one hand, while the capitalist is allowed to realize a handsome return from his charges for the supply of water, the miner is, on the other hand, protected from extortion. Differences do arise, but they are always settled in a rational and peaceable way, either by appeal to the Gold Commissioner of the district, who has the power to take cognizance of such cases, or to the judge of the colony, who acts judicially.

"Whenever the 'bench diggings' have been 'worked' they have paid well. They have been neglected for the greater attractions of the 'placer diggings,' where the gold is found nearer the surface and with less labour. But I consider this class of diggings of great prospective value. They will give employment to two interests—capital and labour. They are generally situated within easy reach of supplies. They are more accessible to all the influences of civilization than more interior localities. They are in the neighbourhood of some good land, which will enable the labourer to alternate his time between mining and husbandry, and where he can make his *home*—the great want which the mines generally do not supply.

RICHNESS OF THE MINES.

"Although now neglected, the 'benches' will be appreciated and come into play when the efflorescence of gold near the surface shall have been exhausted. When this happens they will supply wealth and a profitable living to a mixed population of miners, ditch-owners, traders, and labourers, and that for a long period of time, of which no one can compute the numbers of the one nor the duration of the other.

"The reports of the mining this season on the Fraser in the space between Fort Hope and Fort George, a distance of about 270 miles, give the daily individual earnings at all sums between 3 dollars and 15 dollars. Very little has as yet been done between these two points, and very little will be done so long as the attractions of 100 dollars to 1000 dollars a day continue elsewhere. I will now carry you to other mining localities.

"The Similkameen mines yielded last season 16 dollars to 17 dollars a day to the hand occasionally. A party of three men took 240 dollars in three days' work from 'sluice diggings;' and the 'rocker,' used in 'wet diggings,' yielded 4 dollars, 5 dollars, and up to 8 dollars a day to the hand. Number of miners 200, of whom 150 were Chinese. A waggon road for 25 miles from Hope, and a bridle road of 15 miles in continuation, approach this district.

"Sixty miles further to the southward comes Okanagan. The average yield here was only 4 dollars a day, and the miners were few—some 26 men, some of whom divided their time between mining and husbandry. Okanagan Lake, a beautiful sheet of water, in a rich pastoral district, is from 80 to 100 miles long, and 8 to 10 miles wide, deep, and well suited to navigation. There is a small population in the valley, chiefly French Canadians, and a Catholic mission. There are two small lakes tributary to the great lake, and nineteen streams fall into the latter, of which seven yield gold.

"In the same general direction, and distant from Fort Hope 150 miles, is Rock Creek, close to the American frontier (lat. 49° north), and 60 miles west of the Columbia River. The longitude of Rock Creek is 119° west. This place acquired a temporary reputation in 1860 for the richness of its mines, when a considerable population flocked to it and extemporized a town. In 1861 most of the miners were seduced away by the superior attractions of Cariboo, the latest and richest Eldorado yet discovered, so that only 30 white men and 225 Chinamen remained.

"A party of three white men saved in the season 12,000 dollars that I know of, after paying expenses; 100 dollars a day to the hand was sometimes made. The average earnings are returned at

7 dollars a day per man. There are both 'bench' and 'wet' diggings, and both are productive and extensive. The place is now abandoned.

MINES ON THOMPSON RIVER.

"There being no more mining localities of any note on the southern frontier, we will proceed to the northward and westward for about 120 miles, passing on the way several auriferous streams flowing southward—and, in fact, in every direction—as well as a pastoral and agricultural country of great extent, without comment for the present, and get into the heart of the Thompson River country, as established by the Hudson's Bay Company, in their nomenclature of local divisions of the 'Indian Country.'

"If you could fancy yourself on the banks of the Thompson, you would find it a large, swift-flowing river, rolling with considerable impetuosity between high rocky banks. Near its mouth it is too full, too rapid, and too rocky for mining. Its source is not in the mountains, but comes from the overflow of a series of lakes dispersed over a large extent of the central portion of the country which lies to the eastward of the Fraser, and stretches over more than two degrees of latitude, and as many of longitude. It falls into the Fraser, after running a very tortuous course of perhaps 100 miles, at the small town of Lytton, a mining and trading hamlet on the forks of the two rivers, 75 miles (above) north, and a little to the west of Fort Hope.

"Several streams flow into the Thompson—the Nicaomeen and the Nicola—on its left or east bank. We are now in what may emphatically be called the 'Lake District.' The last-mentioned little river drains two lakes, Nicola Lake and Stump Lake—the first eight miles by three, the other much smaller. The next tributary is the Buonaparte, on the opposite side—a very important river, from its rich auriferous deposits and from the valuable arable soil through which it flows. It drains nine lakes, two of which, Loon and Vert, are each about 12 miles long. After receiving the Buonaparte, the Thompson describes three great tortuous bends, which brings it up to Lake Kamloops, which empties into it (I am describing the river up stream). Lake Kamloops is 20 miles long by five miles wide. From this lake the river continues its course to the east and north, receives the waters of the North River, and extends to Shushwap Lake, which also discharges into the Thompson. Shushwap Lake, a fine sheet of water, situated in a rich pastoral country, 45 miles long, 5 to 10 miles wide, and studded with islands, receives the waters of two other lakes, which discharge by the Barrière River, as well as those of two rivers of considerable length, which rise in the range that divides the valley of the Fraser from that of the Columbia. The lake is a little below the 51st parallel of north latitude, and the 119° of west longitude passes over the east end of it. Kamloops Lake is about a degree further west, and about 12 miles further south. The Tranquille and the Copper River both fall into the latter lake.

"The North River, already mentioned, runs nearly due north for a great portion of its course. Correctly speaking, it runs *from* the north, but I am describing as if I were ascending the river. This river has several tributaries of great length, some rising far to the eastward in the watershed of the great valley of the Fraser, and others draining a long chain of lakes stretching far up into the country beyond the 53rd parallel of north latitude, and embracing nearly three degrees of longitude; while its 'head waters' flow from a range which is the watershed of Swamp River, flowing in an opposite direction into the Cariboo country.

"All the streams which I have mentioned are auriferous—those which are tributary to the Thompson itself, and those which are tributary to its affluents.

"Such portions of the Thompson as run through somewhat level ground are also auriferous. Seven miles from Kamloops, 150 miners worked upon one of such portions, and made 16 dollars a day to the man, 'rocking' on the 'bars' in the bed when the river was low. The banks are very extensive, but require water ditches for 'washing' them, as they run high. Tranquille yielded 7 dollars, 15 dollars, and 20 dollars a day to 'a crowd of Chinamen.' North River gave 8 dollars to 10 dollars a day to the hand; and on the Barrière a community of French Canadians made as high as 50 dollars a day to the hand. Beyond the portions of North River, which have been worked for gold near its embouchure, the country hereabouts has not been prospected. This is about the centre of the colony, and about 80 miles of this space from south to north, by about 100 miles from east to west, have not been developed. It may be auriferous; but its character on the face of the soil is pastoral. It is a high table-land, which produces abundant pasture, free from forest, and only interspersed with timber. Its climate in summer is dry and equable, and in winter cold, but not severe; and noted for its salubrity. In fact, the climate of British Columbia is good throughout the whole extent of the country, and there is no drawback, except from the presence of the mosquitoes in summer. These insects are so numerous as to form a pest while they prevail.

"If we could pursue a straight western course from the Fort to Fraser River for about 100 miles, we should strike the new town of Lillooett, situated at a point where the two great routes of travel into the interior meet that from Hope and Lytton by the river, and that by the Harrison Valley and the Lillooett chain of lake. Lillooett is the great final starting-point to the northern mines, and beyond that there is no made road, and no other means of transport than horses, mules, and what the miners expressively term 'footing it.'

LILLOOETT GOLD-MINE.

"Lillooett is distant from the mouth of the Fraser (on the Gulf of Georgia) by the river route, *viâ* Hope, Yale, and Lytton, 220 miles; and by the Harrison route, *viâ* Harrison Lake, by steamer, Douglas, portages, and four lakes, crossed by steamers, 238 miles. The first route commands steamers up to Yale; the rest of the journey must be ridden or walked. The other route commands steamers to Douglas; a stage coach thence to Williams's Lake, 29½ miles, on a road made along the Harrison River, chiefly by the Royal Engineers; an open boat on the first lake of five miles, steamers on the other three lakes, which are together 49 miles long, and the portages between the lakes and Lillooett, which in the aggregate of the four of them are 33¾ miles long, can be ridden or walked. Both routes afford prospects of beauty and grandeur seldom seen elsewhere; but I dare not trespass on your space so far as to describe them, nor could I do justice to the subject if I tried. From Lillooett to the first or lower Cariboo mines the distance is about 260 miles.

"A few miles beyond Lillooett, and on the same (the west) side, Bridge River falls into the Fraser. Bridge River is very rich in gold. The Indians of the neighbourhood make considerable earnings in it, working in the rudest manner with the most inefficient implements. It was here the Bishop of Columbia found them making an ounce a day to the hand, as I mentioned in my last letter. Nodules of pure copper have been found in the bed of the river, indicating the existence of copper veins in the neighbouring banks.

CARIBOO GOLD RIVER.

"Quesnelle River has two branches, one of which drains Quesnelle Lake, lying a degree and a half to the eastward of the Fraser, and which is 50 miles long. The other branch drains Cariboo Lake, which receives Swamp River and Lower Cariboo Lake, into which Keithley's Creek, one of the Cariboo streams, empties. At the junction of the two branches, a town, the nearest to Cariboo diggings, is built, chiefly for the supply of the latter. The place is called 'The Forks of Quesnelle.'

"Both branches of the Quesnelle are highly auriferous. Mining began here in 1859, and led to the discovery of Cariboo, situate 50 miles further north. The returns for last summer were that nine out of ten of the chains paid over an ounce a day to the hand. The river-banks enable the miners to work in winter. The diggings must be rich to have retained any miners so close to Cariboo, where fortunes were made in the course of a few weeks.

"One grand prominent feature of the country is a chain of mountains, which runs from our southern frontier (on 49° north latitude) in a north-westerly direction through the country, and, in fact, beyond the northern limit of the colony. This range is in many parts very lofty, runs nearly parallel to the Rocky Mountains, and bears the successive names of the Snowy Mountains, the Bald Mountains, and the Peak Mountains, from the height of several of the more elevated portions having induced the belief that these portions were detached mountains, and not parts of a connected chain. It is now known that the different eminences, which at a distance seem to be isolated, in reality form but one vast range subordinate to the Rocky Mountains. It, in fact, forms the watershed of the great basin of the Fraser River, one side of which drains itself into the valley of the Fraser, and the other into that of the Columbia. The whole of this vast range is now known to be auriferous. It has been traced for 400 miles, and 'fine and coarse gold is everywhere found on its western slopes, from Rock Creek in the south to Cariboo in the north.' Cariboo itself is but one point in the range. It is nearly all in British territory, extending, as already remarked, beyond the northern frontier of British Columbia and into the Indian territory of Stickeen, to the east of the Russian possessions on the Pacific. It is the longest stretch of continuous inland gold-bearing country yet discovered in the world. Its value and importance are incalculable both to the mother country and to these colonies; for when it comes to be efficiently worked by tunnelling, it may continue to produce gold for ages, as long, perhaps, as gold retains its value among mankind. Respecting Cariboo, Governor Douglas was good enough to furnish me with the following statement in writing, taken down by himself from a Cariboo miner, Mr. Steele; but I received it after I had finished my letter:—

STEELE'S COMPANY.

"'Steele's company consisted of five partners, of whom Mr. Steele, an American, was one. Their claim was on Williams's Creek (Cariboo, of course). In the summer they sawed the lumber themselves, and made their own sluices. Their claim did not prospect as good as many other claims. Nevertheless, they went at it with a will; made nothing the first three days; persevered, and the fourth day made 4 oz.; the fifth day, 10 oz.; and the sixth day, 41 oz. (the market value of 41 oz. of gold in sterling is £290. 4s. 2d). From that time, after the sixth day's work, when the return rose to 41 oz. a day, it kept increasing, until it reached 387 oz. a day; and the last day's work yielded a return of 409 oz. The five partners employed "four hired hands" to assist them to clear away the tailings. The claim was one of the most difficult to work, as it required eight feet to eighteen feet of top-stripping of superincumbent earth, which covered the auriferous stratum, or "pay dirt." This latter was composed of a blue clay, six feet thick, mixed with gravel and decomposed slate. The whole area of the mine worked was only eighty feet by twenty-five feet, and the yield amounted to 105,000 dollars, equal to £21,875. That so much gold was dug out of so small a space as eighty feet by twenty-five feet is a pregnant fact. It proves that the wealth buried in this remote region lies concentrated in masses thick and plentiful, which is corroborated by the shortness of the period of labour—not over two months' actual work. This is a short period to have earned £21,875 in, certainly, yet the exuberance of the gold of these mines is more clearly demonstrated by the rapidity of the accumulation. I shall show this result more clearly by converting Mr. Steele's gold ounces into American currency. The produce of the labour of the first day that the claim yielded anything was 68 dollars; that of the next day, 170 dollars; of the following day, 697 dollars; and so on, increasing until it reached the astounding sum of 6579 dollars in a day; and culminated in a return of 6953 dollars on the "last day's work."

" 'To prevent any exaggeration in my conversion of the gold-dust, I have taken the money value of the ounce at 17 dollars, although the average value of Cariboo " dust " is 17 dollars 65 cents and 37-1000ths, so that I am under the mark. In other words, this company's gold produced to the partners more money in the market than I have valued it at. Their gold may have been worth 18 dollars the ounce.'

LABOUR IN BRITISH COLUMBIA.

" To show still more clearly to *English* readers the prospects and rewards of labour in British Columbia, I will paraphrase Mr. Steele's statement, which will place it in another and, perhaps, more practical light. I will suppose that the five miners who owned this mining claim were Englishmen, and that they had sent their earnings home. The gold would, by the rule of trade, go to the Bank of England, and be converted into sterling money—say in London. I will deduct all the charges of remitting the bullion (gold-dust), and then see what the miners would have, net money, in London. The fruit of their first day's 'yield' would be £13. 10s. 2d.; of the next day's yield would be £34. 14s. 2d.; the following day's yield, £1343. 4s. 3d.; and the last day's yield would be £1419. 11s. 5d. The mines would have been to them a prolific mother, for the last day's return shows an increase of £76. 7s. 2d. over and above the general run of the yield of 'lucky days,' as the miners term their successful and satisfactory periods. Mr. Steele's return of the gross yield was corroborated by the quantity of gold-dust brought to Victoria, where he remained for some time. Indeed, the miners seldom exaggerate their earnings. Their general reports take the opposite direction. The partners return to their claim in Cariboo in the spring to resume work, and they expect to do much better next season, as the mine is already well opened. To have made the statement complete, I should have mentioned that the four hired men did not share in the profits. They were paid 8 dollars a day wages and 'found;' and they did not work during the whole season.

"I may assert that there are no low earnings. Here is exactly how the matter stands. Some of the Chinamen, while serving their novitiate, are satisfied with such poor diggings as yield only 1 dollar to 2 dollars a day, but they are soon forced by their taskmasters, who paid their expenses from China and San Francisco, and for whose benefit they labour, and who tax them both for repayment of these expenses and for a profit on the venture, to abandon such poor diggings for a richer. And as to white miners, not one of them will work for the small earnings I have mentioned. If a miner cannot fall upon a rich 'claim' he will hire himself to other more fortunate claim-owners, who will pay him from 5 dollars to 10 dollars a day, according to location and circumstances. In this way it comes that no poor diggings are worked. The surface of the mineral region is being 'skimmed'—not efficiently worked. But by-and-by the miners will be satisfied with ground which they now reject. This time is distant, however, owing to the extent of the field, unless the country receives a large addition to its mining population. I suppose it would take half a million of miners to bring the mines into play. It would take a much larger population to develop them efficiently.

"Another cause influences the miner in his conduct. Wages generally are high for all kinds of labour. Common labourers get 3 dollars a day at the lowest; some get more. Farm labourers get £6 a month and are 'found.' I pay an English labourer, whom I found working on the roads, £10 a month, and he 'finds' himself, for looking after my horse and doing odds and ends about the place. This was his pay from the road contractor. Mechanics get 5 dollars (£1) a day. With these rates of wages in competition with mining, and with the prices of provisions very high in the remote mining country, owing to expense of transport, the miner naturally abandons poor diggings which yield a low return; so you understand why there are no *low* returns.

"My advice to emigrants from the old country will be short, and while it can easily be remembered, cannot be misunderstood. British Columbia wants two classes only—men with money, and men with bodily strength—*capitalists and labourers*. Both classes will do well. The one will find lucrative employment for its capital, the other still more profitable employment for its labour. If either fails it will be its own fault. Should either of these two classes be married, let them bring their wives and families; the more numerous the progeny the better."

EXPORT OF GOLD IN 1863.

Allen Francis, Esq., United States Consul at Victoria, Vancouver's Island, states that the export of gold from that port during the year 1863, as obtained from reliable sources, amounted to 2,925,170 dollars 16 cents; and he computes that an equal amount has been taken away in private hands; or about 6,000,000 dollars as the total export.

FERTILITY OF SOIL IN THE GOLD NEIGHBOURHOOD.

Mr. Pemberton says—

"The fertility of the soil in the neighbourhood of the gold-bearing rocks is very remarkable, and is indicated rather by the production from ordinary seed of gigantic roots and vegetables and fruits, than by crops of grains.

"An acre of land planted with 200 apple-trees would, at the end of three years, on a minute calculation, cost a proprietor from £30 to £40, and the lowest selling price of an acre of apple-trees of that age is £200.

"All along the coast of Vancouver's Island the fisheries may be described as beyond value. Salmon and herrings abound to an extent almost unknown elsewhere, and mackerel and cod are also found. There are also sturgeon, halibut, cod, skate, flounders, herrings, dog-fish, and oysters."

PROGRESS OF THE COLONY.

The progress of the colony of British Columbia during the first four years of its organization, will be illustrated by a statement of revenue which is raised almost entirely by customs' duties levied at New Westminster or the mouth of Fraser River, and by a mining licence of 20s. per year for each man. During the first year of the existence of British Columbia as a colony—that is, to the 31st of December, 1859—the customs' duties amounted to £18,464, the receipts from other sources being quite trifling. In the succeeding year, 1860, the customs' receipts were estimated by Governor Douglas at £58,980; other sources, £47,050. One-third of the gross revenue is devoted to the construction of roads and bridges, which are objects of first necessity in a rugged mining country. By the improvement of the roads from the mouth of the Fraser River to stations 300 miles distant, the cost of transport has been reduced to about 20s. a ton, which is 300 per cent. less than in 1860.

VANCOUVER'S ISLAND.

The Island of Vancouver, with its excellent harbourage in Puget's Sound, is in the latitude, and is not unlike the climate of Ireland. The coldest weather of the year is in December; but little snow falls, disappearing usually in a few days. The frosts which precede and follow penetrate the soil but a few inches, and the lakes are covered with ice sufficiently strong to bear the skater only during a few weeks. The climate is mild and equable, but warmer in summer than in England. Cattle, horses, sheep, and hogs, are seldom housed. Probably not more than half the surface of the island is adapted to agriculture, but the soil is of excellent quality, and all other conditions favourable. Wheat, oats, barley, hay, and vegetables are produced, and the almost ever-green turf is well suited to grazing. The section of country now in course of agricultural settlement is within 60 miles of Victoria, the leading town of the island, and is known as the district of Courchan. The conditions on which land may be taken there, as elsewhere in Vancouver's Island, are easy. A single man may pre-empt 150 acres; a married man, with his wife in the colony, 200 acres; and for each child under ten years of age, 10 acres additional. The Government price for the land is 1 dollar an acre. If unsurveyed land be pre-empted, the settler has to pay for it when surveyed. If surveyed, he has three years in which to pay the purchase-money. Another condition makes it incumbent on the pre-emptor to occupy and improve his claim. When 2 dollars an acre are expended in improvements, the Government will make a title; but not so unless the settler has resided on his claim two years.

COAL-BEDS.

Vancouver's Island is the naval station of England in the North Pacific. The harbour of Esquimault, three miles from Victoria and near the Straits of San Júan, is a magnificent haven, fit to shelter a whole navy in safety. The forests of the island are an inexhaustible resource for ship-building, while the coal-mines at Nanaimo, 60 miles from Victoria, on the sheltered navigation of the Gulf of Georgia, are of the best possible quality—bituminous and extensive. The seams now worked at Nanaimo are respectively 3 feet 10 inches, 5 feet, and 2 feet 5 inches, and have been traced to the north-west extremity of the island, where Johnson's Straits furnish excellent land-locked harbours. Up to 1858 the Hudson's Bay Company had, in nine years, taken 63 tons; but during 1863, 22,000 tons have been exported to San Francisco alone, where it found a remunerative sale, though the price at the pit's mouth is 6 dollars per ton. Behind Nanaimo a remarkable natural cleft, known as Albeoni Canal, leads into Barclay Sound, where a London firm have established saw-mills, which, during nine months of 1863, cut and exported 15,000,000 superficial feet of the finest planking from the Douglas and other pines. These details of the coal and lumber trade indicate the great advantages of Vancouver for the construction, repair, and coaling of vessels.

Northward of Puget's Sound the coast of British Columbia is so broken with fiords and inlets, and sheltered by islands, as to present the greatest possible advantages for fisheries and a coasting trade. The salmon, herring, and other fisheries of this region will equal those of Norway.

Table of Imports to Victoria, Vancouver's Island, for the Years 1861, 1862, and 1863.

	1861.	1862.	1863.
	Dollars.	Dollars.	Dollars.
From San Francisco...................	1,288,359	2,345,066	1,880,117
From Washington Territory and Puget's Sound	228,350	224,793	242,781
From Oregon.......................	216,603	75,370	108,603
Total	1,733,212	2,645,229	2,230,501
From England.......................	516,041	694,278	1,432,521
From Sandwich Islands................	54,382	112,108	113,486
From British Columbia................	31,454	32,424	65,870
From China........................		22,268	45,434
From Melbourne....................		32,170	
From Valparaiso		17,000	
Total	601,877	910,248	1,657,311

Statement of Exports from the Port of Victoria, Vancouver's Island, during the Six Months ending December 31, 1863.

TO WHAT PLACE.	July.	Aug.	Sept.	Oct.	Nov.	Dec.	Total.
	Dollars.	Dollars.	Dollars.	Dollars.	Dollars.	Dollars.	Dollars.
San Francisco...	20,673	25,015	16,650	28,112	23,217	25,456	139,123
Port Angelos....	5,970	6,804	6,187	8,863	3,983	10,412	42,024
Astoria..........	945	1,727	637	4,208	2,586	361	10,464
New York		349					349
Total.......	27,588	33,895	23,474	40,983	29,791	36,229	191,960

Statement of the Export of Gold from Victoria, Vancouver's Island, from 1858 to 1863, inclusive.

	Dollars.	Cents.
1858. Wells, Fargo, and Co.	337,765	17
1859. Wells, Fargo, and Co.	823,488	41
1860. Wells, Fargo, and Co.	1,298,466	00
1861. Wells, Fargo, and Co.	1,340,395	72
1862. Wells, Fargo, and Co.	1,573,096	16
1863. Wells, Fargo, and Co.	1,373,443	39
M'Donald and Co., from 1858 to December 31, 1861	1,207,656	00
1862. Not included in Wells, Fargo, and Co.'s statement.	335,379	00
1863. Bank of British North America	585,617	85
1863. Bank of British Columbia	824,876	92
Hudson Bay Company and others, from 1858 to 1863, inclusive, approximate	500,000	00
	10,200,184	64
Shipment of gold by express and on freight during the year 1863	2,935,170	16
Same for the year 1862	2,167,183	18

Captain Mayne, R.N., in his concluding chapter on British Columbia, says:—" As a rule, picking up gold is a mere delusive figure of speech. It has to be dug and worked for hardly—with primitive appliances often, sometimes with all the resources of modern mechanism. Before attempting to describe shortly the various processes of extracting the precious mineral, I may say that they all require the aid of water and, with rare exceptions, quicksilver. It is the abundant natural supply of water that gives British Columbia so great an advantage over California. The country is, as I have before said, and as a glance at the map will show, intersected with streams and rivers, while lakes of various size abound, the majority of which may be easily adapted to the purposes of mining. The very height of the hills also, which may be in other respects a disadvantage, proves in this case of use to the miner, who can divert to his purpose the torrents which course down their sides. In California the want of water has been much felt, and the methods resorted to for melting it illustrate as much as anything else in that marvellous country the enterprise and spirit of the American settler.

PROSPECTING.

"The first task of the miner attracted to a new gold country or district by the report of its wealth, is 'prospecting.' For this purpose every miner, however light his equipment may otherwise be, carries with him a 'pan,' and a small quantity of quicksilver; the latter to be used only where the gold is very fine. Very little experience enables a miner to detect that 'colour' of the earth which indicates the presence of the metallic sand in which the gold is found. Wherever, as he travels through the new country, he sees this, he stops at once to wash a pan of dirt, and thus test its value. Although many diggings are found away from the bank of a stream, the river-sides are the places where gold is generally first looked for and worked. In saying this, of course I except gold in quartz, of which I shall have to speak hereafter. The spots first searched are generally those upon the bank of a river, where the deposit consists of a thick, stiff clay, or mud, with stones. In some cases this is covered with sand, so that the surface has to be removed before the 'pay dust' is revealed. All these workings on river-banks are called 'bars,' and are usually named after the prospector, or from some incident connected with their discovery."

PANNING.

When the prospector comes to dirt which looks as if it would pay, he unslings his pan from his back, and proceeds to test it. This he effects by filling his pan with the earth, then, squatting on the edge of the stream, he takes it by the rim, dipping it in the water, and giving it a kind of rotary motion, stirring and kneading the contents occasionally, until the whole is completely moistened. The larger stones are then thrown out, the edge of the pan canted upwards, and a continual flow of water made to pass through it, until, the lighter portion of its contents being washed away, nothing but a few pebbles and specks of black metallic sand are left, among which the gold, if there be any, will be found. The rotary movement, by which the heavier pebbles and bits of gold are kept in the centre of the pan, and the lighter earth allowed to pass over its edge, requires considerable practice; and an unskilful prospector will, perhaps, pass by a place as not being worth working, that an experienced hand will recognize as very rich. The specific gravity of the black sand being nearly equal to that of the gold, while wet they cannot be at once separated; and the nuggets, if any, being taken out, the pan is laid in the sun, or by a fire, to dry. When dry, the lighter particles of sand are blown away; or if the gold is very fine, it is amalgamated with quicksilver. The miners know by practice how much gold in a pan will constitute a rich digging, and they usually express the value of the earth as "5, 10, or 15 per cent. dirt," meaning that each pan so washed will yield so much in money. Panning, it may be remarked, never gives the full value of the dirt, as may be imagined from the roughness of the process. If the gold should be in flakes, a good deal is likely to be lost in the process, as it will not then sink readily to the bottom of the pan, and is more likely to be washed away with the sand. In panning, as well as, indeed, in all other primitive processes of washing gold, the superior specific gravity of this metal over others, except platinum, is the basis of operations—all depending upon its settling at the bottom of whatever vessel may chance to be used." There are other modes, such as "rocking," or cradling, which is done by placing a box upon rockers. The bottom of the box is provided with cleets, which are placed to arrest the passage of the gold; a continual stream of water runs through the dirt, which has been placed in the box; and it is thus disintegrated. Quicksilver is sometimes placed on a piece of cloth at the bottom, when the gold is fine, and the small particles are thus arrested.

"Hydraulic mining" and "ground sluicing" are of course more intricate, requiring a large capital. To those who desire a comprehensive description of gold-mining in general, we cannot do better than recommend Captain Mayne's book on British Columbia and Vancouver's Island.

AGRICULTURE.

To sum up this chapter, we shall quote the following remarks on Vancouver's Island, contained in the Surveyor's Report for 1860:—" I am firmly persuaded that, under a common judicious system of farming, as good returns can be obtained from these lands as in any part of the continent of America. The climate, it may be noted, is one especially adapted for the pursuits of agriculture, not being subject to the heats and droughts of California, or to the colds of the other British American Provinces and the Eastern United States. The loamy soils everywhere, possessing a depth of two or three feet, and containing a large proportion of the calcareous principle, are especially eligible for fruit-culture; and the oak-plains around the Sanenos and Quamichan Lakes, with a sandy clay subsoil, are exceedingly well adapted for fruit or garden purposes. Among the native fruits, the blackberry, mulberry, raspberry, strawberry, gooseberry, currant, and high bush-cranberry, would require little pains or culture to produce luxuriantly. The varieties of plants are very numerous—a few only were noted growing on the plains or meadow lands, among which are the following:—Wild pea, wild beans, ground-nut, clover, field-strawberry, wild oat, cut grass, wild timothy, reed, meadow grass, long spear-grass, sweet grass, high ostrich-fern, cowslip, crowfoot, winter cress, partridge-berry, wild sunflower, marigold, wild lettuce, nettles, wild angelica, wild lily, broad-leafed rush, and reed-bush. The ferns attain a height of six or eight feet, and the grasses have all a vigorous growth."

We have thus far traced our way from Newfoundland, in the Atlantic Ocean, to Vancouver's Island, on the Pacific coast—a distance of over 3000 miles of territory; and such is the extent of the Confederacy of British North America.

CHAPTER X.

THE RAILWAY SYSTEM OF NORTH AMERICA.

Early Travelling—Steam a Revolutionizer—Length of Railway in England, France, and the United States—Opening of the Ohio and Mississippi Railroad—Professor Mitchell's Testimony as to their Value—Increase in Traffic of American Railways—Railway System of Nova Scotia and New Brunswick—Canadian Railways—The Inter-Colonial Railway—General Review of the Subject—The Duty of England towards the proposed British North American Confederacy.

"Peace has her victories no less renowned than war."

EARLY TRAVELLING.

THERE are a world of pleasant memories connected with the early days of travelling during the first quarter of the present century: the spanking, dashing, blooded four-in-hand—the gorgeous coach, with its artistic decorations—the select and closely muffled quartette that delighted in the exclusiveness of the interior—the good-natured jovial crowd that ornamented the exterior—the burly, purple-faced coachman that so beautifully handled the ribbons—the gorgeously dressed guard in his scarlet and gold. It was a fine sight indeed to see the Royal Mail coaches dash by at the tremendous speed of twelve miles an hour. Merrily did the guardsman peal out his notes from the brightly burnished horn, sharply did the coachman crack his whip at the splendid leaders, and loud were the exclamations of delight that greeted the performances from the throats of the admiring rustics through whose village the coach went rolling on its way. Those were the days when the commercial traveller, with his tidy gig, his well-groomed horse, and his complete surroundings, was the oracle of interior towns; those were the days when a trip to London from the distance of only a hundred miles was an episode in life not to be lightly dealt with. Those were the days when gipsies kept high carnival on Salisbury Plain, and when Dick Turpin, Jack Sheppard, Paul Clifford, and other chivalrous guerillas, relieved gouty millionares of their superabundant cash, and played the cavalier to young and unprotected females with auburn hair and blue eyes; when loving couples rushed in frantic haste to Gretna Green, without the fear of interruption by the electric click that annihilates space; and when news was fresh from across the Atlantic when it was two months old.

STEAM A REVOLUTIONIZER.

Times have changed! The age is utilitarian. Iron hands impelled by steam never exhaust their strength; thought flashes with its intelligence, and electric-lighted tells its story with wings more speedy than the flight of time. Morse has stolen the lightning which blighted and bruised, and made it the dove-like messenger of commerce and the chronicler of daily events. Cugnot, Evans, Symington, Murdoch, Blenkinsop, Brunel, and Stevenson, have revolutionized the system of locomotion, and opened up a means for the absorption of capital, with security for interest, and brought the distant boundaries of England within a day's reach of the metropolis. Steam power and harmonious locomotion have given a throbbing heart to the commodious vessel that speeds over the waves; it has saved the human race a world of exhaustive toil, and, mighty in its strength, it labours on uncomplaining and unexhausted. The engine upon land and upon the sea is the great propeller of commerce and human life. In 1862 there were 9466 steam-vessels, with a total of 3,153,440 tons, entered the ports of Great Britain; and during the same period there were cleared 8588 steam-vessels, with a total of 3,052,960 tons.

LENGTH OF RAILWAY IN ENGLAND, FRANCE, ETC.

Mr. Watkins, M.P., in one of his practical and most sensible statements, made a few days since, said that "Great Britain possessed 12,006 miles of railway, which had cost £400,000,000, that they gave employment to 250,000 men, and that over £12,000,000 was annually distributed in salaries and wages."

France possesses over 9000 miles of railway.

The United States possessed over 33,000 miles of railway on the 1st of January, 1865.

Thirty-five years since the first railway between Manchester and Liverpool was constructed, and in that year Stevenson's "Rocket" astonished the gaping multitude by running thirty miles an hour.

Russia has railways through the arctic climes, India is opening up her country to the iron labourer, whose shrill whistle cowes the lion in his den and the tiger in his jungle. The Red Indian sullenly retires before the advancing smoke that is pushing its way through his hunting-grounds, and nature opens paths and vistas through her choicest abodes.

The cost to England of her railway system is one-half her national debt, yet no one will gainsay every pound spent has not been productive of good.

Great countries, like British North America and the United States, can afford to subscribe one-fourth of the value of their real estate for the purpose of opening up the country; and especially is this the case in interior countries or states.

In considering the value of railways in America, we cannot use their relative value in Europe as a criterion. Distance, to the people of the New World, is as nothing compared to its importance in the Old World. A Canadian or American thinks nothing of packing his carpet-bag after breakfast and leaving Montreal or New York for New Orleans, or with a little more preparation he proceeds to California or British Columbia with less ado than an Englishman makes who proposes visiting Baden-Baden or Wiesbaden.

Europe is the market for the lumber of New Brunswick, Maine, Canada, and Nova Scotia. The cod-fish of Newfoundland; the wheat, flour, and corn of Canada and the Western States, such as Ohio, Illinois, Wisconsin, Michigan, and Minnesota; the beef, pork, and cheese, that the prairies produce in such abundance, all come from the West to the East; and as communication is opened up, and the canal, the steamboat, and the railway pierce the very heart of the interior, so finding a market for the productions of the soil, stalwart men will plough and reap, grow corn, raise cattle, and convert a wilderness into a pasture land, and bring your products

> " From the forests and the prairies,
> From the great lakes of the Northland,
> From the land of the Ojibways,
> From the land of the Dacotahs,
> From the mountains, moors, and fenlands,
> Where the heron, the shu-shu-gah,
> Feeds among the reeds and rushes."

OPENING OF THE OHIO AND MISSISSIPPI RAILROAD.

It is some eight years since we were a guest upon the occasion of the celebration of the opening of the Ohio and Mississippi Railroad, which was to unite the East and the West between St. Louis, Missouri, and Baltimore, Maryland. The celebration was conducted on a scale of princely liberality; the guests amounted to over a thousand. The tickets gave the holder permission to travel for three weeks over a series of lines of railway, which reached 9000 miles. The most eminent men in America composed the happy party, who, during this time, travelled through a dozen different states, meeting on their way festivals and banquets too numerous to mention. Forty-two different lines of railroads were enumerated who had joined in the invitation, and from the 27th of May till the 13th of June, the guests travelled *free*. There was thus an opportunity of seeing the country not often presented, and as Americans are all "born orators from the age of five years and upwards," we enjoyed the occasion to such an extent that we have not ceased to remember it to this day, and many of the incidents have been treasured in our note-book. It may, perhaps, while speaking of the necessity for railways, be proper to quote some of the remarks made by the orators who, upon that auspicious occasion, gave vent to their opinions and thoughts.

The Mayor of Baltimore (Hon. Mr. Swann) said: "There is no expenditure of capital—there is no employment of labour—there is no direction that can be given to the enterprise of your citizens, which contributes, or can contribute, more to the value and prosperity of a country, than the construction of railroads through densely peopled neighbourhoods, or in regions where nature has failed to provide facilities for an easy interchange between convenient markets.

"Situated, as you are here, in the midst of a country unsurpassed in all the elements of substantial wealth, you naturally look to the readiest market and the highest prices for the productions of your soil. Without these, your resources are undeveloped; and your career must be more or less retarded by the contingencies to which you are exposed, in the absence of artificial aids."

TESTIMONY OF PROFESSOR MITCHELL.

Professor Mitchell, the astronomer, related the following incident, in reference to a section of country that at this day teems with agricultural wealth:—

"Well do I remember a family with whom I passed a night in my early explorations on the banks of the little Wabash. On all sides of their cabin stretched the rich and boundless prairie. The fertile soil yielded abundant return for the labour of the hard-working husbandman. But, alas! the crops were even but partly gathered, and a sort of dependent gloom rested on the brow of the sun-bronzed farmer. 'Why don't you gather your corn?' said I. 'What's the use?' was the reply. 'We have gathered and cribbed more than enough for our own use. It is utterly impossible to reach a market: there is no one to buy, and we have no inducement to labour. Our sons and daughters are growing up around us in ignorance. The turnpike road has failed; the State works have failed; and now a last ray of hope has been kindled by the talk of a great railway from St. Louis to Cincinnati. We have enough of everything; all we want is an outlet. But there seems to be no chance, and we are slowly sinking into gloom and despair.'"

And yet from that very region of country which Professor Mitchell referred to only eight years since, and on that railroad whose completion we were celebrating, the report of the Secretary of the Interior of the United States for 1864 proves that there passed, bound to the Atlantic coast, over £10,000,000 worth of freight for the year ending 1863; and that very farmer who complained of his poverty is now one of the largest graziers in the State of Illinois.

When we hear people grumbling, because their city or village subscribed so much towards the construction of some railway that brings luxuries to their doors and carries away every bushel of corn they can grow, we have no patience with them. They don't like the taxes. Why, some men would live without paved streets, gas to light their houses, sewers to carry off the elements of miasmatic fevers, police to protect themselves and their property, courts of justice to decide between right and wrong, and, in fact, an army and navy to sustain the national honour, and even a government to represent them, because of the taxes. Why, there is not a property-holder in Canada or the United States who would not be eventually benefited by subscribing, as we have before remarked, the fourth in value of all his real estate, and in the interior one-half of all his lands, towards the railroads that are under construction. For they may rest assured that the agricultural increase of the country will be upon an equal ratio with the extension of the railway.

Look at the saving in time and in labour, and consider the saving in expense!

INCREASE IN TRAFFIC OF AMERICAN RAILWAYS.

It is only a few years since that the stock of the Erie Railway was as low as 5 per cent. on the face of its value; to-day it pays 8 per cent. in gold on its value at par.

In 1862, the stock of the Hudson River Railroad of New York was 30 dollars a share, and paid no dividend. It now pays 7 per cent. in gold on 130 dollars per share.

The receipts of the New York Central Railroad, in 1854, amounted to 5,918,355 dollars; in 1864, they had increased to 12,997,889 dollars.

The Illinois Central earned, in 1863, 4,571,028 dollars on a capital of 19,000,000 dollars.

The Grand Trunk Railway of Canada, in 1861, on 1090 miles, earned £142,492; while in 1863, on 1174 miles, the road earned £315,036; and for the first half of the year 1864, £181,791, against £133,289 for the same period, from January to June, 1863.

It will thus be seen that the increase of railways is something marvellous in America, and that, however large the expenditure of capital, the interest is certain and rapidly increasing; and we have no doubt that, within the next five years, at the present rate of increase in traffic and passengers, the Grand Trunk Railway will be able to pay a dividend of 7 per cent. on every dollar and pound of its capital. There is no company to-day, either in Europe or America, which is conducted with more careful economy and more splendid ability. The president is one of the most able political economists and financial statisticians of the age, and when we know he is associated with such colleagues as Thomas Baring, M.P., G. C. Glyn, M.P., and Charles J. Brydges, we can have no fears as to the future success of that grand system of railway, which sweeps along from the great lakes to the St. Lawrence River, over whose mighty and tumultuous waters it passes for two miles through the most magnificent tubular bridge in the world; then, hurrying on across the boundaries of Canada, and in sight of the snow-tipped mountains of New Hampshire and the green-plumed forests of Maine, it deposits its gathered treasures on the shores of the Atlantic Ocean, after traversing a distance of 1174 miles.

And this brings us to a consideration of the means whereby this railroad—already completed, with its connexions reaching so far to the west, and with other lines now projected—at one end may be continued to Halifax, Nova Scotia, and at the other may gradually find its way to those shores where India, Japan, China, Australia, and British Columbia are waiting for its coming.

RAILWAY SYSTEM OF NOVA SCOTIA AND NEW BRUNSWICK, ETC.

The system of railways in British North America consists at present of, viz. :—

NOVA SCOTIA.—There are 93 miles of railway in Nova Scotia. The direct line to Truro is 60 miles, and the branch line to Windsor about 33 miles. "The distance from Halifax to Rivière du Loup (the present terminus of the Grand Trunk line) is 530 miles; of this, 60 miles is already made—that is, from Halifax to Truro—which only leaves 470 miles. This is by the north-shore route. By the central route the distance is 478 miles, from which deduct 82 miles already completed, and we have to be built only ·396 miles. Again, there is the St. John River route, which makes the distance from Halifax to Rivière du Loup 593 miles, of which 237 miles is constructed, and which leaves 355 miles to be made."

NEW BRUNSWICK.—The spirit of railway enterprise manifested itself in New Brunswick at an early period of the history of that means of locomotion. As early as 1844 the first railway was commenced, and continued until it was completed from St. Andrew's to Woodstock, a distance of 60 miles. It has been built at less expense than almost any equal number of miles on any known railway, the total cost being 1,402,748 dollars, or about 16,000 dollars a mile, or a little over £3000.

The other railway in New Brunswick reaches from St. John's, on the Bay of Fundy, and extends a distance of 108 miles in length to Shediac, a town on the Gulf of the St. Lawrence. Its cost has amounted to 4,548,564 dollars 59 cents, or 42,116 dollars 34 cents per mile, equal to £8774. 4s. 7d. sterling per mile.

CANADIAN RAILWAYS.

In 1827 the first piece of railway was completed in the United States, and in the State of Massachusetts. In 1828 the first portion of the Baltimore and Ohio Railroad was constructed. In 1830 the first thirty miles of railway in Great Britain were put successfully in operation between Liverpool and Manchester. In 1837 the first sixteen miles of railway were completed in Canada. At the present time she has 1906 miles of railway.

Statement from Report of Inspector of Railways.

GREAT WESTERN RAILWAY.

Name of Section.—Main Line.	Date of Opening.	Miles.
Suspension Bridge to Hamilton	Nov. 10, 1853	43
Hamilton to London	Dec. 31, ,,	76
London to Windsor	Jan. 27, 1854	110
Branches.		
Harrisburg to Galt	Aug. 21, 1854	12
Galt to Guelph	Sept. 28, 1857	15
Hamilton to Toronto	Dec. 3, 1855	38
Komoka to Sarnia	Dec. 27, 1858	51
Total		345

GRAND TRUNK RAILWAY.

Toronto to Guelph	July, 1856	50
Guelph to Stratford	Nov. 17, 1856	39
Stratford to London	Sept. 27, 1858	31
St. Mary's to Sarnia	Nov. 21, 1859	70
Toronto to Oshawa	August, 1856	33
Oshawa to Brockville	Oct. 27, ,,	175
Brockville to Montreal	Nov. 19, 1855	125
Victoria Bridge and approaches.	Dec. 16, 1859	6
Montreal to St. Hyacinthe	Spring, 1847	30
St. Hyacinthe to Sherbrooke	August, 1852	66
Sherbrooke to Province Line	July, 1853	30
Richmond to Quebec	Nov. 27, 1854	96
Chaudière Junc. to St. Thomas	Dec. 23, 1855	41
St. Thomas to St. Paschal	Dec. 31, 1859	53
St. Paschal to Rivière du Loup	July 2, 1860	25
Branch—Kingston	Nov. 10, ,,	2
Total		872

BUFFALO AND LAKE HURON.

Fort Erie to Paris	Nov. 1, 1856	83
Paris to Stratford	Dec. 22, ,,	33
Stratford to Goderich	June 28, 1858	45
From temporary terminus to station in East Street	May 16, 1860	1·27
Total		162·27

But the railroads are so arterial, instead of water, that we must pass them over lightly.

Besides these principal lines, we have the Northern Line, extending a distance of 95 miles from Toronto to Lake Huron.

The London and Port Stanley, from Lake Erie to London.

The Ottawa and Prescott, from the St. Lawrence to Ottawa City.

The Montreal and Champlain, from Montreal to Rouse's Point, a distance of 81 miles.

The Port Hope, Lindsay, and Beaverton, from Lake Ontario northward; the Welland Railway, from Lake Ontario to Lake Erie; and the Brockville and Ottawa.

The total cost of Canadian railways has been about £20,000,000.

The Grand Trunk Railway, consisting of 1090 miles of line, and including the Champlain Railway, of 1174 miles—the longest railway in the world—extends throughout from Portland, State of Maine, and from Quebec and Rivière du Loup, in Canada, to Detroit, Michigan, forming, in connexion with the other railways of Canada and the United States, a direct and continuous route between the Eastern States, Canada, and the entire continent of America.

From Detroit there are three lines converging westward, the Detroit and Milwaukee Railroad, 188 miles in length; the Michigan Central, from Detroit to Chicago, 284 miles in length; and the Michigan Southern, between Toledo and Chicago, 246 miles. From Milwaukee we have the Milwaukee and Minnesota, extending a distance of 199 miles to La Crosse; thus we have reached the extreme western point of that vast network which is in actual operation, but which will soon extend its iron ramifications through Minnesota to Pembina. The advancing footsteps of the moving throng will then cover the valley of the Saskatchewan, mighty as the hosts of the Israelites as they advanced towards Canaan.

THE INTER-COLONIAL RAILWAY.

To unite Nova Scotia, New Brunswick, and the Canadas by a complete and continued railway system, will now be the first duty of the provinces. As we have before stated, there is less than 400 miles required, and the cost is estimated at £3,000,000.

Now, the combined population of Victoria in Australia, which, it must be remembered, has sprung into civilized existence within the last fifteen years, is now 550,000, and we find she has spent £8,000,000 in railways; while Nova Scotia and New Brunswick, with a population of 580,000, have not expended £2,000,000. It really seems that there is a want of that energetic action and vital enterprise that such a continent as America demands. Look at the State of Indiana, in the West. In 1850, she had only 228 miles of railway; in 1864, she possessed 2500 miles.

GENERAL REVIEW OF THE BRITISH NORTH AMERICAN CONFEDERACY.

The magnificent harbour of Halifax is the natural terminus of the products of field and forest, of not only British America, but might be made the ultimate port of debarkation for the mails and passengers of the United States. If we are correct in our knowledge of the history of the various movements made to complete the Inter-Colonial Railroad, Nova Scotia has evinced a willingness to assume more than her share of its entire cost, and she has, through her representatives, proposed various measures, and urged upon her sister colonies the paramount importance of this public work, on grounds not only of military, but commercial and social importance. Millions of acres of land, spread in vast breadth over Nova Scotia and New Brunswick, as untrodden, unploughed, and unproductive, to-day, as they were when they came from the hands of the Creator. In the solitude of their mighty forests, the moose and the elk move in stately grandeur, and the heron and the hawk shriek in their lonely eyries. Why not pledge these lands instead of allowing them to remain idle—why not, at once, without an hour's delay, pledge public credit—legislate among yourselves, and, if necessary, appeal to the Home Government. The developments of the time must operate upon the Ministry at home. They must, if they value the interests and the future welware of the British Crown, see the policy of fostering your interests.

It was but a few days since, and during the time we have been enabled to spare from the hours of business, that we have seen articles which coolly treated of the value of England's colonial possessions, and stated that the people were glad to perceive evidences that Canada could take care of herself. Now, Canada means the whole area in possession of a people extending from the verge of Newfoundland to the Pacific shores. British North America is one in interest, must be one in future purpose; and when we every day have evidence of the gross ignorance which the mass of the people display in reference to America, we are convinced that the greatest boon that can be conferred upon all classes of our people, is a knowledge of the value of possessions whose wealth they must yet learn to appreciate. Man, in his full development, lives— of his stature he is proud—the impulses of his heart tingle to his fingers' end, and every scintillation of his brain lends arrogance to the majesty of his being. Suppose, for one moment, he throws himself back in his chair, and contemplates his existence. The intellectual thinker may say he can do without hands or feet. His brain is filled with wonderful conceptions, and the very pictures that people it—his tongue being the willing instrument—he can delegate to the practical hand of the expert in drawing or in penmanship. Milton, with his eyes dimmed by blindness, and when the poetry of leaf, flower, and sunlight were externally dead to his soul, knew that the garden of his heart was brilliant with sweet flowers of poesy—that his soul was full of the essence of music, and his mind grand with its picture-gallery of thoughts—that his loved daughter would labour to photograph and pen-picture it all to the world. And so posterity possesses an heirloom that all who speak the English tongue refer to with honest pride. But although Milton groped in darkness, he did not think for one moment of murmuring against the poor blind eyes that once pictured to him that world of infinite and varied beauty that lives even after Eden has passed away. Neither does the man who labours to supply with nutritive power every limb of his body question for a moment the relative value of each organ that belongs to him. A bride, splendid in the glittering array of her jewels, that delight the eye with their beauty, does not idly cast them aside. A king does not usually forego the dominion over the least of his subjects. America is to-day engaged in the mightiest war whose artillery has ever shaken the earth or rolled its echoes along the mountains, simply because the United States feels that, in an allegorical sense, her garments would be rent, her giant strength diminished, and the fair face of her beauty marred in the eyes of the watching world, if she allowed a separation of the body politic. And is England, whose colonies are the right-hand maidens that shed radiance along her onward path and scatter treasures beneath her advancing footsteps, to turn the cold shoulder upon those who look to her for protection? Shall she cast aside and thrust from her four millions of people, who speak her language, who glory in her greatness, and would imitate her career? No; rob England to-day of her magnificent principalities, and she is an oak stripped of her luxuriant foliage, a palace shorn of her sculpture, and a jewel marred of the beauty of her surroundings. The future of England is wrapped in the glorious success of her colonies, and she can no more forego her interest in a people who have supported the brightness of her imperial banner, than a father can forego the sympathy and pride which he feels when his children carve a new name of honour upon the escutcheon of his ancestors.

Too many of our people wrap themselves in self-confident surroundings. While reclining beneath the solid arches of their mansions they heed not the progress of time, the advancement of the age, the new lights of discovery. Revolution is turning like a wheel, and eliminating new principles. Wellington, with his smooth-bored muskets that echoed the last shot of victory on the field of Waterloo, would have passed to his grave that same day in respectable regret if three regiments of the opposing force had been armed with Enfield rifles. Nelson, with his invincible fleet, whose guns covered his flag with victory at Trafalgar, would have been quietly ruined by the iron nose of a modern ram. The turning scale at Manassas, the ever comico-serious battle of Bull Run, was won by the additional strength which the South received by the arrival of "the next train." Why, it was a common question to ask twenty years since, "if the Americans were all black." How many people know that potatoes, turkeys, and tobacco first came from Virginia? How many people know that the bacon, cheese, bread, and corn they eat, in a great degree come across the Atlantic? How many know the furs that warm them, the very articles of furniture they sit on, the ships they sail in, and the gold they spend, come from beyond the Atlantic? How many think that tea, coffee, sugar, and spices, and all the cotton and much of the wool, come many thousands of miles, from lands that they know but little of? The peoples of Europe are pressing on circumscribed limits, and it is better to provide a habitation and a home for them with a link still binding them to early memories, early associations, and early ties, than it is to allow them to go forth dissatisfied, murmuring, and discontented, when they look back, with no pleasant reminiscences of the "spot where they were born."

The newspapers of the day educate the masses in reference to the general history of the time better than any other means that we know of, and the present war in America has attracted a more general attention to that country than heretofore. The late movements of the various colonies in North British America have also added to that interest, and we believe it impossible that those in power at this moment can fail to see the vital advantages which will accrue to our noblest sisterhood by tying them together with iron bands, and making them one in the great object they seek to obtain.

PART II.

CHAPTER I.

THE UNITED STATES OF AMERICA.

Progress and Extent of Territory—Her Natural Beauties, Lakes, Rivers, Prairies, and Mountains—English Appreciation of America, and her Sympathy—Her Poets, Orators, Historians, and Artists—Peace and Reciprocity—The Blessings of Peace—The Reciprocity Treaty—Its Results and Mutual Benefits—Its Continuation desirable.

PROGRESS AND EXTENT OF TERRITORY.

ON that continent where four millions of people flourish under the dominion of British authority, and extend their sway across from one oceanic shore to the other, speaking the same language, actuated by the same impulses, and looking forward with like fervour to a glorious career in the coming centuries—so there is another body of people occupying a vast tract of territory, which extends from the southern shores of the St. Lawrence River and the lakes to the Gulf of Mexico, and from the Atlantic Ocean to the Pacific Ocean. They number over thirty millions, their commerce floats on every sea, their products find their way into every land, they speak the same language, they possess almost the same judiciary, and their habits and customs closely assimilate with their more northern neighbours. Their career has been the most splendid of any that adorns the page of history during the last eighty years. From a population of three millions they have increased to thirty millions; from eleven states to thirty-four, besides territories, which will soon obtain the dignity of sending senators and representatives to the marble chambers of the capitol. Their country is a boundless mine of wealth; their resources inexhaustible; their climate varied and delightful; their people progressive, intelligent, inventive, brave, and ambitious. If they are vain, they have much to be vain of; for if you speak to them of the beauty of other lands, they point with honest pride to their own. Speak of the Thames, the Rhine, or the Seine; they tell you of the Mississippi, commencing as a rivulet in Minnesota, yet stretching 2000 miles in length from its source to the sea. They tell you of the varied and delightful country through which it passes—of the charming pictures of Minnesota—of the forest-crowned cliffs of Missouri—of the wide fields of golden wheat and corn, and the flowering prairies of Illinois—of the white-plumed cotton and the nodding sugar-cane of Louisiana, and the crimson cactus and perfumed magnolia that ornament the shores of Arkansas—of the Alabama River, that passes through a wilderness of tropical beauty—of the Hudson, whose palisades, whose receding shores, whose abrupt and overhanging rocks, whose gentle pastoral slopes, and whose lovely nooks Washington Irving and N. P. Willis, in their love of poetry and its surroundings, made their home. Speak you of mountains! The navigator who seeks her shores beholds the snow-clad caps of the White Mountains, from whose lofty peaks he may survey such a panorama of world-wide beauty, that language fails to describe. The Blue Mountains of Vermont are the pride of all eyes whose vision reaches their extent. The Cattskill Mountains afford a feast of Nature's wayward loveliness, that, once seen, lives in the mind a dream of joy for ever. The Alleghanies—jagged, yawning with chasms, a mountain of confused masses of iron, stone, and slate thrown with inextricable confusion into a shapeless line, and forming a catalogue of pines, precipices, rocks, torrents, ledges, overarching trees, and all the elements that make one "feel the sublimity of stern solitude." We know them all. Those beautiful glades, or mountain meadows, are not connected in a level field like the western prairies, but lie in unbroken outlines, with small wooded ranges between them, or jutting out from their midst in moderate elevations. But all is wealth—there is wealth everywhere in America. Tip the eastern edge of the Alleghanies; descend, and enter the highland basin of the old mountain lakes, which extends over many thousand acres, and is known as the "Glades." There the Tonghigheny takes its rise, while the dividing ridge of the great Backbone sends the water on one side into the Gulf of Mexico, and on the other into the Chesapeake River. Travel half way across the continent, and the Sierra Nevada proudly raises its head, a king among the minor mountains that dwell around her.

Look at her lakes! Bulwer would never have wasted his word-picturing on the Lake of Como (though Byron wooed his Maid of Athens there) if he had seen Lake George or Lake Champlain. Then when you speak of vastness and extent: the great lakes of the interior are rocked by storms as mighty as those that disturb the ocean, and drive the canvas-winged vessel on the pitiless rocks.

Talk of territory! Breadth, extent, and depth are to be found in all their meaning here. The prairies are a rolling sea of varied beauty, wide-sweeping in excellence. The Indian corn, that so gracefully bends its serried phalanx to the toying wind, presents a scene not easily to be forgotten. The forests are royal with oaks, beeches, walnuts, and magnolias. The rivers and lakes are alive with trout, and waste themselves in cascades and falls after furnishing pools for the fish. The cities are the centres of commerce and civilization, vital with a moving throng of men, and alive with queenly beauty.

Talk of gold! California, Colorado, and Arizona have sent their golden tributes to make up the sum of the world's auriferous wealth.

The progress of America has been a marvel; and while she

carried in her right hand as emblems the symbols of progressive civilization, who so proud as we to watch her increasing prosperity?

ENGLISH APPRECIATION AND SYMPATHY.

America does the people of England a gross wrong when she accuses her of a jealousy of her success; on the contrary, we have hailed every new stride in her onward career with pride and satisfaction. If she has referred to England as the England of Shakespeare, Raleigh, and Sidney; to England as the grand old mother of bards, heroes, and sages, who has sat crowned among the nations a thousand years—when her orators have said they were proud to speak our tongue, to re-enact our laws, to read our sages, to sing our songs, and to claim our ancient glory as part of their own; and spoke of her as the stormy cradle of their nation, the sullen mistress of the angry western seas, and said that their hearts went out to her across the ocean, across the years, across old wars, and in love and reverence—we were proud of their language, of their sentiments, of their lingering love for all that made us noble. Remember the Hudson was named after one of our heroic navigators; the commercial centre of their country was called after the city of York. There are Kings' and Queens' Counties in their States, while one of the richest corporations that extends the benefits of Christianity over that country is supported to-day by the bounty of Queen Anne.

The Smithsonian Institute at Washington, that annually scatters abroad the results of scientific discovery, is the gift of an Englishman. Virginia is surrounded with a web of romance. Here Sir Walter Raleigh gave its title after Elizabeth the memorable and the mighty. Here the gentle Indian Princess Pocahontas won the life of the gallant Smith by touching the heart of Powhattan. Here Washington was born, and here, on the banks of the Potomac River, in the sacred precincts of Mount Vernon, his ashes repose. The hawthorn hedge blossoms here in pink and white; the holly ornaments herself with coral berries in the deep recesses of her shaded pines, and the mistletoe showers her pearl-shaped berries, though she clings from many a tree in blood-stained, war-stricken Virginia.

Tell us the time, the day, or the hour, that we have failed to appreciate all that is good and noble in American character. If Tennyson is our poet-laureate, are not the beauties of Longfellow as much appreciated, and are not their works found equal one with the other in the select libraries of our land? Yes! and Bryant, Lowell, Willis, Holmes, and Whittier, occupy an honourable position wherever poetry finds her devotees.

In law, Kent, Story, and Tancy, are respected as monuments of legal acumen.

As orators, Patrick Henry, Clay, Webster, and Calhoun, hold an equal place with Burke, Sheridan, Fox, and Pitt, on the tablet of fame.

There is not an educated Englishman who does not accord, and most willingly, his appreciation of every contribution to science, history, or the arts, made by America. Washington Irving and Hawthorne are as widely read by the hearthstones of old England as they are by the firesides of the people of New York or Massachusetts. Have we failed to do honour to the greatness and goodness of George Washington? Are not Bancroft, Prescott, Sparke, and Motley, respected as historical authorities?

Amid the congregated works of art that adorned the Palace of Industry in 1851, who received from our people a higher meed of praise than Powers? We know his "Greek Slave," his "Eve," his "Fisher Boy," and all his other cunning art-chisellings; and we know Palmer's "White Captive," and have ourselves lingered many an hour over its perfect beauty.

In the National Gallery, in the Palace of St. James, and the Castle of Windsor, whose works hold a higher place than those of Benjamin West?

Cole's "Voyage of Life" and his "Dream of Arcadia," Gigrioux's "Niagara," Church's "Niagara," his "Heart of the Andes," and his "Icebergs," have drawn crowds of our people, who have lingered long and lovingly over these pictures on the canvas.

Did not our own Queen show her appreciation of a noble gift when she accepted in person from Lieutenant Harsteine the last ship that went in search of Franklin? Do we fail to mention in terms of respect the names of Kane, of Maury, or of Peabody? Have the great newspaper representatives of Europe allowed any national prejudice to bias them, when every sheet they send broadcast to the world passes over Hoe's American press?

England is not, nor ever has been, jealous of the increasing power or the splendid prosperity of America. Why, the whole heart of England beat with joy when her people, from the palace to the humblest cottage, read of the magnificent reception accorded to the Prince of Wales. America then was the refuge of the expatriated; her land was as free as the flight of the eagle; her prosperity approached the marvellous; her wealth was increasing beyond parallel; her people multiplied and spread from one ocean to the other; her flag that floated on every sea was the symbol of the mightiest Republic that ever swayed power; and her future was a theme that her orators could not find language brilliant enough to picture. Alas! the sky became overcast—the sun of her prosperity travelled behind the gathering clouds. The scythe of death was about to gather in her fearful harvest, and the wail of the widow and orphan was soon to be heard in places where mirth and gladness had long held their dwelling-places. The roll of the drum, the heavy tread of armed men, the ringing of alarm bells, the rattle of musketry, the roar of artillery, and the flaunting of defiant banners, announced the nation was in arms.

PEACE AND RECIPROCITY.

For four long years a terrible and dreadful war has desolated and devastated the fair face of her beauty. Its details have been read with sorrow and regret, and to-day no announcement would be received with more unselfish pleasure than the news of peace.

Oh! how peace would bless the land again. The shouts of thankful voices would rush in great echoes through the valleys and along the mountain's side until its music pierced the very sky; mothers' hearts would beat quick with tremulous joy as they welcomed back their bronzed hero-sons; sisters would proudly lean upon the arm of brothers whose deeds crowned them with glory; wives would clasp to heart the long and weary absent one, warm kisses would glow upon his hungry lips, and, while bright smiles irradiated his face, fond arms would fold him in safety and peace, and kind soothing words would fall as soft as sweetest music on his listening ear. Dear children—God's ungrown angels—would shout hosannas of welcome. The desolate valleys, where the tread of armed men had crushed down all vegetable existence, would again teem with verdant life. Violets would slily peep out from beneath some fallen leaf and gaze bright-eyed upon the sun. Persecuted wanderers would return home from their hiding-places in the mountain. Poor suffering and maimed warriors would raise themselves from their cots and thank God in brief but earnest prayer. The dark and profound dungeons would be bathed in light, and the gates would open wide for freedom to step in. Soldiers would return crowned with bays and laurels. Banners, war-torn and bullet-rent, would be laid aside until the dust of time obliterated their memory. The rifle, the cannon, and the sword would be but curiosities adorning the farmhouse, the villa, and the museum—reminders of the past and warnings for the future. The plough would be guided by the soldier, once more the peasant, and the birds would warble their songs as music for him all the day long.

BLESSINGS OF PEACE.

Peace on the battle-field; peace on the mountains, plains, and valleys; peace on the vast ocean, where the great ships may sail in security; peace on the lakes, where the barque and the steamer may bear the products of the soil; peace all over, blessing the labourer, the mechanic, the merchant, and the mariner. We shall rejoice to see its advent, and to see corn and cotton kiss each other; and we would live in peace with America—we would see our colonists growing, increasing, and prospering by the side of their great neighbour, and carrying on a generous rivalry with a cordial reciprocity not only of commerce, but of honest, sincere, and lasting friendship.

THE RECIPROCITY TREATY.

It is with feelings of profound regret—and we are sure these feelings are shared in by all who desire the kindly relations which have existed so long between the United States and the British American Colonies to continue—that we have observed the late evidences of misunderstanding, that have called forth crimination and recrimination between them. The causes which have operated to engender the bitter feeling lately displayed by the United States towards Great Britain, as well as Canada, we are assured have been, or will soon be removed; and that, as a result, the hasty legislation which has characterized the Government of the United States will be followed by that enlarged policy which should actuate a great and friendly people. The Reciprocity Treaty, which for ten years has existed between them, we think the figures will show to be mutually advantageous; and we are supported in this belief by the resolutions of the Chamber of Commerce in New York, Chicago, and Detroit, and by the statements of United States Senators.

LEADING POINTS OF THE TREATY.

The following are the leading points of the treaty:—

I. The inhabitants of the United States possess, under the Reciprocity Treaty, the right to take fish of any kind, except shell-fish, on the sea-coast and shores, in the bays, harbours, and creeks, of any of the British Provinces, without being restricted to any distance from the shore, with permission to land upon the coasts and shores of those provinces for the purpose of drying their nets and curing fish.

II. British subjects possess, in common with the citizens of the United States, the liberty to take fish of any kind, except shell-fish, on the eastern sea-coasts and shores of the United States north of the 36th parallel of north latitude, with the same privileges as to landing on the sea-coast as are enjoyed by American citizens in the British Provinces.

III. Certain articles, being the growth and produce of the British Colonies, or of the United States, are admitted into each country free of duty respectively. (The most important of these articles are—grain, flour, bread-stuffs, animals; fresh, smoked, and salted meats; fish, lumber of all kinds, poultry, cotton wool, hides, ores of metals, pitch, tar, ashes, flax, hemp, unmanufactured tobacco, rice, &c.)

IV. The right to navigate the river St. Lawrence and the canals of Canada is equally enjoyed by the citizens of the United States and the British Provinces. This right extends also to Lake Michigan; and no export duty on lumber cut in Maine, and passing through New Brunswick to the sea, can be levied.

ITS MUTUAL ADVANTAGES.

Now no candid observer will fail to perceive the advantage to the United States over that which the British Provinces possess in regard to the fisheries. The best fishing-grounds on the American coast are certainly in the neighbourhood of Newfoundland, Nova Scotia, and New Brunswick; and a more generous provision was never accorded in any treaty than the throwing open of fishing-grounds which have been so long a mine of wealth to the provinces. It also put an end to a question of right or property which was fruitful of mischief. The Hon. Charles Sumner, United States Senator from Massachusetts, lately said, " The fisheries have been a source of anxiety throughout our history. Even from the beginning, and for several years previous to the Reciprocity Treaty, they had been the occasion of mutual irritation, verging at times in positive outbreak. The treaty was followed by entire tranquillity, which has not been for a moment disturbed. This is a plain advantage which cannot be denied." Why seek, then, to disturb these pleasant and harmonious relations by abrogating the treaty?

INCREASE OF TRADE.

The increase of trade has been wonderfully influenced by the Reciprocity Treaty. Between the years 1857 and 1862, the shipping of the United States which cleared for the British Provinces was 10,056,183 tons, and the foreign shipping which cleared during this same period was 7,391,399 tons; while the shipping of the United States which entered at the United States custom-houses from the British Provinces was 10,056,183, and the foreign shipping which entered was 6,453,520 tons.

Exports from the United States to both Canada and the Provinces, with the total Imports from both.

Fiscal Year ending—	Domestic Exports.	Foreign Exports.	Total Exports.	Imports.
1853	7,404,087	5,736,555	13,140,642	7,550,718
1854	15,204,144	9,362,716	24,556,860	8,927,560
1855	15,806,642	11,999,378	27,806,020	15,136,734
1856	22,714,697	6,314,652	29,029,349	21,310,421
1857	19,936,113	4,326,369	24,262,482	22,124,296
1858	19,638,959	4,012,768	23,651,727	15,806,519
1859	21,769,627	6,384,547	28,154,174	19,727,551
1860	18,667,429	4,038,899	22,706,328	23,851,381
1861	18,883,715	3,861,898	22,745,613	23,062,933
1862	18,652,012	2,427,103	21,079,115	19,299,995
1863	28,629,110	2,651,920	31,281,030	24,025,423

In the three years immediately preceding the treaty, the total exports to Canada and the other British Provinces were 48,216,518 dollars, and the total imports were 22,588,577 dollars. In the ten years of the treaty the total exports to Canada and the British Provinces were 256,350,931 dollars. The total imports were 200,399,786 dollars. The total exports to Canada in the three years immediately preceding the treaty were 31,866,865 dollars, and the total imports were 6,587,674 dollars, while the whole exports to Canada alone, during the ten years of the treaty, were 176,371,911 dollars, and the total imports were 161,474,347 dollars. It will be perceived by these figures that the British Provinces have consumed and paid the United States 56,000,000 dollars, or over £11,000,000 sterling, during the ten years, over the amount they exported to the United States. During the year 1863 the British Provinces paid 6,555,485 dollars in gold coin, instead of paper money, which is current in America.

RAILWAY TRAFFIC.

Look again at the traffic upon the American railways from Portland and Boston to the Canadas. It shows that over one-third of the import trade of Canada enters now at United States ports, and is transported over their railroads under bond.

	Imports via United States.	Imports via St. Lawrence.
1855	4,463,774 dollars.	12,738,373 dollars.
1856	4,926,922 ,,	16,989,513 ,,
1857	5,582,643 ,,	14,378,094 ,,
1858	2,057,024 ,,	10,768,161 ,,
1859	4,546,491 ,,	11,472,754 ,,
1860	3,041,877 ,,	13,527,160 ,,
1861	5,688,952 ,,	16,726,541 ,,
1862	5,508,427 ,,	17,601,019 ,,
1863	6,172,483 ,,	16,439,930 ,,

Speaking in reference to this subject, Mr. Sumner said:—" There are also railroads furnishing prompt and constant means of intercommunication which have gone into successful operation only since the treaty. It would be difficult to exaggerate the influence these have exercised in quickening and extending commerce. *I cannot doubt the railroad system of the two countries has been of itself a Reciprocity Treaty more comprehensive and equal than any written parchment.*" Then why allow the passion and the excitement of the moment to control your judgment, and why attack a treaty which is increasing and will increase railway communication every hour. Consider for a moment the produce and passengers that pass each day across the boundaries of the two countries, and which will continue if the two peoples can live in harmony. Not only will there be a railway system between

Maine, New Brunswick, Nova Scotia, and Canada, between New York, Boston, and Montreal, Ogdensburg and Ottawa, Buffalo and Hamilton, Toronto and Rochester, Toronto and Detroit and Chicago; and not only will the St. Lawrence and the Niagara be bridged by the Grand Trunk and the Great Western Railway, but St. Paul, Pembina, and the Red River Settlements, British Columbia and Washington Territory, Oregon and California, will alike have their system of railways, canals, and river navigation interlinking one with the other, until freight, starting first in American territory, and passing up the Columbia River, will reach British Columbia, thence, crossing the Rocky Mountains, it will be carried across the fertile plains of Central British America again across the boundary-line at Pembina, through the State of Minnesota, to Fond du Lac, and thence, by the Great Lakes and the St. Lawrence, reach the ocean, or continue by railroad through Wisconsin and Michigan, till it again reaches British territory, and the Grand Trunk line hurries it along either to Portland in Maine, or Halifax, Nova Scotia.

But the importance of reciprocity of trade is mutual in every respect; it not only involves national comity, but it suggests equality, exchange, and equity. It is urged by the United States that Canada receives the larger amount of custom; but the reason is because, as we have before stated, Canada has taken in excess 56,000,000 dollars of goods and produce within the last ten years. Is it nothing for the United States to have the free navigation of Canadian canals, the St. Lawrence River, and an equal right to the unsurpassed fishing-grounds of Newfoundland? The Canadian people were the people that grumbled in the beginning; they believed the provisions were entirely in favour of the United States, and that belief is shared in by the people of the United States most interested. Ask the people of Maine, Vermont, Wisconsin, Michigan, and Minnesota. Senator Ramsay, of Minnesota, and Senator Howe, of Wisconsin, strongly opposed its repeal.

TRAFFIC ON THE CANALS.

Let us now glance at the exchange of traffic on the canals. The table of trade through the Canadian canals shows that in 1861 there passed through from the lakes to the Canadian ports a total of 217,892 tons; to United States ports, 427,521 tons. In 1862, to Canadian ports, 285,192 tons; to United States ports, 471,521¼ tons. In 1863, to Canadian ports, 298,436 tons; to United States ports, 441,862 tons. The Westward or Upward trade shows that in 1861 there was a total of 10,185 tons to Canadian ports, while during the same period there was 116,240 tons to American. In 1862, to Canadian ports, 14,908½ tons; United States, 171,673½ tons. In 1863, to Canadian ports, 67,478 tons; to United States ports, 323,244 tons.

Exports to Canada of Wheat, Flour, Indian Corn, and Meal, for the Fiscal Years 1849 to 1863, inclusive.

YEARS.	WHEAT. Bushels.	WHEAT. Value.	WHEAT FLOUR. Barrels.	WHEAT FLOUR. Value.	INDIAN CORN. Bushels.	INDIAN CORN. Value.	Meal, Rye, &c., Value	Total Value.
1849	140,696	$ 112,086	19,127	$ 78,129	49,621	$ 20,265	$ 5,355	$ 215,835
1850	78,610	56,968	29,138	132,509	89,604	42,113	3,813	237,403
1851	208,130	150,288	51,716	191,750	88,306	39,158	6,873	387,764
1852	360,405	238,808	38,888	127,068	98,898	38,681	8,684	413,241
1853	40,434	26,835	46,835	175,648	151,416	72,462	303	275,248
1854	125,525	155,635	82,028	472,274	1,206,207	729,927	17,107	1,374,973
1855	240,874	365,772	58,993	494,081	1,074,869	708,426	30,761	1,599,040
1856	991,648	1,370,971	102,611	1,341,743	1,736,131	1,057,222	110,162	3,880,098
1857	1,655,641	1,867,457	118,857	717,245	1,161,088	673,989	160,185	3,418,846
1858	2,673,947	2,082,648	326,045	1,681,072	486,999	296,879	135,683	4,198,292
1859	1,352,252	1,178,560	287,772	1,666,546	663,918	439,125	226,407	3,510,638
1860	1,120,975	1,010,681	246,359	1,253,278	827,621	522,693	126,487	2,913,139
1861	4,146,029	3,871,233	83,617	444,803	1,891,740	810,346	46,206	5,172,588
1862	4,538,472	3,801,515	118,643	536,756	3,218,438	1,010,243	68,339	5,416,853
1863	6,512,801	6,717,098	232,160	1,103,171	4,211,897	1,622,825	145,301	9,588,390

Exports to Canada, 1863.

PLACES.	WHEAT. Bushels.	WHEAT. Value.	WHEAT FLOUR. Barrels.	WHEAT FLOUR. Value.
		Dollars.		Dollars.
From Lake Ports of Ohio	1,428,511	1,505,015	895	3,769
„ Detroit	345,075	363,746	39,059	220,940
„ Chicago	1,519,396	1,502,575	78,749	340,850
„ Milwaukee	2,880,791	3,029,649	40,069	172,020
	6,173,773	6,400,985	158,772	737,579

Imports from Canada, 1863.

PLACES.	WHEAT. Bushels.	WHEAT. Value.	WHEAT FLOUR. Barrels.	WHEAT FLOUR. Value.
		Dollars.		Dollars.
At Vermont	26,739	27,691	112,557	590,741
„ Champlain	17,877	18,120	11,585	53,641
„ Cape Vincent	135,628	133,933	15,993	90,998
„ Ogdensburg	75,521	78,651	46,718	249,298
„ Oswego	360,405	375,308	47,303	248,081
„ Genesee	54,104	60,544	52	264
„ Niagara	20,652	21,076	81,822	383,267
„ Buffalo	267,328	291,896	93,323	557,189
	958,254	1,007,219	393,360	2,173,479

GOOD FEELING.

Let us continue these peaceful relations. If there are clauses in the treaty which seem unjust or inequitable, let a proper commercial convention revise them. Do not, for a mere minor consideration, abrogate entirely a treaty whose general provisions are enlightened, fairly reciprocal, and mutually beneficial. There is not a clause which is ineradicable. If in the temple erected we have used a few worthless stones, remove them and replace them by others more worthy to compose it, but do not tear down a structure which has stood so long, and which was not the labour of an idle hour.

Cousin Jonathan, you are angry! Domestic quarrels have irritated your feelings. You think that Old England has permitted and countenanced evil doings on Canadian soil. Lord Palmerston says you have cause to be irritated, that the causes shall be removed and reparation made. Now it will be all right. It is no use tearing down each other's fences and letting stray cattle and poachers in. Let existing treaties remain. Canada will protect her soil, and she will see that in future her hospitality is not abused. We don't want gunboats on lakes, we don't want a passport system, and we don't want old customs restored in this enlightened age. But we want to carry on and continue that mighty interchange of commercial products which mutually enriches and strengthens us; we want to see the whole continent of America moving along in harmonious fellowship, and governed by reason, dignity, and justice.

CHAPTER II.

THE UNITED STATES.

Primary Object of the Book—Captain Palisser's Testimony—Route wholly through British Territory impossible—The only feasible Route, by way of Michigan and Minnesota to Hudson's Bay—Wealth of the Western States—OHIO: Products of Agriculture; Railways—INDIANA: Area, Population, Progress of the State, Agricultural Products, Manufactures, and Railways—MICHIGAN: General Statistics, Products of Agriculture, the Cereal Products, Miscellaneous Crops, and Railroads—WISCONSIN: Topographical Features, Railroads, Products of Agriculture, Valuation and Taxation—IOWA: Agricultural Wealth, Increase, Railroads—ILLINOIS: Agricultural Progress, Valuation and Taxation, Railways, and Number, Extent, and Cost of all the Railways in the United States.

PRIMARY OBJECT OF THE BOOK.

THE primary object of writing the present volume was to gather and collect all the information which various authorities presented in reference to the future prospects of the proposed British North American Confederation, and to point out the importance of at once constructing a road across the continent to British Columbia. It being impossible to do this wholly and entirely within the boundaries of the Canadas, the natural and physical features presenting insuperable obstacles, and there being no population which could maintain the cost of such a road, and no soil adapted to support a population for hundreds of miles until you reach the region of the Lake of the Woods, it becomes necessary to consider the most practicable manner of doing it, and what territories possess the best means of assisting in the burden of its construction till we reach the splendid region of the Red River country and the prairies of the Saskatchewan.

CAPT. PALISSER'S TESTIMONY.

Capt. Palisser states in his Report, under date July 8, 1860 (page 22 of Blue Book):—

"The difficulty of direct communication between Canada and the Saskatchewan country, as compared with the comparatively easy route through the United States by St. Paul's, renders it very unlikely that the great work of constructing a road across the continent can be solely the result of British enterprise."

When asked by the Duke of Newcastle to state his opinion in reference to the direct continuation of a railway through British territory, he answers:—" As a line of communication with the Red River and the Saskatchewan prairies, the canoe route from Lake Superior to Lake Winnipeg, even if modified and greatly improved by a large outlay of capital, would, I consider, be always too arduous and expensive a route of transport for emigrants, and never could be used for the introduction of stock, both from the broken nature of the country passed through, and also from the very small extent of available pasture. I therefore cannot recommend the Imperial Government to countenance or lend support to any scheme for constructing or, it may be said, forcing a thoroughfare by this line of route either by land or water, as there would be no immediate advantage commensurate with the required sacrifice of capital; nor can I advise such heavy expenditure as would necessarily attend the construction of any exclusively British line of road between Canada and the Red River Settlement."

"As regards the fitness for settlement of the district traversed by the canoe route, I beg to state that there are only very few and isolated spots where agriculture could be carried on, and that only by the discoverer." We must, therefore, look to the United States for a railway passage for a portion of its route.

STATE OF OHIO.

We shall present important statistics in reference to some of the Western States, with which Canada is so intimately connected.

Ohio was settled in 1788, and is one of the largest and most important of the great Western States. It extends over an area of 200 miles in length and 195 miles in breadth, or 39,964 square miles, being equal to 25,570,960 acres. She was admitted into the Union November 29, 1802. The population in 1861 was 2,539,202. The capital is Columbus.

PRODUCTS OF AGRICULTURE.

	1850.	1860.
Lands improved	9,851,493 acres	12,665,587 acres
Value of farms	358,758,603 dols.	666,564,171 dols.
Value of farming implements and machines	12,750,585 „	16,790,226 „
Horses	463,397 No.	622,829 No.
Asses and mules	3,423 „	6,917 „
Milch cows	544,499 „	696,309 „
Working oxen	65,381 „	61,760 „
Other cattle	749,067 „	901,781 „
Sheep	3,942,929 „	3,063,887 „
Swine	1,964,720 „	2,175,623 „
Value of live stock	44,121,741 dols.	80,433,780 dols.
Wheat	14,487,351 bshls.	14,532,571 bshls.
Rye	425,918 „	656,146 „
Indian corn	59,078,695 „	70,637,140 „
Oats	13,472,742 „	15,479,133 „

	1850.	1860.
Barley	354,358 bshls.	1,601,082 bshls.
Tobacco	10,454,449 lbs.	25,528,972 lbs.
Buckwheat	638,060 bshls.	2,327,005 bshls.
Wool	10,196,371 lbs.	10,648,161 lbs.
Peas and beans	60,168 bshls.	105,219 bshls.
Irish potatoes	5,057,769 „	8,752,873 „
Sweet „	187,991 „	297,908 „
Value of orchard products	695,921 dols.	1,858,673 dols.
Wine	48,207 gals.	562,640 gals.
Butter	34,449,379 lbs.	50,495,745 lbs.
Cheese	20,819,542 „	23,758,738 „
Hay	1,443,142 tons.	1,602,513 tons.
Maple sugar	4,588,209 lbs.	3,323,942 lbs.
Value of animals slaughtered	7,439,243, dols.	14,293,972 dols.

The report of the auditor for 1862 shows the following ratio of increase :—

Wheat	Acres sown	1,931,002
	Bushels produced	20,055,424
Rye	Acres sown	69,374
	Bushels produced	779,829
Barley	Acres sown	60,501
	Bushels produced	1,255,049
Corn	Acres sown	2,266,129
	Bushels produced	74,858,378
Buckwheat	Acres sown	51,389
	Bushels produced	696,623
Oats	Acres sown	728,722
	Bushels produced	17,798,794
Meadow	Acres sown	1,461,018
	Tons of hay produced	1,708,201
Potatoes	Acres sown	80,949
	Bushels produced	6,556,901
Butter	Pounds produced	35,442,858
Cheese	Pounds produced	20,637,235
Stone-Coal	Bushels mined	24,541,843
Sheep killed by dogs	Number	32,061
	Value	63,868 dols.
Sheep injured by dogs	Number	24,301
	Value	23,224 dols.
Sheep killed and injured by dogs.—Number and value		87,092

RAILWAYS.

In 1850, Ohio possessed 575·27 miles of railway, which cost

10,684,400 dollars. In 1860 she possessed 2999·45 miles of railway, which had cost the State 111,896,351 dollars.

T. Addison Richards, speaking of Ohio, says: "Ohio owes her wonderful prosperity—her almost marvellous growth, in the period of half a century, from a wild forest track to the proud rank she now holds among the greatest of the great American States—mainly to the rich capabilities of her generous soil and climate. Nearly all her vast territory is available for agricultural uses. In the amount of her products of wool and of Indian corn, she has no peer in all the land—while she is exceeded by only one other State in her growth of wheat, barley, cheese, and live stock; by only two States in the value of her orchards, oats, potatoes, buckwheat, grasses, hay, maple sugar, and butter. Tobacco also is one of her staples, and among other articles which she yields abundantly, are hops, wine, hemp, silk, honey, beeswax, molasses, sweet potatoes, and a great variety of fruits. Her vines, which are known and esteemed everywhere, have yielded, in the vicinity of Cincinnati alone, half a million gallons of wine in a year."

INDIANA.

Its area is 38,809 square miles, or 21,637,776 acres, its length being 270 miles from north to south, and its breadth, from east to west, about 150. Its northern boundary is Michigan, and the lake of that name, its eastern is Ohio, its southern the Ohio River, which separates it from Kentucky, and its western, Illinois. The face of the country is nowhere mountainous; the nothern is quite level, and is prairie land to a considerable extent. It is well timbered, the soil is fertile, and the climate mild and healthy. The State was originally territory belonging to the Indians, whose title was extinguished by treaties, and purchases made from them by the United States. Its population in 1860 was 1,850,428, and its rate of increase decennially is nearly 50 per cent. It contains ten principal cities and towns, Indianapolis being the capital, with about 20,000 inhabitants, the remainder having a population ranging from 5000 to 15,000 each.

PRODUCTS OF AGRICULTURE.

Its improved lands amount to 8,161,717 acres, and the unimproved to about the same number.

The value of the farms in 1860 was 344,902,776 dollars, and of the implements of husbandry used upon them 10,420,826 dollars.

The live stock consisted of 409,504 horses, 18,627 mules and asses, 491,038 milch cows, 95,982 working oxen, 582,990 other cattle, 2,157,375 sheep, 2,498,522 swine.

Their products and those of its busy bees were as follows:—

Butter, 17,931,767 lbs.; cheese, 569,574 lbs.; wool, 2,466,264 lbs.; animals slaughtered produced 9,592,322 dollars, and the wax and honey amounted to 1,221,939 lbs.

The cereal products were of wheat, 15,219,120 bushels; rye, 400,226 bushels; Indian corn, 69,641,591 bushels; oats, 5,028,755 bushels; barley, 296,374 bushels; buckwheat, 367,797 bushels.

The commercial crops were 1219 lbs. of rice, 7,246,132 lbs. of tobacco, 75,058 lbs. of hops, 73,112 lbs. of flax.

The miscellaneous crops were returned as follows:—

Peas and beans	79,701 bushels.
Irish potatoes	3,873,130 ,,
Sweet ,,	284,304 ,,
Wine	88,275 gallons.
Hay	635,222 tons.
Clover seed	45,321 bushels.
Grass seed	31,886 ,,
Flax seed	155,159 ,,
Maple sugar	1,515,594 lbs.
Maple molasses	203,028 gallons.
Sorghum do.	827,777 ,,
Silk cocoons	959 lbs.

The value of the orchard products the same year was 1,212,142 dollars, of market gardens 288,070 dollars, and of home-made manufactures 847,251 dollars.

The value of the principal articles of production was as follows:—

Flour and meal	11,292,665 dollars.
Lumber	3,169,843 ,,
Spirits (8,358,560 gallons)	1,951,530 ,,
Boots and shoes	1,034,341 ,,
Leather	800,387 ,,
Agricultural implements	709,645 ,,
Woollen goods	695,370 ,,
Cotton goods	349,000 ,,
Furniture	601,124 ,,
Steam engines	426,805 ,,
Malt liquors (66,338 bls.)	328,116 ,,
Soap and candles	256,535 ,,
Iron castings	168,575 ,,
,, rolled (2000 tons)	105,000 ,,
,, pig (375 tons)	9,375 ,,
Coal (15,161 tons)	27,000 ,,
Printing	135,415 ,,
Gas	96,012 ,,
Fish (white fish)	17,500 ,,

The steam tonnage employed in the State is estimated at 5000 tons, the latest returns being only up to 1858.

The number of banks in 1860 was 39, with a capital of about five millions. The number has been slightly increased under the National system.

The Indiana railways in 1850 were but 228 miles in length, but in 1860 they were extended to 2200. Their cost was 72,795,000 dollars. They are about 26 in number.

The Indiana canals are but two in number, the Wabash and Erie, between Evansville on the Ohio River to the Ohio State Line 379 miles, and the White Water between Lawrenceburg on the same river and Cambridge City, 74 miles. The mails are carried over routes to the extent of 7960 miles.

The value of the real and personal property was in 1860 528,835,371 dollars, having increased about 300 per cent. in ten years.

The number of manufacturing establishments was 5120, with a capital of 18,875,000 dollars, using annually raw material of the value of 27,860,000 dollars, employing 21,000 operatives, and producing fabrics of the value of 43,250,000 dollars.

The school fund pledged to the support of the public schools is about 5,000,000 dollars, of which one-half is productive of revenue for that purpose, and the residue is becoming so.

The income of the State from other sources than taxes is about 1,500,000 dollars.

The State debt was in 1860, 10,286,855 dollars, and the canal debt 7,017,807 dollars.

In 1800 the population of the territory now the State of Indiana was but 4875, and it was admitted into the Union in 1816.

There is not one of the Northern States which offers greater advantages to immigrants than Indiana.

MICHIGAN.

Settled in 1670. Admitted into the Union, January 26, 1837. Capital, Lansing. Area, 56,243 square miles, or 35,995,520 acres. Population, 749,113. The lands of Michigan are well adapted for emigrants, and the soil is productive and rich in substance.

PRODUCTS OF AGRICULTURE.

In 1860 there were 1,929,160 acres under cultivation, and 2,454,780 unimproved but surveyed. In 1860 there were 3,419,861 acres of land under cultivation, and 3,511,581 acres unimproved lands. The cash value of the farms in 1850 was 51,872,446 dols.; in 1860 the value was 163,279,087 dols. In 1850 the value of farming implements and machinery in the State was 2,891,371 dols., and in 1860, 5,855,642 dols. The live stock consisted in 1850 of horses, 58,506; mules, 70; milch cows, 99,676; working oxen, 55,350; other cattle, 119,471; sheep, 746,425; swine, 205,847; value of live stock, 8,008,734 dols. In 1860 there were of horses, 154,168; asses and mules, 359; milch cows, 200,635; working oxen, 65,949; other cattle, 267,683; sheep, 1,465,477; swine, 374,664; value of live stock, 23,220,026 dollars.

The cereal products for 1850 were of wheat, 4,925,889 bushels; rye, 105,871 bushels; Indian corn, 5,641,420 bushels; oats, 2,866,056 bushels; barley, 75,249 bushels; buckwheat, 472,917 bushels. The cereal products for 1860 showed the following extraordinary increase:—Wheat, 8,313,185 bushels; rye, 494,197 bushels; Indian corn, 12,152,110 bushels; oats, 4,539,132 bushels; barley, 305,914 bushels; and buckwheat, 123,202 bushels.

The products of industry for the year ending 1860:—Number of establishments, 2530; capital in real and personal estate in the business, 24,000,000 dols.; value of raw material, including fuel, 19,000,000 dols.; average number of hands employed, 22,860 males, 1260 females; value of annual product, 35,200,000 dollars.

The real estate and personal property in 1850 were valued at 59,787,255 dols., in 1860 at 257,163,983 dols.; the increase being 197,376,728 dols., or 330·13 per cent. in ten years.

The miscellaneous crops were as follows:—

	1850.	1860.
Butter	7,834,359 lbs.	14,704,837 lbs.
Cheese	1,011,492 ,,	2,009,064 ,,
Wool	2,043,283 ,,	4,062,858 ,,
Animals slaughtered	8,008,734 dols.	23,220,026 dols.
Wax and honey	359,232 lbs.	770,872 lbs.
Orchards	132,650 dols.	1,137,678 dols.
Peas and beans	74,254 bshls.	182,195 bshls.
Irish potatoes	2,359,897 ,,	5,264,733 ,,
Sweet ,,	1,177 ,,	36,285 ,,
Wine	1,654 gals.	13,733 gals.
Hay	404,934 tons.	756,908 tons.
Clover seed	16,989 bshls.	49,480 bshls.
Grass seed	9,285 ,,	6,555 ,,
Maple sugar	2,429,794 lbs.	2,988,018 lbs.

RAILROADS.

THE PRINCIPAL RAILROADS.	Mileage.		Cost of Construction.	
	1850.	1860.	1850.	1860.
Bay de Noquet and Marquette		20·50		410,000
Chicago, Detroit, and Canada Grand Junction		57·00		1,710,000
Detroit and Milwaukee	25·00	188·00	408,000	9,118,219
Detroit, Monroe, and Toledo		51·00		1,522,821
Flint and Père Marquette		33·00		1,000,000
Iron Mountain (Northern Michigan)		25·00		590,000
Michigan Central	226·00	284·80	6,339,667	13,158,058
Michigan Southern and Northern Indiana (with branches)	103·00	484·60	2,378,082	15,590,952
	354·00	1,143·90	9,125,749	43,010,950
Deduct—				
Michigan Southern, in Ohio, Indiana, and Illinois	12·00	279·60	180,000	8,995,291
Michigan Central, in Indiana and Illinois		65·00		3,003,260
	12·00	344·60	180,000	11,998,551
Total in Michigan	342·00	799·30	8,945,749	31,012,399

WISCONSIN.

Organized as a territory in 1836. Admitted into the Union, May 29, 1848. Capital, Madison. Area, 53,924 square miles, or 34,511,360 acres. Population (1850), 305,391 ; in 1860, 775,873.

The topographical aspect of Wisconsin is very similar to that of other portions of the north-west section of the Union, presenting, for the most part, grand stretches of elevated prairie land, sometimes 1000 feet higher than the level of the sea. Though there are no mountains in this State, there are the characteristic plateau ridges of the latitude, formed by depressions, which drain the waters, and afford beds for the rivers and lakes. The descent of the land towards Lake Superior is very sudden, and the streams are full of falls and rapids.

A writer, speaking of the progress of the State, refers to Madison, and remarks : " There was no building, except a solitary log cabin, upon the site of Madison, when it was selected in 1836 for the capital of the State; yet in 1860 the population had reached nearly 7000. The streets of this beautiful city of the wilderness drop down pleasantly towards the shores of the surrounding lakes." Its high lakes, fresh groves, rippling rivulets, shady dales, and flowery meadow lawns, are mingled in greater profusion, and disposed in more picturesque order, than we have ever elsewhere beheld.

RAILROADS.

Wisconsin contains several hundred miles of railroads, and is progressing with others.

The Chicago and Milwaukee extends along the western shore from Lake Michigan (85 miles from Chicago) to Milwaukee, connecting with various routes to other towns in the State.

The Milwaukee and Minnesota Railroad extends the entire breadth of the State south from Milwaukee to La Crosse. The Milwaukee and Mississippi Railroad extends to Prairie du Chien (200 miles), with branch to Janesville. The Milwaukee and Horicon, from Horicon to Stevens' Point, on the Wisconsin. Racine is connected with Beloit by railway, 65 miles. Kenosha, Sheboygan, and Manitowoc, are each building railways westward; and the Chicago, St. Paul, and Fond du Lac route is being urged forward northward from Fond du Lac to Lake Superior. Besides these main lines there are others in operation.

The census of 1860 shows the following progress in railways in this State:—

RAILROADS.	MILEAGE.		COST OF CONSTRUCTION, &c.	
	1850.	1860.	1850.	1860.
Wisconsin Central....................	....	10·00	Dollars.	Dollars. 250,000
	20·00	810·61	612,382	27,711,759
Add— Chicago and North-Western from Illinois	....	147·00	....	7,123,282
	20·00	957·61	612,382	34,835,041
Deduct— Racine and Mississippi, in Illinois......	....	35·00	....	1,279,435
Total in Wisconsin......	20·00	922·61	612,382	33,555,606

In 1864 there were nine railway companies, with 1010 miles of railway, costing 37,165,000 dollars.

PRODUCTS OF AGRICULTURE, ETC.

The number of acres of land improved in 1850 was 1,045,499; in 1860, 3,746,036; unimproved, but owned and surveyed, in 1850, 1,931,159 acres; in 1860, there were 4,153,134 acres. The cash value of farms in 1850 was 28,528,563 dollars; while in 1860 they amounted to 131,117,082 dollars. The value of farming implements and machinery in 1850 was 1,641,568 dollars; in 1860, 5,758,847 dollars.

The assessed value of real and personal estate in 1860 was— real estate, 148,238,766 dollars; personal property, 37,706,723 dollars.

The true value of real estate and personal property, according to the seventh census (1850) and the eighth census (1860) respectively, was—real estate and personal property in 1850,

42,056,595 dollars; while in 1860 it was 273,671,668 dollars showing an increase of 231,615,073 dollars, or 550·72 per cent.

The value of live stock in 1850 was 4,897,385 dollars; in 1860 17,807,366 dollars.

AGRICULTURAL PROGRESS.

In agriculture, Wisconsin shows the following returns:—Wheat, in 1850, 4,286,131 bushels; in 1860, 15,812,625 bushels. Rye, in 1850, 81,253 bushels; in 1860, 888,534 bushels. Indian corn, in 1850, 1,988,879 bushels; in 1860, 7,565,290 bushels. Oats, in 1850, 3,414,672 bushels; in 1860, 11,059,270 bushels. Irish pototoes, in 1850, 1,402,077 bushels; in 1860, 3,848,505 bushels. Butter, in 1850, 3,633,750 pounds; in 1860, 13,651,053 pounds.

The value of flour and meal produced during the year 1850 was 3,536,293 dollars; in 1860, 8,161,183 dollars, showing an increase of 130·7 per cent. The value of planed and sawed lumber in 1850 was 1,218,516 dollars; while in 1860 it was 4,836,159 dollars, or an increase of 297 per cent.

VALUATION AND TAXATION IN 1863.

Number of acres of land assessed	16,945,374 dollars
Value of lands, exclusive of town lots	91,596,750 ,,
Value of town lots	29,936,932 ,,
Aggregate value of real estate	121,533,682 ,,
,, ,, as equalized	127,590,133 ,,
Value of personal property	25,481,640 ,,
Aggregate of all property	153,071,773 ,,
State tax charged on the above	382,130 ,,

INCOME AND EXPENDITURE.

The report of the Secretary of State (*ex officio* auditor) dated Oct. 1, 1863, shows:—

Balance in the Treasury, Sept. 30, 1862	312,217 dollars
Receipts to Sept. 30, 1863, on account of all funds	2,658,095 ,,
	2,970,312 ,,
Disbursements on all accounts to the same time	2,602,386 ,,
Balance in the Treasury, Oct. 1, 1863	367,926 ,,

IOWA.

Organized as a territory, June 12, 1838. Admitted into the Union, December 28, 1846. Capital, Des Moines. Area, 55,045 square miles. Population (1860), 674,948.

AGRICULTURE OF IOWA.

William Duane Wilson, Esq., secretary of the Iowa Farmer's College, has courteously furnished the following statistics of the agriculture of Iowa for 1862 (and partly for 1863), in advance of its official publication. All the information thus given is three years later than that contained in the United States Census returns, and some of it is *four* years later:—

TABLE *showing the following particulars concerning the Agriculture of Iowa from 1850 to 1863 inclusive—viz., the Number of Acres of Improved Land, the Number of Acres sown in Wheat and Corn, the Total Product of each for each year, and the Average Number of Bushels of each Produced per Acre in each year.*

Year.	Population.	Acres of Improved Land.	WHEAT.			CORN.		
			Acres.	Bushels Produced.	Average Per Acre.	Acres.	Bushels Produced.	Average Per Acre.
1850	192,514	824,682	117,729	1,530,581	13·10	192,373	8,656,799	45·00
1856	519,414	2,043,958	388,080	5,469,516	14·10	737,213	31,163,362	42·33
1858	633,547	3,109,436	779,909	3,119,239	4·00	986,096	23,366,684	24·00
1859	*674,913	3,445,394	974,886	8,433,205	8·60	1,109,358	41,116,994	37·00
1862	+702,374	4,784,886	1,119,836	8,795,321	7·64	1,733,503	63,883,916	36·85
1863		4,902,000	1,200,000	14,592,000	12·16	1,800,000	39,000,000	21·44

AGRICULTURAL RETURNS FOR 1862.

These statistics are from the official returns made in the spring of 1863, embracing the whole State, excepting six small counties:—

Acres enclosed	4,784,886
Acres unimproved, attached to farms	4,135,613
Acres of sorgo and imphee	36,667
Gallons of sorgo syrup	3,012,396
Pounds of sorgo sugar	21,469
Acres of Hungarian grass	36,410
Tons of Hungarian grass	71,091
Acres of tame grasses for mowing	224,187
Acres of tame grasses for pasture	70,565
Tons of hay from tame grasses	328,042
Tons of hay from wild grasses	633,420
Bushels of grass seed	55,173
Acres of spring wheat	1,098,998
Bushels of spring wheat harvested	8,052,684
Acres of winter wheat	50,838

---

* The population placed here is that of 1860, but the products on the same line are for 1859. The population opposite 1862 and 1863 is that of the State census, taken early in the spring of 1863.

† The products opposite 1863 are the only items not based upon official data, but they are based upon reliable information from all sections of the State.

Bushels of winter wheat harvested.	742,637
Acres of oats.	336,137
Bushels of oats harvested.	7,582,060
Acres of corn.	1,733,503
Bushels of corn harvested	63,883,916
Acres of Irish potatoes.	35,535
Bushels of Irish potatoes harvested	2,362,918
Acres of rye.	36,963
Bushels of rye harvested.	474,675
Acres of barley.	18,679
Bushels of barley harvested.	385,067
Acres of flax.	6,317
Bushels of flax seed harvested.	36,168
Pounds of flax lint.	158,918
Gallons of linseed oil.	22,728
Acres in all other crops.	44,004
Bushels of sweet potatoes.	37,498
Fruit-trees in orchard, bearing.	503,943
Fruit-trees in orchard, not bearing	1,833,651
Hogs of all ages.	1,743,865
Value of hogs of all ages.	2,886,170 dols.
Cattle of all ages	897,247
Number of milch cows	292,025
Number of working oxen	56,596
Value of cattle of all ages.	7,689,852 dols.
Pounds of butter manufactured.	13,675,500
Pounds of cheese manufactured.	902,701
Sheep at shearing-time in 1862.	406,408
Sheep on hand in 1863	599,938
Pounds of wool shorn in 1862.	1,429,209
Horses of all ages.	275,697
Value of horses of all ages.	11,492,147 dols.
Mules and asses of all ages.	12,032
Value of mules and asses of all ages.	596,671 dols
Hives of bees.	84,731
Pounds of honey.	1,052,685
Pounds of beeswax.	40,762
Pounds of grapes raised.	294,755
Gallons of wine from tame grapes.	13,163
Pounds of hops raised.	41,738
Pounds of tobacco raised.	517,194
Acres planted for timber.	8,360
Rods of hedging	306,728
Value of domestic manufactures not before included.	967,979 dols.
Value of general manufactures.	2,951,805 ,,
Value of agricultural implements and machinery, including waggons.	5,178,049 ,,

The average product of wool per head of sheep, at the shearing of 1862, was 3·51 pounds. This rate for 1863 would yield, from the 599,938 sheep on hand in that year, a wool-clip of 2,099,783 pounds. Mr. Wilson estimates the number of sheep in Iowa, for the shearing of 1864, at 900,000—which number, at 3¼ pounds per head, will yield a product of wool amounting to 3,150,000 pounds.

Railways in Iowa in 1860.	Miles.	Value.
		Dollars.
Burlington and Missouri	93·30	2,492,758
Cedar Rapids and Missouri	25·35	612,359
Chicago, Iowa, and Nebraska	82·11	1,860,251
Dubuque and Pacific	111·18	2,836,833
Dubuque, Marion, and Western	51·00	1,351,790
Keokuk, Fort Des Moines, and Minnesota	92·00	2,879,615
Keokuk, Mount Pleasant, and Muscatine	25·20	1,022,306
Mahaska County	12·00	120,000
Mississippi and Missouri (with branches)	187·63	6,318,721
Total in Iowa	679·77	19,494,633

In 1864 the number of railway companies was 10, with 804 miles of railway, with a total value of 25,498,000 dollars.

ILLINOIS.

Settled in 1749. Admitted into the Union, Dec. 3, 1818. Capital, Springfield. Area, 55,409 square miles. Population (1860), 1,711,951.

AGRICULTURAL PROGRESS.

The amount of lands improved in 1850 was 5,039,545 acres; in 1860, 13,251,473.

The cash value of farms in 1850 was 96,133,290 dollars; in 1860, 432,531,072 dollars. While the value of farming implements and machinery in 1850 was only 6,405,561 dollars, in 1860 it had increased to 18,276,160 dollars. The total value of live stock in 1850 was 24,209,258 dollars; in 1860 it was 73,434,621 dollars.

		1850.	1860.
Wheat	bushels,	9,414,575	24,159,500
Rye	,,	83,364	981,322
Indian corn	,,	59,646,984	115,296,779
Oats	,,	10,087,241	15,336,072
Wool	lbs.	2,150,130	2,477,563
Peas and beans	bushels,	82,814	112,624
Irish potatoes	,,	2,514,861	5,799,964

M

		1850.	1860.
Sweet potatoes	bushels,	157,433	341,443
Barley	,,	110,795	1,175,651
Buckwheat	,,	184,504	345,069
Value of orchard products	dollars,	446,049	1,145,936
Wine	gallons,	2,997	47,093
Value of productions of market-gardens	dollars,	127,494	418,195
Butter	lbs.	12,526,543	23,337,516
Cheese	,,	1,278,225	1,595,358
Hay	tons,	601,952	1,834,265
Value of animals slaughtered	dollars,	4,972,286	15,159,343

VALUATION AND TAXATION.

TABULAR STATEMENT *of Number of Horses, Cattle, &c., Carriages, Watches, Pianos, &c., their number and assessed value, in 1861; also valuation of all other Personal Property for same year; also valuation of Real Property for same year; and Taxes levied and Number of Acres in cultivation in Wheat, &c., in 1860.*

	Number.	Value	
Horses	625,242	21,064,138	dols.
Neat cattle	1,428,362	11,494,803	,,
Mules and asses	39,278	1,708,530	,,
Sheep	731,379	747,437	,,
Hogs	2,196,581	4,032,874	,,
Carriages and waggons	209,247	4,859,507	,,
Clocks and watches	169,779	715,768	,,
Pianos	3,467	248,677	,,
Goods and merchandise	...	9,104,949	,,
Bankers' property	...	2,009,611	,,
Manufactured articles	...	1,111,127	,,
Moneys and credits	...	13,781,843	,,
Bonds, stocks, &c.	...	443,329	,,
Unenumerated property	...	11,549,953	,,
Total value of personal, after all deductions were made	...	80,720,918	,,

REAL ESTATE.	Number.	Value.	
Town lots	...	41,454,142	dols.
Lands	...	107,404,607	,,
Railroad property	...	11,243,722	,,
Total value of real and personal property	...	330,823,479	,,
Amount of taxes charged	...	2,523,536	,,
Amount of taxes abated, commissions, &c.	...	323,136	,,
Net amount of taxes	...	2,200,400	,,

Number of acres in cultivation in wheat . . 1,963,328
Number of acres in cultivation in corn . . . 4,119,620
Number of acres in other field products . . 1,035,673

RAILWAYS IN ILLINOIS.

RAILROADS.	Mileage. 1850.	Mileage. 1860.	Cost of Construction. 1850.	Cost of Construction. 1860.
			Dollars.	Dollars.
Chicago, Alton, and St. Louis		220·00		10,000,000
Chicago, Burlington, and Quincy	13·00	138·00	195,000	7,468,926
Chicago and Milwaukee		45·00		1,884,344
Chicago and North-Western		213·00		10,684,922
Chicago and Rock Island		181·50		6,913,554
Elgin and State Line		32·20		581,317
Galena and Chicago Union (with branches)	42·50	261·25	695,507	9,352,481
Great Western (with branch)	55·00	182·00	550,000	5,086,206
Illinois Central		738·25		27,195,391
Illinois Coal		4·00		100,000
Joliet and Chicago		35·80		1,000,000
Logansport, Peoria, and Burlington		171·00		5,000,000
Mount City		3 00		60,000
Ohio and Mississippi		148·00		4,870,686
Peoria and Bureau Valley		46·60		2,106,000
Peoria and Oquawka		94·00		3,769,889
Quincy and Chicago		100·00		1,978,550
Quincy and Toledo		34·00		750,000
Rockford		28·00		560,000
Rock Island and Peoria		11·00		220,000
Sycamore and Cortlandt		5·00		75,000
Terre Haute, Alton, & St. Louis (with branches)		208·30		8,865,252
Warsaw and Peoria		13·00		300,000
Totals	110·50	2,912·90	1,440,507	108,822,518

In 1864 there were 26 companies, 3156 miles of railway, the aggregate cost of which was 120,417,000 dollars.

RAILWAYS OF THE UNITED STATES.

The number of companies, miles of railway, and aggregate cost of all the railways in the United States, up to the 1st of January, 1865, were as follows:—

	No. of Companies.	Miles.	Aggregate Cost.
Alabama	10	804	18,161,000 dols.
Arkansas	1	38	1,155,000 ,,
California	3	116	5,790,000 ,,
Connecticut	13	629	23,014,000 ,,
Delaware	4	126	4,500,000 ,,
Florida	6	401	8,628,000 ,,
Georgia	17	1419	29,389,000 ,,
Illinois	26	3156	120,417,000 ,,

	No. of Companies.	Miles.	Aggregate Cost.
Indiana	19	2195	71,296,000 dols.
Iowa	10	804	25,496,000 ,,
Kansas	1	40	1,400,000 ,,
Kentucky	12	566	21,062,000 ,,
Louisiana	9	334	12,021,000 ,,
Maine	13	505	12,669,000 ,,
Maryland and District of Colorado	8	408	22,737,000 ,,
Massachusetts	49	1285	59,051,000 ,,
Michigan	10	898	35,091,000 ,,
Minnesota	4	157	3,850,000 ,,
Mississippi	5	862	24,682,000 ,,
Missouri	7	924	50,046,000 ,,
New York	42	2820	135,887,000 ,,
New Hampshire	17	660	22,489,000 ,,
New Jersey	26	864	38,892,000 ,,
North Carolina	10	983	19,120,000 ,,
Ohio	30	3310	117,583,000 ,,
Oregon	2	19	700,000 ,,
Pennsylvania	85	3359	170,080,000 ,,
Rhode Island	3	125	4,588,000 ,,
South Carolina	10	973	22,053,000 ,,
Tennessee	14	1295	33,533,000 ,,
Texas	8	451	16,239,000 ,,
Vermont	9	587	23,852,000 ,,
Virginia	17	1378	42,905,000 ,,
West Virginia	1	360	21,985,000 ,,
Wisconsin	9	1010	37,165,000 ,,
Totals	510	33,877	1,261,526,000 ,,

CHAPTER III.*

MINNESOTA.

Extent of Territory—St. Paul, the Capital—Physical Districts—Falls of St. Anthony and its Water Power—Mineral Resources—Sandstone, &c.—Salt Springs—The Relations of Minnesota in Reference to Internal Commerce—Rapid Progress of Cultivation—Agricultural Productions—Progress of Population—The Future of Minnesota—Testimony of Hon. W. H. Seward—Conclusion—Railway through Minnesota—Illinois Central Railroad—The Value of the Lands—Value of Illinois Lands.

" Here is the place—the central place—where the agriculture of the richest region of North America must pour out its tributes to the whole world."—*Speech of Hon. Wm. H. Seward, delivered at St. Paul, Minnesota.*

EXTENT OF TERRITORY.

The territory of Minnesota, as organized by the Act of Congress, of March 3, 1849, is an extensive region, being about four times as large as the State of Ohio, and is 675 miles in extent from its south-eastern to its north-eastern border. It extends from the Mississippi and St. Croix Rivers, and the western extremity of Lake Superior on the east, to the Missouri, and White-Earth Rivers on the west a distance of over 400 miles ; and from the Iowa line (latitude 43° 30') on the south to the British line (latitude 49°) on the north, also a distance of over 400 miles—the whole comprising an area of 166,000 square miles, or 106,000,000 acres.

A large portion of its territory has since been ceded west of the Red River to form the territory of Dacotah. The present number of square miles is 83,531, or 53,459,840 acres. Minnesota was admitted into the American Union, and permitted to enjoy the rights of a sovereign State in 1857. Since that time her increase in population and her progress, in every sense, has been without a parallel. Why, she has sent an army of 15,000 stalwart men to bear arms in the present unfortunate war ; yet her population has increased between 1859 and 1864 to 350,000, and during the last year she has produced 2,000,000 bushels more wheat than any preceding year. Her tax levy shows property to the amount of 40,000,000 dollars, or £8,000,000 sterling. She has a college and numerous schools, which are supported by grants of land In the year 1862, 38,147 acres were sold, yielding a sum of 242,532 dollars.

---

* This chapter is condensed from the admirable reports of the Hon. J. A. Wheelock and the Hon. James W. Taylor, Commissioners of Statistics for the State of Minnesota.

ST. PAUL, THE CAPITAL.

St. Paul—latitude 44° 52' 46", longitude 93° 4' 54"—is a port of entry, the county seat of Ramsey County, and the seat of government of the territory of Minnesota. It is pleasantly situated on the east bank of the Mississippi River, eight miles from the Falls of St. Anthony, and five miles from Fort Snelling; about 2070 miles from the mouth of the Mississippi River, and near its confluence with the Minnesota River, and is elevated about 800 feet above the Gulf of Mexico. It is near the geographical centre of the continent of North America, in the north temperate zone, and must eventually become a central nucleus for the business of one of the best watered, timbered, and most fertile and healthy countries of the globe. It is surrounded in the rear by a semicircular plateau, elevated about forty feet above the town, of easy grade, and commanding a magnificent view of the river above and below. Nature never planned a spot better adapted to build up a showy and delightful display of architecture and gardening, than that natural terrace of hills. The town has sprung up, like Minerva full armed from the head of Jupiter, and now contains 10,000 inhabitants; its whole history of four years forming an instance of Western enterprise, and determined energy and resolution, hitherto unsurpassed in the history of any frontier settlement.

PHYSICAL DISTRICTS.

The Superior basin of the St. Lawrence is terminated on the west and north by an immense development of the primary rocks, complicated by local disturbances, and stretching from Labrador and James's Bay in broad granitic and trappean ranges, overlaid by huge deposits of clay and drift, and disappearing to the west under the argillaceous drift deposits of the Red River Valley, and on the south, in the Silurian sandstones and limestones of the Mississippi Valley. This range of transverse rocks, with all its diluvial covering, does not rise over 1680 feet above the sea, while its average elevation is not over 1450 feet above the sea, or 450 feet above the general level of the State.

The immense diluvial sand dunes which cover the uplift of this formation, west of Lake Superior, constitute the height of land which skirts the summit level of the Mississippi, and give origin, between latitudes 47° and 49°, to the three great river systems of the continent. This highland district is the watershed of North America—the fountain head of that radiating efflux of inland waters which clothe the vast circle of the continent with their gorgeous intertexture of physical and commercial life, and in return gather back to their sources the centripetal movements of American development. The surface of Minnesota is thus made up of the culminating acclivities of the three great hydrographical divisions of the North American plain. It is a pyramid formed by the slanting basins of the St. Lawrence, of the Mississippi, and of Lake Winnipeg, converging respectively from the east, south, and west upon this central ridge.

Three-fifths of this surface slopes south and south-eastwardly, with the waters and plains of the Mississippi; the rest is nearly equally divided between the low savannahs of the Red River, in the north-west, and the broken highlands of the north-east, which are drained by the precipitous streams of Lake Superior and Rainy Lake. These three great hydrographical slopes have the following estimated areas respectively :—

   The Mississippi slope . . . . . . 49,000 square miles
   The Red River slope 17,000   ,,
   The Superior and Rainy River slope . 15,000   ,,

Each of these slopes constitutes a distinct physical district, with its characteristic structure and physiognomy—the nuclei of the broad differences which their diverging basins carry to the opposite extremities of the continent :—

1. The name of the Superior or Highland district belongs not only to the volcanic uplift of the Superior basin, but to all the great northern block of drift stratum on its borders, which encloses the summits of the Mississippi and the Red River, and the valley of Rainy Lake River. This whole district forms a singular exception to the general character of the State. Its elevation, about 1400 or 1500 feet above the sea, is only about 450 feet above the general level of the country; but the rugged and comparatively barren aspect of its surface, broken by numerous transverse ridges, with its low curves of summer temperature and subarctic flora, entitle it to be designated the "mountain district of Minnesota." Its whole area, about 20,000 miles in extent, is covered with a compact forest growth, of which the pine, spruce, and other conifers, are the prevailing forms. The hills and knolls, which rise only from 85 to 100 feet above the surrounding waters, ramify throughout its whole extent, so as to determine the basins of the innumerable lakes and streams which so peculiarly characterize this region of country. These hills are generally sandy and sterile. In the valleys the soil is alluvial and rich. The climate here is from 5° to 12° colder than in the rest of the State, being comprehended between the summer temperature of 60° on its northern and 65° on its southern boundary. With these general features in common, this region embraces three subordinate districts, marked by distinct characters—

(1.) *The Superior declivity*, which is distinguished by its bold ranges of granitic and trappean hills, and their imbedded wealth of mineral deposits—by the immense expanse of its lake excavation, with a water area of 32,100 square miles, and a depth of 600 feet, and by the number and picturesqueness of the cascades and lakes into which its rivers break in their passage across the transverse chains of hills;

(2.) *The Rainy Lake Valley*, whose waters flow into Hudson's Bay, and form, between the Lake of the Woods and Rainy Lake, a navigable aqueduct nearly a hundred miles in length, along our northern boundary, and whose banks Sir George Simpson describes as a gentle slope of greensward, crowned in many places with a plentiful growth of birch, poplar, beech, elm, and oak, resembling the banks of the Thames in fertility; and

(3.) The *summit level of the Mississippi*, with its immense system of lacustrine reservoirs, pressing around the sources of the Mississippi and its tributaries, with its interminable labyrinth of streams and rice lakes, meadows, ponds, bogs, and cranberry swamps. Instead of the rugged hills of the Superior district, the country is here broken into low oblong sandy knolls and ridges covered with pine, and separated by low savannahs, while the rivers are fringed with low alluvial bottoms, covered with a dense growth, chiefly of hardwoods.

This forest highland region, which has its southern limit about latitude $46\frac{1}{4}°$, extends westward a little over half the breadth of the State, when its forests and sandy hills, suddenly disappear to the west, and its line of elevation sinks by a terraced descent of 500 feet to the low, alluvial, almost woodless levels of the Red River basin. To the primary rocks which underlie this north-eastern Adirondack with its sandy covering, succeeds a bed of limestone, concealed under a deep deposit of clay. Instead of a sterile soil of sand, we have a deep, dark, argillaceous alluvium, exceedingly rich and grassy. The poplar, the alder, and willow, take the place of the pine and the spruce. Both districts are imperfectly drained, but in the one case the swamps and surface waters are accumulated by the flatness of the country, and in the other by its broken and hilly conformation. Though the Red River Valley spans the same latitude as the north-eastern Adirondack, its mean summer temperature is from $5°$ to $10°$ higher, and by a still more curious contrast its winters are colder. Both districts belong nearly to the same rain belt, having a summer fall of about ten inches. These contrasted districts, lying, as it were, back to back, occupy the section of Minnesota lying north of latitude $46\frac{1}{2}°$, embracing together about 38,000 square miles. The region south of this line, comprising all the rest of the State, 46,000 square miles in extent, belongs geologically, and in its forms of relief as well as hydrographically, to the Mississippi Valley, whose summit we have assigned in accordance with its geological and botanical affinities to the Superior or Highland district.

The general character of the Mississippi slope is that of a rolling prairie, whose undulations dip down on all sides to the cool margin of beautiful lakes and streams. It is everywhere covered with a warm, dark, and fertile siliceo-calcareous soil, enriched with organic remains and alluvial deposits, and resting either on the Silurian limestones or sandstones, or a drift stratum overlying these rocks. The pine, spruce, and other conifers, which characterize the Superior district, abruptly disappear between the 46th and 47th parallel, with its compact forest mass, and the sudden transition from the pine belt to the deciduous forms, distributed in groves and belts, conspicuously mark the important change of climate and soil which is expressed in the whole physiognomy of this district. While the surface of this part of Minnesota partakes of the general character of the prairie districts of the Mississippi Valley, it possesses a marked individuality in the picturesque cast of its surface forms. Its rivers, cutting deep troughs in the plain, and mingling with the bold and angular outline of their bluffs with the rounded and graceful sweep of their valleys, afford, with a thorough drainage, and an immense extent of inland navigation, some of the most animated scenery on the continent, while the innumerable lakes scattered over its surface, the number and beauty of its groves and belts of timber, which crown the undulations of the upland, or shadow the margins of streams, break up the monotony of the prairie into forms of infinite variety and beauty, and unite all the elements, not only of successful husbandry, but of delightful landscape, in the limits of almost every farm. The Mississippi slope below the parallel of $46\frac{1}{4}°$, or the pine belt, is enclosed between the summer temperature of 65° on the north, and 73° on the south.

FALLS OF ST. ANTHONY.

1. Minnesota possesses a more ample and effective water power than New England. The Falls and Rapids of St. Anthony alone, with a total descent of 64 feet, afford an available hydraulic capacity, according to an experienced and competent engineer,[*] of 120,000-horse power. This is considerably greater than the whole motive power—steam and water—employed in textile manufactures in England in 1850, and nearly seven times as great as the water power so employed.

That is to say, the available power created by this magnificent waterfall is more than sufficient to drive all the 25,000,000 spindles and 4000 mills of England and Scotland combined. The entire machinery of the English Manchester and the American Lowell, if they could be transplanted here, would scarcely press upon its immense hydraulic capabilities. But as compared with those great industrial centres, the Falls of St. Anthony possess one decisive advantage, which is to a great extent illustrative of the functions of

---

[*] See a pamphlet by the Hon. David Heaton, on "The General Interests of Manufacture and Trade connected with the Upper Mississippi," to which is appended a report on the hydrography and geology of the Mississippi River, by T. M. Griffith and Dr. C. L. Anderson.

the State as a commercial and manufacturing emporium. This splendid cataract forms the terminus of continuous navigation on the Mississippi, and the same waters, which lavish on the broken ledges of limestone a strength almost sufficient to weave the garments of the world, may gather the products of its mills almost at their very doors, and distribute them to every part of the great valley of the Mississippi.

The St. Croix Falls, which are only second to St. Anthony Falls in hydraulic power, are similarly, though somewhat less advantageously situated at the head of navigation upon a tributary of the Mississippi. Except the Minnesota, nearly every tributary of the Mississippi, in its rapid and broken descent to the main stream, affords valuable mill sites. The Mississippi itself, in its descent from its Itasca summit to Fort Snelling, in which it falls 836 feet, or over 16 inches per mile, is characterized by long steps of slack water, broken at long intervals by abrupt transitions in the character of the rocks which form its bed, and forming a fine series of falls and rapids available for hydraulic works. Pokegoma Falls, Little Falls, Sauk Rapids, and St. Anthony Falls are the chief of these. But the Elk, Rum, St. Croix, and numberless smaller streams on the east slope of the Mississippi, the Sauk, Crow, Vermilion, Cannon, Zumbro, Minneiska, Root, and their branches, nearly all the tributaries of the Minnesota, and a multitude of streams besides, in their abrupt descent over broken beds of limestone or sandstone, through long and winding valleys or ravines, with a fall of from 3 to 8 feet per mile, afford an unlimited abundance of available water power to nearly every county in the State. This diffusion of hydraulic power throughout the whole State is a feature whose value as an element of development can scarcely be over estimated, as it gives to every neighbourhood the means of manufacturing its own flour and lumber; and affords the basis of all those numerous local manufactures which enter into the industrial economy of every northern community.

2. Passing to the second point of comparison with New England, already incidentally touched upon, the commercial position of Minnesota upon the termini of the three great water-lines of the continent, not only gives it an immensely wider capacity of interior trade, but a far easier access to the sources of supply of raw material. A region six times as large as all New England, as yet undeveloped, but already starting on the swift career of western growth, and capable of supporting many millions of population, is directly dependent upon Minnesota for all the manufactured commodities it may consume. Its position, relative to these northwestern valleys, invests its manufacturing capabilities with an importance greater than those of any other of the interior districts of the continent. For the future manufacture of cotton and woollen fabrics, it has decided advantages of position over New England. The Mississippi River brings it into intimate relation with the

sources of cotton supply, and it lies in the midst of the great wool zone of the continent. To the development of textile manufactures, however, large aggregations of population, and a thorough organization of labour are necessary, and we may confidently resign the task to the sure operation of the laws of growth and political economy.

3. But it is especially its internal resources of raw material, of which New England is to a great extent destitute, which give Minnesota its physical superiority over that district in manufacturing capacity.

MINERAL RESOURCES.

To enumerate these in the order of their importance, we possess in the mineral ranges of Lake Superior deposits of *iron* and *copper*, which have been shown by the severest tests to be superior to any on the continent, and fully equal in tenacity and malleability to the best Swedish and Russian iron.*

The completion of a railroad from Lake Superior to the Mississippi River, for which a grant of lands was made this year (1861) by the State Legislature, and which will undoubtedly be pushed forward as soon as the pressure of the war is removed from business enterprises, will enable us to turn these rich ores to account as a basis for the important class of manufactures of which they form the staple.

With these facilities at her command, Minnesota may be reasonably expected, with her projected systems of internal improvement completed, to control the manufacture of iron and copper products for the Mississippi Valley. Agricultural and mechanical implements, railroad iron, locomotives, stoves, bolts, nuts, screws, cutlery, edge tools, safes, scales, now imported at an immense cost by railroad, could be produced here and supplied to every part of the Mississippi Valley above the Ohio, at least as cheaply as in Pennsylvania.

But iron and coal, though the most important, are not the only useful minerals which the rock formations of Minnesota hold in reserve for her future manufactures.

Roofing and ciphering *slates* of excellent quality are found in Carlton County, near the St. Louis River, directly on the surveyed line of the Superior railroad.

SANDSTONE, ETC.

A *fine white sandstone*, peculiar to Minnesota, forms the base of the bluffs at Fort Snelling, and along the Mississippi from Red Rock to St. Paul. This sandstone is made up of grains of limpid and colourless quartz. Nicollet suggests its utility for the manufac-

---

* Beds of nodular ironstone, of great value, also exist at a number of localities on the Blue Earth and Le Sueur Rivers, yielding 31 per cent. of iron from the raw ore.

ture of glass. Norwood says it is even purer than the celebrated Linn sand used by the Scotch manufacturers of flint glass. Treated in the same way, it yielded a glass of similar quality.

The *limestone*, which crops out near the surface along the banks of the Mississippi, affords an exhaustless supply of building material of excellent quality. The upper stratum of this limestone formation is a greyish, buff-coloured rock, lying in layers of from 4 to 12 inches in thickness, easily quarried and worked, though not capable of a high polish. Under this lies a beautiful blue shell limestone, which is quarried extensively at West St. Paul, St. Anthony, and elsewhere—hard, close-grained, durable, and admirably adapted to architecture. These limestone formations, at various localities, contain a large per centage of *carbonate of lime*. Lime-kilns are numerous all over the State, but the best lime is said to be manufactured at the mouth of the Cottonwood, and at Shakopee on the Minnesota, the former yielding 90 per cent. of carbonate. Furthermore, this blue or shell limestone, as the result of experiments made by Dr. C. L. Anderson, promises to furnish an excellent *hydraulic cement*.

The bluish *clay* which underlies the soil in a large portion of the State, is used for the manufacture of *bricks* of a good quality. The white marl, of which beds occur at St. Anthony, yields a beautiful and durable buff-coloured brick, resembling the celebrated Milwaukee brick, but of more variable colour. This clay, I believe, forms the material employed in the *pottery* at that place.

Similar marl and clay beds yield fine materials for bricks and pottery at Carver, Chaska, Stillwater, St. Paul, and other parts of the State. A bed of fine porcelain clay is reported in Wabashaw County.

SALT SPRINGS.

Not the least important of the indigenous raw material, which Minnesota possesses for profitable manufactures, are the numerous *salt springs* of the Red River Valley, the beginning of the immense salines which stretch westward along the international boundary to the Rocky Mountains. These large reservoirs of salt, of which twelve belong to the State under a grant of Congress, are destined to form a considerable source of wealth. Reference has already been made to the manufacture of salt in the British settlements of the Red River. A few years ago the supply of salt for these settlements was obtained in North-eastern Dakota, near Pembina. With the imperfect apparatus employed by the half-breeds who are engaged in its manufacture, the springs near Lake Manitoba are said to yield 1 bushel of good salt to 24 gallons of brine, or $33\frac{1}{3}$ per cent. The immense consumption of salt in the north-west in the packing of beef and pork, and other purposes, gives a peculiar value to this resource. In 1839 the Chicago market was supplied with 19,000 barrels. In 1858 there were imported into Chicago for the north-western trade, from the salt-factories of New York alone, 1,669,000 bushels. The whole yield of the New York salt springs in 1858 was 7,033,000 bushels. There are also numerous salt springs in Virginia and Pennsylvania. Recently a valuable spring has been opened at East Saginaw, Michigan, yielding the same proportion of salt to brine as at Lake Manitoba. Nearly all the product of these springs goes to the supply of the north and of the north-west, which possesses in Minnesota and Dakota abundant resources for supplying itself.

THE RELATIONS OF MINNESOTA TO THE MOVEMENTS AND CHANNELS OF INTERNAL COMMERCE.

A complete analysis of the commercial position of Minnesota would embrace a geographical description of the continent.

The contiguous basins of the St. Lawrence, the Mississippi, and of Lake Winnipeg form an immense triangular plain, throughout which every diversity of soil and vegetation covers an uniform geology of the successive series of sedimentary rocks. This vast interior basin, enclosed by the mountain chains of the ocean coasts —with an area of 2,500,000 square miles—culminates in Minnesota, as the apex from which its great divergent valleys slope to their ocean outlets, the common source and centre from which these three great rivers radiate to the ocean.

The Mississippi River, originating in the lacustrine steppes of Northern Minnesota, in latitude 47° and longitude 95°, gives 900 miles of its waters to its mother State, of which 400 miles are navigable, with only two interruptions, before it reaches the head of continuous navigation below the Falls of St. Anthony; whence, starting at a more majestic pace, and gathering in its bosom the commerce of fifteen States, it empties into the Gulf of Mexico, at a distance, by its course, of 2187 miles from St. Paul, embracing in its basin an area of 1,217,562 square miles, a population of 13,000,000, and an aggregate shore-line of 35,644, of which seven-eighths belong to its navigable tributaries.

The St. Lawrence, of which the St. Louis River may be regarded as the source, rises north of the Mississippi summit. Of the great fresh-water lakes which form the reservoirs of this majestic stream, the largest and furthest inland, the Superior, forms a portion of the north-eastern boundary of Minnesota. Their collected waters, flowing eastward, with a channel wide and deep enough to float the navies of the world, reach the Gulf of St. Lawrence on the Atlantic Ocean, at a distance of 2400 miles from the head of Lake Superior in Minnesota. Its basin has an area of 1,000,000 square miles. The Red River, rising in Elbow Lake, near the sources of the Mississippi, flows south-westwardly to the western border of Minnesota, whence it runs for 520 miles with a narrow and winding but navigable current, through a rich alluvial plain, due north to Lake

Winnipeg, when it interlocks with the waters of the Saskatchewan, whose great branches rise in the Rocky Mountains, and extend this chain of navigation 1000 miles further to the northward. Lake Winnipeg, which unites the waters of these streams, is 264 miles long and 35 miles wide. These waters drain a fertile area of nearly 400,000 square miles in the form of a parallelogram, between the 49th and 50th degrees of latitude. Such are the gigantic arms with which Minnesota grasps the extremities of the continent. These three great channels of internal commerce, converging from the opposite extremes of the great plain, unite all its infinite gradations of climate and production in one simple and integral geographical and social mass, having their common link of inter-communication in Minnesota. Nevertheless, each of these component basins constitute a distinct physical district, with a distinct climate, a distinct physiognomy, and characteristic productions. According to the present distribution of industrial interests, the St. Lawrence Basin, or the north-east, is the seat of manufactures and maritime commerce. The Mississippi Valley is spanned by three successive belts of production, of which cotton, sugar, and rice characterize the southern; corn, tobacco, and fruits the middle; and wheat, provisions, wool, hay, and the products of the dairy the extreme northern belt, including Minnesota and Wisconsin.

The Saskatchewan Basin is the continuation of this northern belt to the north-west, constituting the north-west delta of the great triangular plain, as the middle and southern belts of the Mississippi valley constitute its southern delta, and the St. Lawrence Basin its north-eastern delta. These well-defined sections are all reciprocally dependent upon each other.

The bread and provisions of the north-west go to feed the manufacturer and merchant of the north-east and the cotton-planter of the south. In return it receives from the north-east the fabrics of domestic or foreign manufactures, and from the south its sugar, rice, fruits, tobacco, &c.

Here are four distinct commercial movements arising between these several districts, each having its corresponding channel of transit, and all having their common point of *internexus* in Minnesota. Each of these movements involves two transhipments within her borders upon her eastern and western water-lines, and imposes, therefore, a double tariff on through freightage over her territory, to swell the commercial revenues of her people.

These movements, moreover, constitute two transverse commercial currents, the first having a general direction north and south, and the other a general direction east and west. Each has its corresponding water-line, and a belt of continuous plain or railway bed.

1. The north and south current represents the normal tendency of commercial movement in the direction of the great contrasts of climate and production between the opposite sides of the temperate zone.

The Mississippi and Red River valleys constitute the north and south belt, which nearly spans the temperate zone, and on which are exhibited the whole scale of its physical diversities, on a surface of nearly uniform elevation. This north and south movement has its appropriate channel in the magnificent reaches of navigable waters which constitute what we may call the axis of this belt, of which the Hudson's Bay and the Gulf of Mexico are the opposite poles. The Mississippi, the Minnesota, the Red River, and Lake Winnipeg form a nearly continuous chain of navigation, 3300 miles in length, or, if we include the Saskatchewan, 4300 miles, interrupted only by a low and narrow portage across the western levels of Minnesota, crossing 25 degrees of latitude, while numerous lateral tributaries permeate their valleys in all directions.

2. The east and west, or maritime current, has its corresponding belt in the St. Lawrence, Upper Mississippi, Red River and Saskatchewan valleys, which form a continuous level plain, with a general direction north-west and south-east, coinciding with the isothermal belt, between the mean summer temperatures of 60° and 70°, which defines the grass, wheat, and wool zone of the continent, and extending from the Rocky Mountains to the Atlantic, across 55 degrees of longitude. It has also its corresponding channel in the water axis of this plain, formed by the St. Lawrence, the Red River, and Saskatchewan, two continuous chains of navigation, east and west of Minnesota, whose aggregate length is 3412 miles, extending three-quarters of the distance across the continent.

RAPID PROGRESS OF CULTIVATION.

In 1854, we had less than 15,000 acres under cultivation with an aggregate product of less than 500,000 bushels of grain and potatoes, so that the breadth of tillage and quantities produced have, on the average, nearly doubled every year for six years. The following comparison with the census results of 1850 will show the enormous advance of agricultural production in Minnesota since its first organization and settlement:—

	No. Acres Improved.	No. Acres Tilled.	No. Bushels Grain and Potatoes produced.
1850	5,035	1,900	71,709
1860	546,951	433,267	14,693,517

In 1859, according to the census, we produced 9,232,566 bushels of grain and potatoes, though to this at least 10 per cent. must be added for deficient returns. By a laborious calculation—founded upon a comparison of the assessors' returns of the crop of 1859, with the assessors' returns of the same crop for 20 counties—I am able to give a close approximation to the area tilled for 1859. The result corrected for deficient returns* as compared with that of 1860 is as follows:—

* That is adding 10 per cent. to the census returns for 1859, and 20 per cent. to the assessors' returns of 1860.

	Area Tilled.	No. Bushels of Grain and Potatoes produced.
1859	345,000	10,155,822
1860	433,267	14,693,517

This does not however exhibit the whole agricultural growth, for while only 34 per cent. of the tilled area of 1859 was in wheat, 53 per cent. of that of 1860 was in this crop; so that the relative increase in the quantity of grain produced is much less than the increase in its value and weight.

To show how far cultivation has advanced in Minnesota, notwithstanding the newness of the country, beyond the ordinary standards—taking population as a measure—let us compare it with other States in this respect.

First—As to cultivation—

		No. Acres Tilled.	No. Acres to each Inhabitant.
Minnesota	1860	433,267	2·6
Ohio	1858	5,000,000	2·2
New York	1855	4,072,000	1·7

Second—As to product of grain and potatoes—

	No. Bushels.	No. Bushels to each Person.
Minnesota, 1860	14,693,517	143¼
Ohio, average, 1857-58	112,883,870	49
New York, 1855	76,639,910	21¾
Austrian Gallicia	67,409,145	14¾

Such a degree of agricultural development as is here shown in a State, which eight years ago was a wilderness, has certainly not been witnessed before in so short a period in any American State, and it is doubtful if history affords its parallel.

GENERAL RESULTS OF AGRICULTURE.

Adding 20 per cent. for deficient returns, the following table exhibits the area and product of each crop and the proportion of each 100 acres of the whole cultivated area which was occupied by each crop in 1860:—

Crop.	No. Acres in each Crop.	Ratio per Cent. of Tilled Area.	No. of Bushels produced.	Average yield per Acre.
Wheat	230,315	53·38	5,101,432	22·05
Rye	13,276	3·06	286,125	21·56
Barley	9,073	2·09	301,539	33·23
Oats	68,714	15·85	2,912,857	42·39
Buckwheat	3,618	83	56,929	15·73
Corn	88,126	20·34	3,143,577	35·67
Potatoes	16,687	3·85	2,303,308	138·00
Beans	694	15	10,932	15·7
Sorghum	159	03	*11,830	*72·5
Timothy	1,597	32	2,779	..

* Gallons of syrup.

Staple Agricultural Productions.

		1849.	1859* Census.	1860† Assessors' Returns.
Bushels of	wheat	1,401	2,154,017	5,001,432
,,	rye	123	142,877	286,125
,,	oats	30,582	2,131,333	2,912,857
,,	Indian corn	16,725	2,794,318	3,143,577
,,	barley	1,216	125,104	301,539
,,	buckwheat	515	25,195	56,929
,,	potatoes	21,145	1,859,632	2,303,308
,,	peas and beans	10,002	18,371	No returns.
Tons of hay		2,019	249,974	300,000

Miscellaneous Agricultural Products.

	1850.	1860.
Pounds of tobacco	..	34,955
Bushels of sweet potatoes ‡	200	897
Bushels of clover seed	..	159
Bushels of grass seed	..	3,506
Pounds of hops‡	..	83
Tons of hemp	..	272
Pounds of flax	..	1,529
Bushels of flax seed	..	211
Pounds of maple sugar§	2,950	353,633
Gallons of maple syrup	..	24,403
Gallons of sorghum syrup	..	7,048
Pounds of beeswax	..	1,838
Pounds of honey	..	20,290
Pounds of beeswax and honey	80	29,128
Gallons of wine	..	833
Value of orchard products	..	7,475 dols.
Value of produce of market gardens.	150 dols.	160,108 ,,
Value of home manufactures	..	6,394 ,,

Live Stock.

	1850.	1860.
Horses	860	16,879
Asses and mules	14	384

---

* I have before given the reasons for the belief that at least 10 per cent. must be added to the census returns of agricultural productions, as here given, to obtain the closest approximation to the actual result.

† In this column I have added 20 per cent. to the assessors' returns to correct the deficiencies already explained. The returned results by counties are given in the table annexed.

‡ These articles are generally grown in market gardens, and, when these are not attached to farms, are not enumerated specifically in the census schedules, but are probably included in the item "Value of produce of market gardens." Wild hops grow in great luxuriance in the timber.

§ This includes only the maple sugar made by the farmers. As much again, probably, is made by the Indians and others.

	1850.	1860.
Horses, asses, and mules	874	17,263
Working oxen	655	17,290
Milch cows	607	38,938
Other cattle	740	49,781
Total neat cattle	2,002	106,009
Sheep	80	12,595
Swine	734	104,479
Value of live stock	92,859 dols.	3,210,769 dols.

Animal Products.

	1850.	1860.
Pounds of butter	1,100	2,839,500
Pounds of cheese	. .	186,527
Total dairy products	1,100	3,026,027
Pounds of wool	. .	19,306
Value of slaughtered animals	2,840 dols.	480,162 dols.

PRICES OF AGRICULTURAL PRODUCTS.

Prices are fluctuating, but range as follows:—
Wheat, from 50 cents to 65 cents.
Rye, from 20 cents to 25 cents.
Barley, from 30 cents to 40 cents.
Oats, from 12 cents to 18 cents—22 to 30 in the fall of 1861.
Corn, from 30 cents to 40 cents.
Butter, from 7 cents to 8 cents, or from 10 cents to 12 cents for choice rolls.
Pork, from 2 cents to 4 cents.
Eggs, from 6 cents to 10 cents.
Cheese, from 9 cents to 10 cents.
Beef, from 1 dollar 75 cents to 2 dollars 75 cents.
Potatoes, from 15 cents to 18 cents in the fall, and from 20 cents to 25 cents in the summer.
Cranberries, from 90 cents to 1 dollar 50 cents per bushel.
Flour, from 3 dollars to 3 dollars 50 cents for superfine; and from 3 dollars 75 cents to 4 dollars for extra.

VALUE OF AGRICULTURAL PRODUCTS OF 1860.

Wheat, at 55 cents.	2,805,787 dols.
Rye, at 23 cents.	65,808 ,,
Oats, at 20 cents.	582,571 ,,
Corn, at 35 cents.	1,110,251 ,,
Barley, at 35 cents.	105,538 ,,
Buckwheat at 60 cents.	34,157 ,,
Potatoes at 18 cents.	414,595 ,,
300,000 tons of hay at 2 dollars per ton.	600,000 ,,

200,000 lbs. of cheese at 10 cents. per lb.	20,000 dols.
3,000,000 lbs. of butter at 8 cents. per lb.	240,000 ,,
Value of produce of market gardens . .	175,000 ,,
Value of animals slaughtered	500,000 ,,
25,000 lbs. of wool at 20 cents. . . .	5,000 ,,
400,000 lbs. of maple sugar at 10 cents. .	40,000 ,,
Miscellaneous products	50,000 ,,
Total value of agricultural products of 1860	6,748,707 ,,

The shipments of St. Paul for 1861, as compiled for the daily newspapers, exclusive of transhipments, not landed at the levee, from the Minnesota River, were stated as follows in the *Press*, of Jan. 1, 1862:—

Flour, bbls.	25,600
Wheat, bush.	527,087
Oats ,, ...	12,000
Barley ,, ...	7,260
Beans ,, ...	500
Pork, bbls.	2,430
Bacon, lbs.	105,566
Lard, bbls.	800
Cranberries, bush.	4,542
Butter, lbs.	9,000
Dry and Green hides, number . . .	27,109
Ginseng, lbs.	208,650
Potatoes, bush.	3,000
Deer skins	3,000
Onions, bush.	500
Wool, lbs.	3,000
Furs, amount	200,000 dols.

TABLE SHOWING THE GROWTH OF PROPERTY IN TEN YEARS.

Year.	No of Assessed Counties.	Valuation of Real and Personal Estate.	Ratios of Increase per Cent.	Population.
1849	1	514,936 dols.	—	4,049
1850	6	806,437 ,,	56	6,077
1851	3	1,282,123 ,,	59	7,000
1852	8	1,715,835 ,,	33	10,000
1853	6	2,701,437 ,,	51	14,000
1854	13	3,508,518 ,,	29	32,000
1855	18	10,424,157 ,,	197	40,000
1856	24	24,394,395 ,,	134	100,000
1857	31	49,336,673 ,,	102	150,037
1858	37	41,846,778 ,,	15	156,000
1859	40	35,564,492·70	15	162,000
1860	41	36,753,408 ,,	3	172,022
1861	41	38,712,427 ,,	5	200,000

PROGRESS OF POPULATION.

By the Territorial census of 1849, the population of the territory of Minnesota, embracing what is now Dakota, was 4780. Of this number, the returns show 723 for settlements now outside of the State, leaving the population of the State, as now bounded, 4057. The United States census of Minnesota territory for 1850, showed a population of 6077. Subtracting therefrom the number given the previous year for Dakota, not otherwise ascertainable, the result for the State, as now bounded, would be 5354.

The following table, then, exhibits the growth of population in Minnesota for ten years, within the limits of the present State:—

Year.	Authority.	Number.
1849	Territorial census	4,057
1850	United States census	5,354
1857	Territorial census	150,037
1860	United States census	172,022
1865	Computed	350,000

The following table will show the movement of population in eight States of the north-west in the last decade, as compared with Minnesota:—

	Population. 1850.	Population. 1860.	Actual Increase.	Increase per Cent.
Minnesota	5,330	172,022	166,692	3,127
Iowa	192,214	674,948	482,734	251
Wisconsin	305,391	775,873	470,472	154
Illinois	851,470	1,711,753	860,283	101
Michigan	397,654	749,112	251,458	88
Indiana	988,416	1,350,479	362,063	36
Ohio	1,980,329	2,339,599	359,270	18
Kansas	...	107,110	107,110	
Total	4,720,804	7,880,896	3,180,082	

THE FUTURE OF MINNESOTA.

(Testimony of Hon. Wm. H. Seward.)

"I find myself now, for the first time, upon the highlands in the centre of the continent of North America, equi-distant from the waters of Hudson's Bay and the Gulf of Mexico—from the Atlantic Ocean to the ocean in which the sun sets. Here upon the spot where spring up almost side by side, so that they may kiss each other, the two great rivers, the one of which, pursuing its strange, capricious, majestic, vivacious career through lake, cascade, and river rapid, and lake after lake, and river after river, cataract and bay, and lake and rapids, finally, after a course of 2000 miles, brings your commerce half-way to Europe; the other, after passing through highlands and prairie, a distance of 2000 miles, taking tributary after tributary from the east to the west, bringing together waters from the western declivity of the Alleghanies, and from those which trickle down the eastern sides of the Rocky Mountains, finds its way into the Gulf of Mexico.

"Here is the place—the central place—where the agriculture of the richest region of North America must pour out its tributes to the whole world. On the east, all along the shore of Lake Superior, and west, stretching in one broad plain, in a belt quite across the continent, is a country where State after State is yet to arise, and where the productions for the support of human society in other old crowded States must be brought forth.

"This is, then, a commanding field; but it is as commanding in regard to the destinies of this country, and of this continent, as it is in regard to their commercial future; for power is not permanently to reside on the eastern slope of the Alleghany Mountains, nor in the seaports. Seaports have always been overrun and controlled by the people of the interior, and the power that shall communicate and express the will of men on this continent is to be located in the Mississippi Valley, and at the sources of the Mississippi and St. Lawrence.

"In our day, studying perhaps what might have seemed to others trifling or visionary, I had cast about for the future and ultimate central seat of the power of the North American people. I had looked at Quebec, New Orleans, at Washington and San Francisco, at Cincinnati and St. Louis, and it had been the result of my conjecture that the seat of power for North America would yet be found in the valley of Mexico, and the glories of the Aztec capital would be surrendered, in its becoming ultimately and at last the capital of the United States of America. But I have corrected that view; I now believe that the *ultimate last seat of government on this great continent will be found somewhere within a circle or radius not very far from the spot on which I stand at the head of navigation on the Mississippi River.*"

CONCLUSION.

Such are the facts in reference to Minnesota, the "North Star" of the Western States. We have in the dry details and facts presented to the reader, striven to give an idea of the future from a contemplation of a history of the past. Through that State must pass the railway on its way to the Pacific. We are only on the threshold of the splendour of American history; its future, judged by the past, is beyond all conjecture.

THE RAILWAY THROUGH MINNESOTA.

The United States and the State of Minnesota have granted

lands for the purpose of building the railways of that State; and without specially referring here to their amount, or entering into any detail as to the plan or arrangement necessary for their completion, we propose to consider the value of these lands by contrasting the grant of the Illinois Central Railroad.

ILLINOIS CENTRAL RAILROAD.

The grant of land to the Illinois Central Railroad Company embraces 4055 square miles, or
The grant thus bestowed was . . . . 2,595,000 acres.
Of which there have been appropriated to secure the payment of 17,000,000 dollars of Construction Bonds . 2,000,000 acres.
To secure the payment of interest on said Bonds . . . 250,000 acres.
To secure the payment of 3,000,000 dollars of Free-land Bonds . . . . . 345,000 acres.
                                                              ─────────
                                                              2,595,000 acres.

Hence, the Company's lands are respectively designated as CONSTRUCTION, FREE LANDS, and INTEREST LANDS.

The Indenture with the Trustees prescribes that there shall be set apart,—

50,000 at 20 dols. per acre, until there be realized 1,000,000 dols.
350,000 at 15   „   „   „   5,200,000 „
1,300,000 at 8   „   „   „   10,400,000 „
300,000 at 5   „   „   „   1,500,000 „

The Company have already sold about 1,200,000 acres of land, comprised in this grant, for the sum of 15,600,000 dollars; this is less than one-half of the grant, and the unsold portion will undoubtedly bring a sum equal to that of the portion sold.

During the last two years upwards of 6000 buyers have taken an average of less than 60 acres, and therefore owe less than 1000 dollars each. With one or two good harvests many of them will repay this small amount, which meantime is running at 6 per cent. interest. There are still 1,282,626 acres of land for sale. Of the Company's lands 1,312,373 acres have been sold; 6,749,814 dollars 88 cents have been collected from these sales in cash, leaving 9,914,008 dollars 56 cents balance due on contracts in hand, which relate to 928,429 acres; the payments in full have been made on 383,944 acres only. Thus the sales embrace—

Acres.		Dollars.
383,944. 59 . . Cash . .		6,749,814. 88
928,429. 17 . . Contracts .		9,914,008. 56
─────────		─────────
1,312,373. 76		16,663,823. 44

Now, the cost of the Illinois Central Railroad, including everything connected with the road, has been 28,610,229 dollars, and the sale of lands will amount to at least 35,000,000 dollars. Thus the lands pay in the end for the road. Suppose Minnesota grants lands as a basis for the structure of her railroads, and suppose European capitalists have the common sense to view correctly the lesson which the history of Illinois teaches, the prospect for bond-holders and property-holders, for merchants, financiers, speculators, and emigrants holding land in Minnesota, is without an equal.

There is no State like Minnesota; her climates, her forests, her rivers, her prairies, her position at the head of great watercourses is something marvellous. She points fearlessly to the map—she knows where she stands in the geographical centre. Through her paths, her forest openings, across her rivers, and onward moving, the line of emigration will pursue its course towards the Rocky Mountains.

FROM MINNESOTA TO BRITISH COLUMBIA.

The Secretary of the Treasury for the United States says, "The necessity of more than one highway between the Mississippi States and the Pacific coast will appear from an enumeration of the railroad lines which are indispensable to the commerce between the Atlantic and interior States. These are seven well-defined thoroughfares: (1) From Portland, by the Grand Trunk, to Detroit, and thence, with a traverse of the State and Lake of Michigan, to Milwaukee and La Crosse; (2) by the New York Central, the Great Western of Canada, and the Chicago and North-Western Railroad, to Prairie du Chien; (3) by the New York and Erie, the lines of Ohio and Indiana south of the great lakes, and the Illinois Central, to Galena; (4) the Pennsylvania Central and its western connexions, to Rock Island; (5) the Baltimore and Ohio, by way of Cincinnatti to St. Louis; (6) from Richmond, through the Cumberland Valley, to Memphis; and (7) from Charleston and Savannah, traversing the States of Georgia, Alabama, and Mississippi, to Vicksburg and New Orleans. All these highways are thronged and prosperous, and, with the wonderful impulse to colonization and commerce induced by mining investments, a period of 25 years will probably witness the completion of four great continental communications within the limits of the north temperate zone, and upon the following lines:—

"1. Through the southern tier of States, on or near the parallel of 35°, which is central to the region of cotton, the sugar-cane, and the vine, and which will be supported by the populations of Louisiana, Arkansas, Neosho (or the territory occupied by the Cherokee and Choctaw Indians), Texas, New Mexico, Arizona, Sonora, and Southern California. This may be called the Gulf route, from its relation to the Gulfs of Mexico and California.

"2. The Central, which is now in course of construction, on the average latitude of 40°. With its present prestige and aid from the Federal Government, soon to be increased by the intervention of State governments in its behalf, the speedy construction of this road may be anticipated. If in operation at the present moment, the road would be financially successful. All the resources of Kansas, Nebraska, Colorado, Utah, Nevada, and, in a great degree, of Missouri and California, are pledged to such a result.

"3. The Lake route, hitherto designated in Congressional debates as the Northern Pacific route, connecting the western coast of the great lakes, and the navigable channel of the Columbia River, by the most direct and feasible communication with which the territories and future States of Dakota, Montano, Idaho, and Washington, as well as the States of Minnesota and Oregon, are identified.

"4. The International route, or an extension of the Canadian railway system across the peninsula of Michigan, and through Wisconsin and Minnesota, to the English colony of Selkirk, in latitude 50°, and thence, through the valleys of the Saskatchewan and Upper Fraser Rivers, to the Pacific coast in latitude 54°.

"The prediction is hazarded that the year 1890 will witness the consummation of the 8000 miles of interior railroad above indicated. A more accurate statement would be, that whenever, along either of these routes, a population shall be assembled of 2,000,000 of souls, then will follow, by an irresistible social law, the construction and support of 2000 miles of railroad. The probability of that aggregate of population by the year 1870 has been considered on the central line. The situation of the more southern communication has been also referred to, and some space will now be given to the probabilities that, by the year 1890, the great lakes will be connected by railroad with the Columbia River and Puget's Sound, while 1880 is likely to witness the completion of the international railroad upon the average latitude of 52° north."

Now, the United States is lending all the aid she possibly can towards a direct route through her territories, but the natural obstacles to be surmounted are not to be forgotten. She has appropriated enormous amounts of money for exploration and surveys, and for their publication, and her people have pushed their way westward, and populated and developed regions that require hardship, self-denial, and great perseverance, to make habitable.

Look at the territories of Utah, Nevada, Colorado, Kansas, and Nebraska.

COLORADO.

Colorado territory, with a white population of 34,231 in 1860, and an estimated area of 100,000 square miles, or 66,880,000 acres, has nearly doubled in population during the first three years of the current decade. The population in January, 1864, may be fairly stated at 60,000. The production of gold in 1862 was 10,000,000 dollars, which will probably reach 15,000,000 dollars during 1864.

KANSAS AND NEBRASKA.

The census of 1860 returned the population of the interior districts, which are connected with the overland trade west of the Missouri River as follows:—

New Mexico	83,009
Colorado	34,277
Utah	40,273
	157,559

In 1860 a special correspondent of the *New York Herald* furnished the following statement:—

Table showing the Amount of Freight forwarded across the Plains from the various Ports on the Missouri River during the Year 1860, with the required Outfit.

Where from.	Pounds.	Men.	Horses.	Mules.	Oxen.	Waggons.
Kansas City	16,439,134	7,084	464	6,149	27,920	3,033
Leavenworth	5,656,082	1,216	. .	206	10,925	1,003
Atchison	6,097,943	1,591	. .	472	13,640	1,280
St. Joseph	1,672,000	490	. .	520	3,980	418
Nebraska City	5,496,000	896	. .	113	11,118	916
Omaha City	713,000	324	377	114	340	272
Grand total,	36,074,159	11,601	841	7,574	67,950	6,922

In 1863 a population of 60,000 in Nevada employs for the transportation of machinery, merchandise, provisions, &c., from the Pacific coast, a number of men, animals, and waggons fully half as great as the foregoing exhibit of overland transportation west of Kansas and Nebraska. That this table is inadequate to express the traffic of 1864, may also be inferred from the consideration of the present population of the mountain territories, viz.:—

New Mexico (no increase)	83,009
Colorado	60,000
Utah	80,000
Montana	12,000
	235,009

It is not an excessive estimate that the present transportation is 50,000,000 pounds, employing 10,000 trains, and at a cost of 5,000,000 dollars annually. In consequence of the war and other causes, a considerable diversion of the traffic across the plains has taken place in favour of the northern points of departure from the Missouri River; Kansas City by no means leading in the degree indicated in 1860. Whether the traffic will resume its former proportions, depends altogether upon the railway construction of the next twelve months.

NEVADA.

The population of Nevada territory by the census of 1860 was 6857. At the close of 1863 it had reached 60,000, of which nearly 20,000 was concentrated at Virginia City, the centre of the most productive silver district. Within four years 5,000,000 dollars have been expended in erecting quartz-mills and reduction works; another 5,000,000 dollars have been laid out in opening the mines, and three times as much in various kinds of improvement. In waggon roads alone, leading into and through the territory, 500,000 dollars have been spent—an investment that has paid from 40 to 80 per cent. per annum. The tolls collected on these roads during the year 1863 reached at least the sum of 200,000 dollars. The money paid on freights coming into the territory from the Pacific coast amounted to fully 3,000,000 dollars. About 3000 teams of various kinds are employed in this business, besides numerous pack trains.

UTAH.

The settlements of Great Salt Lake City, and elsewhere in Utah territory, have directed their industry exclusively to agriculture and domestic manufactures. Their ecclesiastical rulers, by giving such a direction to the labour of the people, have shown great sagacity, for not only is society organized on surer foundations than in mining districts, but the demand for all the products of Utah has been so constant and remunerative as to furnish an advantageous home market. Simultaneously with the first settlement at Salt Lake the overland emigration to California commenced, and has increased from year to year until in 1863 it meets a return column of adventurers who are pushing eastward and northward to the gold-fields of Colorado, Idaho, and Montana. The consumption by the crowds in transit, both east and west, sustains the prices of provisions and manufactures at rates which encourage population and accumulate wealth.

By the census of 1860 the population of Utah was 40,273, an increase of 253·89 per cent. since 1850. The total valuation o. property was 986,083 dollars in 1850, and 5,596,118 dollars in 1860, or an increase of 467·50 per cent. If these proportions continue during the present decade, the population of Utah will be 142,525, and the valuation of property 31,757,966 dollars in 1870.

SOUTH PACIFIC RAILWAY.

Estimated Cost.

SECTIONS.	Distance.	Preparation of Road-Bed	Superstructure.	Equipment.	Engineering & Contingencies.	Amount.
		Dollars.	Dollars.	Dollars.	Dollars.	Dollars.
Fort Smith to head of Pajarito Creek	706	5,294,472	11,192,690	2,747,500	1,923,466	21,158,128
Head of Pajarito Creek to Isleta	144	5,995,800	2,769,764	706,000	947,156	10,418,720
Isleta to Campbell's Pass	116·7	1,564,500	2,558,540	570,500	469,354	5,162,894
Campbell's Pass to mouth of Rio Puerco of the West	121	1,840,070	2,808,814	670,500	531,438	5,845,822
Valley of Flax River	35	371,000	774,856	142,400	128,826	1,417,082
Flax River to Leroux's Spring	81	4,401,400	1,713,662	434,300	654,936	7,204,298
Leroux's Spring to Aztec Pass	87	5,281,174	1,787,544	478,900	754,762	8,302,380
Aztec Pass to Cross Mountain	23·3	351,580	476,424	113,300	94,130	1,035,434
Cross Mountain to Big Sandy	27·5	1,207,000	563,556	169,100	193,966	2,133,622
Big Sandy to Rio Colorado	53·7	599,100	1,090,132	431,800	426,006	2,556,038
Rio Colorado to Soda Lake	96·8	1,380,800	2,006,062	731,700	823,712	4,941,274
Soda Lake to point of leaving Mojave River	70·5	822,400	1,448,345	380,900	265,165	2,916,810
Point of leaving Mojave River to Tah-ee-chay-pah Pass	63	856,200	1,263,621	513,000	263,282	2,896,103
Through Tah-ee-chay-pah Pass	38·5					8,465,000
Tah-ee-chay-pah Pass to San Francisco	268					14,400,000
From Fort Smith to San Francisco	1,952					93,853,605
Average						48,081

INTERNATIONAL PACIFIC RAILWAY.

In reference to a route beyond Pembina, we shall throw out no suggestions of our own, but simply give the testimony of Captains Palisser and Blakiston, who were specially delegated by the British Government to survey this whole region, with reference to its adaptability for a railway. Captain Palisser says :

" The connexion, therefore, of the Saskatchewan Plains, east of the Rocky Mountains, with a known route through British Columbia, has been effected by the expedition under my command, without our having been under the necessity of passing through any portion of United States territory. Still, the knowledge of the country on the whole would never lead me to advocate a line of communication from Canada across the continent to the Pacific, exclusively through British territory. The time has now for ever gone by for effecting such an object, and the unfortunate choice of an astronomical boundary-line has completely isolated the Central American possessions of Great Britain from Canada in the east, and also almost debarred them from any eligible access from the Pacific coast on the west.

" The settler, who will always adopt the shortest and least expensive route, will undoubtedly follow the line of traverse indicated by the formation of the country.

" He will travel by steamer along the Canadian lakes through Saut Ste. Marie to Superior City, situated at the extremity of the ' Fond du Lac,' or most western extremity of Lake Superior; and he will then be only 70 or 80 miles distant from Crow

Wing, on the high road between St. Paul's and the Red River Settlement.

"American squatters and lumberers are rapidly settling up Red River, and the railway communication (now nearly complete to St. Paul's) will soon be completed to Pembina, in which case the establishment of a branch line to Superior 'Fond du Lac' would be a positive certainty. Thus, easy and rapid communication would be established between Lake Superior and the frontier of Red River Settlement.

"In the event of railway communication being extended as far as Pembina, it would not be unreasonable then to entertain the prospect that the Imperial Government might feel justified in encouraging the extension of such railway on the British side of the line to the northward and westward, through the southern portion of the 'Fertile Belt' to the Rocky Mountains; at all events, as soon as the country showed symptoms of becoming sufficiently populated to warrant such an effort.

"As the case at present stands, all communication with the colony at Red River is through the States. Soon after the publication of my despatch, declaring the navigability of the Red River for steamers, American enterprise established one there; this, as I now understand, plies the whole way from Lake Winnipeg to Graham's Point, above the forks of the Shienne, and, now that the results of the expedition lately under my command. are known, even the Hudson's Bay Company have adopted the route *via* St. Paul's and Pembina, for bringing their merchandise into this country. As for the importation of horses, cows, and any other species of live stock, all such traffic would be impossible either *via* Hudson's Bay or by the canoe route.

"There is, however, another means of proceeding from the Columbia to the westward, in a more northern latitude, which I can advocate upon excellent authority,* although I cannot describe it from personal observation.

"The Columbia River, north of the boundary-line, is navigable by steamers the whole way up the Great Columbia Lakes, and above the most northern one to an extensive plain or table-land, along which my informant has taken heavily laden horses with ease round both the northern and the southern shores of the Great Okanagan Lake to the forks of the Fraser and Thompson Rivers.

"A steamer here would not only serve for effecting communication between the Saskatchewan Plains and the west coast of British Columbia, but would also form an additional link to that chain of American steamers already along the Columbia from Astoria on the Pacific coast.

---

* Namely, that of Mr. Angus McDonnell, one of the gentlemen in charge of Fort Hope, and subsequently of Fort Colville, where he had been long resident, and in the constant habit of travelling backwards and forwards through the country.

"From Astoria, ocean steamers can ascend the Columbia River up to the point where it cuts the Cascade range, a distance of 135 miles; here a boarded portage and tramway, about 2 miles long, enables the traveller to reach a second steamer which runs up to the Dalles, distant about 48 miles. At this place a steep waggon road, which is kept in good order, takes the traveller on to the Des Chutes, a distance of 12 miles, whence a third steamer runs up as far as old Walla Walla, and when occasion requires up to Priest's Rapids, distant from the Des Chutes 180 miles."

TESTIMONY OF CAPTAIN BLAKISTON, R.E.

"Being now at the western extremity of the Kootanie Pass, I will pause to point out the capabilities it affords for a railway across the mountains within the British possessions. I should premise that I have not sufficient evidence to be able to state that the Kootanie Pass is absolutely the most advantageous place for the crossing of a railroad from the Saskatchewan Plains to the Pacific, because the mountains to the north have not yet been sufficiently explored; but I am able to say that it is the most southern line within the British territory, and, as yet, by far the shortest; moreover, I have every reason to believe that the most suitable portion of the mountains for the passage of a railroad will be found to the south of Bow River.

"The Kootanie Pass crosses the Rocky Mountains from the Great Saskatchewan Plains on the east, to the Tobacco Plains on the west, its extremity on the former side being 40 and on the latter 18 English miles to the northward of the international boundary, the 49th parallel of north latitude. Its length is 40 geographical or nearly 47 English miles, extending from longitude $114° 34'$ to $115° 24'$ west. It leaves the Saskatchewan Plains where they have an altitude of about 4000 feet above the sea, rises 2000 feet to the watershed of the mountains, descends to Flathead River, again rises to an altitude of 4000, follows up this river to its head waters, then crosses a precipitous ridge, reaching an altitude of 6000 feet; it then descends the great western slope, falling 2000 feet in 2 miles of horizontal distance, after which, by a nearly uniform grade of 100 feet per geographical mile, it gains the Tobacco Plains at the point where the Wigwam branch enters Kootanie or Elk River.

"By reference to Section No. 1, it will be seen that there are three obstacles to the passage of a railroad—namely, two mountains and one steep slope. As to the mountains, they could, I consider, without difficulty be pierced by tunnels. The great western slope is a more serious obstacle; however, in the following details I hope to show that it also may be overcome.

"From the forks of Belly River, on the east side the line would traverse the gradually ascending prairie to the entrance of the pass where Railway River issues from the mountains. This river would be followed up with a grade of 1 in 180, or 34 feet per geographical mile for 7½ miles, the 'river levels' affording considerable advantages; leaving this river it would follow the course of my track marked on the map. A cutting of about 3½ miles would lead to a tunnel of nearly 5 miles in length, which would pierce the Watershed Mountain, and come out in the valley of Flathead River, the whole having a grade of 1 in 130, or 47 feet per geographical mile. On emerging into the valley, the line would skirt the base of the mountains to the north of the track, thereby avoiding a steep descent, then following up the river with a grade of 40 feet per geographical mile, it would reach the rise of the western ridge at a height of 5100 feet above the sea. This would be the culminating point of the line, from which in a distance of 10 geographical miles it has to fall 1900 feet to the North and South Bluff, and after that, by a slope of 54 feet per geographical mile for 5 miles, to reach the Tobacco Plains, crossing the Kootanie Fork by a bridge. This I propose to accomplish in the following manner:—From the culminating point, to pierce the ridge by a tunnel of 3 geographical miles, and continue the line along the side of the hills to the north of the track reaching the North Bluff, the whole with a grade of 190 feet per geographical mile. This portion of the line of 10 geographical miles would have to be worked by a wire rope, and one or more stationary engines. Regarding the remaining 5 miles to the west of the North and South Bluffs, a careful survey is required to determine whether a grade not too steep for locomotives can be made. My measurements, taken with so uncertain an instrument as an aneroid barometer, must not be depended on to a few feet; they give a fall of 54 feet per geographical mile, or 1 in 112.

"As regards the country to the west of the Kootanie Fork I can say nothing, but that no mountains were visible to the distance I could see, neither have I any personal knowledge of the Saskatchewan Plains to the eastward of the forks of Belly River; but it is probable that these great prairies stretch without break from this point to the Red River Settlement, and that in the construction of a railroad, little more labour would be required than that of laying down the rails. The following statement of distances to be traversed by a railroad to the Pacific within the British territories may be of interest:—

	Geo. Miles.
Lake Superior to Red River Settlement	320
Red River Settlement, *viâ* Elbow of South Branch of Saskatchewan to Rocky Mountains	700
Kootanie Pass	40
West End of Kootanie Pass to Mouth of Fraser's River, Gulf of Georgia	300
Total, Lake Superior to Pacific	1360

Probable length of railroad, 2300 miles English.

"Thus it will be seen that out of the whole distance **one-half is** over level prairies, and but 40 miles through mountains.

"There are now two steamers on the Red River of the North. With our present news there will be a necessity, in July, for a propeller through Lake Winnepeg, and a river steamer on the Saskatchewan. These furnished with a water communication from Georgetown, in Minnesota, would transport an emigrant to the new Eldorado in the Rocky Mountains, from which the Fraser flows to the Pacific, the Peace River to the Arctic Ocean, and the Saskatchewan to Hudson's Bay."

"The conception of an Inter-Oceanic Railway (writes an able correspondent of the *Times*), commencing at Halifax, and after passing in its entire length of 3200 miles, terminating at the new Liverpool, which, we may confidently hope, will, in a few years, rise up on the southern shore of Vancouver Island, is one the magnitude and importance of which cannot be over estimated. As compared with the route to British Columbia *viâ* Panama, the Inter-Oceanic line would effect a saving of 22 days, while the position of Vancouver Island, as contrasted with Panama, in relation to China and Australia, is also very significant.

	Miles.
Panama to Canton, about	10,000
Vancouver Island to Canton	9,000
Panama to Sydney	8,200
Vancouver Island to Sydney	7,200

"This proximity to Australia," continues the writer, "is especially worthy of note at a time when the transmission of the mails across the Pacific is again being prominently advocated. It will be apparent from the aforegiven distances, that by transmitting the Australian mails from England to the Pacific across British North America *viâ* Vancouver Island, instead of *viâ* Panama, a saving of five days is effected between England and the Pacific, and of 1000 miles, or say five days more, in the passage across that ocean—ten days saved in all.

"The advantages to Great Britain which would accrue consequent upon the entire service being performed through British territory are beyond all calculation. The construction of the railway would not merely open up to civilization a large territory in British North America hitherto almost unexplored, but it would open up to the cultivators of the soil in that territory and in Canada a means of transit to all the markets of the Pacific, and an open passage to the China seas and to our possessions in the East Indies. In every aspect, whether viewed politically, socially, or commercially, the establishment of the proposed railway would give a progressive impulse to the affairs of the world, which, in its results, would eclipse anything which has been witnessed even amid the extraordinary development of the present century. That the railway will infallibly be made is as certain as that now is the time to undertake it. One does not require to be a prophet to predict that when the resources of British Columbia are fully opened up, and a communication established between the Atlantic and the Pacific, there will be enough traffic for a dozen steamers as large as the *Great Eastern* on both oceans. The British empire has now the opportunity of securing that position which it has hitherto occupied without dispute as the greatest commercial nation in the world."

Speaking on this subject, T. D. M'Gee (quoted in the *Canadian News*, of the 31st of October, 1861) remarks: "But there is a more important consideration connected with the territory of the Hudson Bay Company, for we know that through its prairies is to be found the shortest and best *railroad* route to the Pacific. Every one can understand that the American route from Western Europe to Asia, which lies farthest to the north, must be the most direct. Any one glancing at a globe will see where the 46th degree parallel leads the eye from the heart of Germany, through the British Channel, across to the Gulf of St. Lawrence, and from our gulf westward to the Saskatchewan, to Vancouver's Island—the Cuba of the North Pacific—and from Vancouver to the rich and populous archipelago of Japan. This course was demonstrated by Captain Synge to be 2000 miles shorter between London and Hong Kong than any other in existence; it has but one formidable engineering difficulty to be overcome—an elevation of 6000 feet above the sea-level in crossing the Rocky Mountains into Columbia. Such at least is the carefully-guarded statement of Mr. Stevens, the late American Governor of Washington territory, and such is said to be the result arrived at by Captain Palisser's more recent explorations. By a short tunnel at the favourable pass, the elevation may be reduced to 5000 feet, ' whose gradients,' it has been calculated, ' need not exceed 60 feet per mile, from the head of Lake Superior to Puget Sound.' An elevation of 5000 feet is not an insuperable obstacle, as has been shown at Mount Cenis and the Alleghanies. (On the Philadelphia and Pittsburg Road at Altona the gradient of 96 feet to the mile has been found practicable.) The name—' Rocky Mountains '—is more formidable to the ear than to the engineer; as the latitude has misled us with regard to climate, so the latitude has been overrated with regard to cost; but the science of this age once entering upon any experiment, it will neither be deterred by regions represented as uninhabitable, nor by mountains reputed to be impassable."

overwhelming majority (70,000) proceed to the United States. This result is not, of course, equal to that of the years 1853-56, when an average of 200,000 Germans emigrated from their native country. But those were extraordinary and exceptional times. It is, however, the published opinion of the two great authorities on German emigration—we refer, of course, to Consul-General Sturz and Dr. Carl von Scherzer—that the stream* of emigration will in future direct itself more exclusively, and in larger numbers than ever before, to the United States of America. It is also worth mentioning that the Brazilian Government has never been able to tempt the German emigrant again to its shores, although it has lavished vast sums for that purpose.

LAWS OF MIGRATION.

Australia and New Zealand have only recently succeeded, by the fictitious lure of gold, in diverting a small part of the European emigration, and there is no proof that these colonies will form any exception to the destiny of fruitless decay which has marked all attempts to naturalize the northern races in southern or tropical climates. It is only in North America that the principle of social life and growth has survived the transplantation of the Germanic and Celtic populations of Northern Europe, and not only has the singular social energy been able to perpetuate itself here alone, but here alone has it found the physical conditions which call forth the full measure of its powers.

North America contains to-day over 30,000,000 of Europeans and their descendants. Outside of North America and their native seats in the north temperate zone, there are not five millions of the offspring of Europe in all the rest of the world, though it was in the South that the first and grandest historic attempts at conquest and colonization have been made. Moreover, of the vestiges of European migrations which still exist in more southern zones, for the most part sunk with all their nobler characteristics in a degrading amalgamation with the native tribes, the larger proportion was planted by the southern nations of Europe—the Spanish, Portugese, and Italians. On the other hand, North America has been peopled almost entirely from Northern Europe, from the British Islands, Germany, the Netherlands and France, and latterly from Norway and Sweden. Of the thirty million white inhabitants of North America, over nine-tenths came from these countries occupying the district or belt of Northern Europe between the parallels of 48 and 58 degrees, and of these same thirty millions of North Americans, twenty-two millions, or 73 per cent., dwell in the northern districts or belts between the parallels of 38 and 46 degrees. In 1850 there were 1,942,000 persons of European birth resident in the United States. Of these 93 per cent, were from the *northern districts of*

Europe above mentioned, and of the whole foreign population of the United States, less than 7 per cent. were in the Southern States—that is to say, over 93 per cent. were in the Northern States—and including the foreign population of Canada, over 96 per cent. of the whole European emigration to North America have sought homes between the parallels of 38 and 46 degrees. It is evident then that the sources and general flow of emigration is within this northern belt of climate, having a breadth of about 10 degrees in Europe and of about 8 degrees in America. This isothermal belt which we have arbitrarily defined by lines of latitude, is nearly conterminous in Western Europe and Eastern America with Maury's upper thermal band between the lines of mean annual temperature of 32 and 52 degrees. In Western America the belt rises northward to enclose the valley of the Saskatchewan and British Columbia. In Eastern Europe it sinks southward to Southern Russia and the Caspian basin, enclosing in Western Asia the primitive seats of the Caucasian race, and all the ancient pathways of its victorious career. An interior and fundamental operation of the same law which concentrates within this belt the cities, the commerce, the railways, the prosperous and liberal civilization of the world, also collocates within it the governing, civilizing, organizing and progressive races of the world.

INDUCEMENTS TO SETTLE IN AMERICA.

To a young farmer just starting in life, and with a capital of 1000 dollars, there is no better field for him to enter upon. At home he has to encounter active competition, and work for unremunerative wages. If he cultivate the paternal acres, after years of toil, and after having reared and educated a family of children, he finds himself, at the close of life, about where he started. Very many of the farms in New England do not yield 5 per cent. on the capital invested. They are so small as to make it undesirable to sub-divide them among the children of the owner; and hence the farmer, in his declining years, so apportions his estate that one retains the homestead, while the others go out into the world to seek their fortunes. Let such an one, with his good common-school education and his habits of thrift, go to the broad prairies and select a quarter-section, or 160 acres, at say 10 dollars per acre, on the terms of seven years' payment. For four years he pays interest in advance, the first instalment being 96 dollars. He buys a yoke of oxen and a plough, which shall cost him 100 dollars. He erects a house to shelter him from the storm for 350 dollars, and encloses 40 acres with a two-board fence, to turn cattle, which shall cost him 150 dollars. If he join with a neighbour, he pays one-half. In May he turns over the sod of one-half of the tract enclosed, and puts in a crop of corn which shall yield him 15 bushels to the acre; but if he can rent some old land from a neighbour, it is better. In June, he breaks the other half, and early in September he harrows in his wheat. With his remaining means, let him buy a few pigs and calves, or yearlings. The former he should pen up, but the latter may roam over the prairie. A few tons of hay mown from some neighbouring meadow, together with his sod-corn, will carry his stock through the winter.

The second year, his 20 acres of corn-land will be mellow and ready to be re-planted. He encloses another 40 acres, at a cost of 112 dollars 50 cents, or if he remove the division fence, his expenses for additional materials will be 75 dollars. He breaks an additional 40, going through the same routine. In July his wheat is harvested, which will yield him 400 bushels, worth from 300 dollars to 400 dollars, and in October he finds himself in possession of 800 or 1000 bushels of corn, half a dozen fatted hogs, and others coming on to supply their places; his calves will have increased 50 per cent. in value, his steers will be ready to break, and one-half of his farm, or 80 acres, will be in a high state of cultivation, and his first broken land in a condition to put out in orchards, and everything will have assumed an air of comfort. The worst is now over. One-half of his farm is subdued, and will from henceforth prove remunerative. The third year he fences the whole 160 acres, by purchasing 75 dollars' worth of new materials, and removing the divisional fences. If he wishes to make a fence to turn hogs, he must add about 33 per cent. to the first cost. Again he breaks, and again goes through the same processes before described. He reaps his wheat, and gathers his corn. His calves have grown to cattle, his trees have taken root, his farm is now subdued and fenced, and he looks over his broad acres with a feeling of satisfaction, "I HAVE MADE MYSELF A HOME." The fourth year he commences his payment of principal, and in the soil he finds himself possessed of ample resources to meet it.

Such is an outline of what a man of energy and a little capital can accomplish on these lands. The proprietor in his own right of a farm of 160 acres, properly fenced and cultivated, with a neat house, surrounded with gardens and orchards, and flocks and herds, he need not repine at his lot.

STOCK-BREEDING AND RAISING IN ILLINOIS.

The prairies are well fitted for stock-raising in two essential particulars—the cheapness with which Indian corn can be grown, and the almost unlimited amount of natural pasturage. Jacob Strahn, who came to this country 25 years ago a poor man, when in the full tide of enterprise has been known to turn off 10,000 head of cattle a year. There are other graziers who range from 1000 up to 5000. One individual sends cattle to the eastern market to the value of 500,000 dollars per annum. Many of the Kentucky and Ohio farmers are securing stock-farms on the lands. One gentleman from the latter State has a tract of 22,000 acres, which he is rapidly converting into a stock-farm, and another still larger, which he proposes to treat in the same way.

In the vicinity of Bloomington there are two stock-growers, brothers, who came to this State more than 30 years ago. They had nothing to rely upon but their strong hands and their far-seeing sagacity. One of them now owns 7000 acres of land, 2700 of which is in a high state of cultivation; and the yearly products of his farm, in cattle and hogs, often reached 50,000 dollars.

The other brother has 27,000 acres of land, 4000 of which are in cultivation; and his annual sales of pork and beef reach 65,000 dollars.

These are examples of what industry and sagacity can accomplish upon these lands.

Referring again to the State of Minnesota, where will centre all the lines of railway, and from whence they will converge to the various sections now so rapidly developing, and also the importance of a wise and liberal legislation on the part of the British Home Government, we append certain letters and papers:—

Letter from the GOVERNOR OF MINNESOTA *to* THOMAS RAWLINGS, *Esq., Gresham House, Old Broad Street, London.*

"*State of Minnesota, Executive Department,*
"*St. Paul, Nov. 28, 1862.*

"* * * I regard the road in question as a central outlet to these extensive and fertile districts of Northern Minnesota, and the lands in its vicinity must materially appreciate as its construction extends. I enclose you documents indicating my estimation of the future progress of the region with which the St. Paul and Pacific Railroad is closely connected. I also forward a memorial of the last Minnesota Legislature bearing on the same subject, of which I have recorded my official approval."

Extract of a Memorial presented to the Congress of the United States.

"It is now well known that north of latitude forty-nine degrees (49°), and west of longitude ninety-four degrees (94°), there extends to the Rocky Mountains a district which may be properly styled Central British America.

"This region, at least to latitude fifty-four (54°)—five degrees of latitude in width and eleven degrees of longitude in length—is connected with Minnesota by internal river and lake navigation, and is capable of sustaining as dense a population as the States of Michigan, Wisconsin, and Minnesota.

"The climate and soil invite a similar agriculture. Selkirk Settlement, with a population of ten thousand souls, immediately joins Minnesota, and is a key to the future occupation and development of the fertile valleys and navigable rivers which converge to Lake Winnipeg. One of these streams, the Red River of the North, is navigable for four hundred miles by its course within the United States, forming the north-west boundary of Minnesota.

"It was a favourite policy of the Derby Ministry, and especially of Sir Edward Bulwer Lytton, Colonial Secretary, to organize a Crown Colony of Central British America, with the seat of Government at Selkirk.

"A draft of a bill for that purpose has not been pressed during the Palmerston Administration, greatly to the dissatisfaction of the people most interested.

"Meanwhile the revenue and postal system of the United States has been extended to Pembina, and beyond; and, with the aid of steamboat navigation (transferred to the Red River from the adjacent sources of the Mississippi, by the enterprise of the citizens of Minnesota), has rapidly removed former prejudices to commercial, and even political association with the United States. It is not too much to say, that if England shall not immediately take measures in behalf of the Red River and Saskatchewan districts, by a political organization, and effective measures of colonization, that the Americanization of a grain region as large as six States of the size of Ohio cannot long be postponed. Hitherto the people of Minnesota have desired no other relations with their northern neighbours than the concord of international treaties; they still seek no other, satisfied with the political frontier entrusted to their keeping, although claiming to be central to a vast division of physical geography."

From Hon. HENRY M. RICE, *U. S. Senator, to* E. B. LITCHFIELD *Esq., New York.*

"*Senate Chamber, Washington, D.C.,*
"DEAR SIR, "*Nov.* 27, 1862.

"The lands belonging to the St. Paul and Pacific Railroad, on the main line from Stillwater to Breckinridge, are among the most valuable in the State; and, since the grant was made by Congress, and the route surveyed and selected, the country through which the line passes has been densely settled by industrious farmers. Many communities, villages, and towns have sprung up. * * * * The railroad lands will average (so soon as the road is built) at public sale 20 dollars, equal to £4 sterling, per acre. * * * * It is seldom that a line of only ten miles in length pays, but such is the case with the road between St. Paul and St. Anthony; the business upon it will astonish all who are not personally acquainted with the resources of the valleys of the Upper Mississippi, Lank, and Red Rivers.

"Owing to the troubles in the Border States, North and South, thousands will leave in the spring for Minnesota. I am just in receipt of a letter from the Hon. B. B. Meeker, then in Kentucky, saying that a large number of his acquaintances in that State, among the wealthiest inhabitants, would do so. "Very truly yours,
"HENRY M. RICE."

From J. W. TAYLOR, *Esq., to* THOMAS RAWLINGS, *Esq.*

"*St. Paul, Nov.* 21, 1862.
" * * * * I consider that railroad enterprise as having the same prospects before it which the first railroad north-west of Chicago had in 1852.

" What ten years have accomplished for the Chicago and Galena Railroad, both in business and the value of lands near the road, I anticipate for the railroad north-west of St. Paul in 1872. * * * * The northwest, beyond St. Paul, and extending through British America to the Rocky Mountains, is destined to a development, which is my warrant for the foregoing opinion. * * * *

" Lord Dunmore, who spent the summer of 1862 in British territory, north-west of Minnesota, lately passed through St. Paul on his way to London. Here he fully confirmed the intelligence of gold discoveries on the Saskatchewan River, east of the Rocky Mountains. In his own language, ' A rush may be expected from England and Canada next summer (1863).'

" An overland emigration in that direction has already commenced, and will pass from St. Paul to Red River, over the route of the St. Paul and Pacific Railroad."

From the COMMISSIONER OF THE STATE OF MINNESOTA LAND OFFICE *to* EDMUND RICE, *Esq., President of the St. Paul and Pacific Railroad Office.*

" *St. Paul, Jan.* 24, 1863.

" I have the honour to inform you, under the Act of the Legislature of March 10, 1862, that not less than 100,000 acres of school lands shall be appraised and offered for sale at public auction, on or before the 1st day of November, 1862; eighty-seven thousand eight hundred and thirty-two and 93/100 (87,832$\frac{93}{100}$) acres were offered for sale, of which thirty-eight thousand one hundred and forty-seven and 13/100 (38,147$\frac{13}{100}$) acres sold for two hundred and forty-two thousand five hundred and thirty-one and 60/100 dollars (242,531$\frac{60}{100}$ dollars); the average price per acre being over six and 35/100 dollars (6$\frac{35}{100}$ dollars). The average distance of the lands from any public conveyance to market is not less than twenty-five miles.

" I would also state that the demand for these lands is such that the State will have another general sale as early as May in the present year."

From the Hon. EDMUND RICE, *President of the St. Paul and Pacific Railroad, to* THOMAS RAWLINGS, *Esq., of London.*

" *St. Paul, Jan.* 30, 1863.

" I have the honour to send you herewith a map of the State of Minnesota, with the lands certified to this Company indicated thereon. These are the 307,200 acres mortgaged to trustees to secure the payment of 1,200,000 dollars, of 7 per cent. bonds, dated June 2, 1862.

" You will observe their proximity to the railroad and to the Mississippi River, none of them being more than fifteen miles therefrom.

" Their identity is certified under the seal of the Department of the Interior.

" I enclose also an official description of the lands embraced in each township, as returned by the Surveyor-General's Office by the Government Surveyors, who are sworn officers. I also enclose an official statement of the Commissioner of the State Land Office, showing the amount realized for school lands sold by him at public auction in October last.

" These lands were granted by the United States for the purpose of maintaining schools, and consist of the 16th and 36th sections in each township.

"Of course, they can be no better than the railroad lands, and in one respect they are not so valuable, because they extend to all parts of the State, whereas the railroad lands are all within fifteen miles of the line. * * * *

"You must be aware that there is a thriving population all along the valley of the Mississippi, from St. Paul's to Crow Wing, and that thereby the Company's lands are rendered altogether more valuable and more desirable to emigrants and others than they otherwise would be."

In confirmation of the value of the lands as in comparison with the school lands, we have received the following from the Senators of Minnesota:—

"*Senate Chamber, Washington, D.C.,*
"*Feb.* 19, 1863.

"From personal knowledge, we are satisfied that the lands belonging to the St. Paul and Pacific Railroad are as valuable and as well located as the school lands, and some of them more valuable, in consequence of their proximity to the road and the numerous dépôts or stations upon the line. "M. S. WILKINSON, U.S. Senator.
"HENRY M. RICE, U.S. Senator."

Thus, in conclusion, quoting the words of an eminent writer, from whose volume on Minnesota we have gathered much useful information—"Through Minnesota, the sole pathway of westward emigration, must flow the great exodus now dashing itself in vain against the shores of Europe through the passes of the Caucasus. Every advancing wave of population lifts higher and higher this gathering flood of American life, which, the moment that it begins to press upon the means of subsistence, must pour all its vast tide through this narrow channel into the inland basins of the northwest—till the Atlantic and Pacific are united in a living chain of populous States. Behold, then, the geographical circle of American development completed! Henceforth, the energies thinly dispersed in the vast movement of territorial expansion are concentrated in the upward career of civilization and social growth. This is but the outline, faintly limned upon the canvas, of the empire into which is to be wrought the glory and the grace of all historic civilizations. Progress is no longer a superficial diffusion, but an inward growth, of which not width but depth is the measure. The movement of life is turned from the circumference to the centre. The reciprocal dualism of the east and west, of the north and south —their action and re-action—becomes a continental economy. The social life of the New World ceases to be a fragment—a broken echo of Old-World traditions—and becomes a complete and rounded continental organism, at once independent and supreme, of which Minnesota is the vital centre—the heart from which all its arteries pulsate to the majestic systole and diastole of the commerce of the world."

APPENDIX "A."

THE BRITISH AMERICAN FEDERATION.

THE following Resolutions were adopted at a Conference of Delegates from the Provinces of Canada, Nova Scotia, and New Brunswick, and the Colonies of Newfoundland and Prince Edward Island, held in the City of Quebec on the 10th of October, 1864, as the basis of a proposed Confederation of those Provinces and Colonies:—

"That the best interests and present and future prosperity of British North America will be promoted by a Federal Union under the Crown of Great Britain, provided such Union be effected on principles just to the several provinces.

"That in the Federation of the British North American provinces the system of government best adapted under existing circumstances to protect the diversified interests of the several provinces, and secure efficiency, harmony, and permanency in the working of the Union, would be a general government charged with matters of common interest to the whole country, and local governments for each of the Canadas and for the provinces of Nova Scotia, New Brunswick, and Prince Edward Island, charged with the control of local matters in their respective sections—provision being made for the admission into the Union, on equitable terms, of Newfoundland, the North-West Territory, British Columbia, and Vancouver.

"That in framing a constitution for the general government, the Conference, with a view to the perpetuation of our connexion with the mother country, and to the promotion of the best interests of the people of these provinces, desire to follow the model of the British constitution so far as our circumstances will permit.

"That the executive authority or government shall be vested in the Sovereign of the Kingdom of Great Britain and Ireland, and be administered according to the well-understood principles of the British constitution by the Sovereign personally or by representative duly authorized.

"That the Sovereign or representative of the Sovereign shall be Commander-in-chief of the land and naval militia forces.

"That there shall be a General Legislature for the Federated Provinces, composed of a Legislative Council and House of Commons.

"That for the purpose of forming the Legislative Council the Federated Provinces shall be considered as consisting of three divisions—1st, Upper Canada; 2d, Lower Canada; 3d, Nova Scotia, New Brunswick, and Prince Edward Island, with equal representation in the Legislative Council.

"That Upper Canada be represented in the Legislative Council by 24 members, Lower Canada by 24 members, and the three Maritime Provinces by 24 members, of which Nova Scotia shall have 10, New Brunswick 10, and Prince Edward Island 4 members.

"That the colony of Newfoundland shall be entitled to enter the proposed Union, with a representation in the Legislative Council of four members.

"The North-West Territory, British Columbia, and Vancouver shall be admitted into the Union on such terms and conditions as Parliament shall deem equitable, and as shall receive the assent of Her Majesty; and in the case of the province of British Columbia or Vancouver, as shall be agreed to by the Legislature of such province.

"That the members of the Legislative Council shall be appointed by the Crown under the Great Seal of the General Government, and shall hold office during life; provided that absence from the Legislature for two consecutive Sessions shall render such seat absolutely vacant.

"That the members of the Legislative Council shall be British subjects by birth or naturalization, of the full age of 30 years, shall possess a continuous real property qualification of 4000 dollars over and above all incumbrances, and shall be and continue worth that sum over and above their debts and liabilities, except in the case of Newfoundland, where the property may be either real or personal.

"That if any question shall arise as to the qualification of a Legislative Councillor, the same shall be determined by the Council.

"That the first selection of the members of the Legislative Council shall be made from the Legislative Councils of the various provinces, with the exception of Prince Edward Island, so far as a sufficient number be found qualified and willing to serve; such members shall be appointed by the Crown at the recommendation of the General Executive Government, upon the nomination of the respective local Governments, and that in such nomination due regard be had to the claims of the members of the Legislative Council of the Opposition in each province, so that all political parties may as nearly as possible be fairly represented.

"That the Speaker of the Legislative Council (until it is otherwise provided by the Legislature) shall be appointed by the Crown from among the members of the Legislative Council, and hold office during pleasure, and he shall only be entitled to a casting vote on an equality of votes.

"The 24 Legislative Councillors representing Lower Canada in the Legislative Council of the Federal Legislature shall be appointed to represent each one of the 24 electoral divisions mentioned in Schedule A of Chap. I. of the Consolidated Statutes of Canada, and such councillor shall reside or possess his qualification therein.

"That the basis of representation in the House of Commons shall be population, as determined by the official census every ten years; and that the number of members at first shall be 194, distributed as follows:—

Upper Canada	..	82	New Brunswick ..	15
Lower Canada	..	65	Newfoundland ..	8
Nova Scotia	..	19	Prince Edward Island	5

"That each section shall distribute its representatives in such electoral divisions as it deems best.

"That until the official census of 1871 has been made up there shall be no change in the number of representatives from the several sections.

"That immediately after the completion of the census of 1871, and immediately after every decennial census thereafter, the representation from each section shall be readjusted on the basis of population.

"That for the purpose of such readjustments Lower Canada shall always be assigned 65 members, and each of the other sections shall, at each such readjustment, receive for the ten years then next succeeding the number of members to which it will be entitled on the same ratio of representation to population as Lower Canada will enjoy according to the census then just taken by having 65 members.

"That no reduction shall be made in the number of members returned by any section unless its population shall have decreased relatively to the whole population of the whole Union to the extent of 5 per centum, or over.

"That in computing at each decennial period the number of members to which each section is entitled, no fractional parts shall be considered, unless when exceeding one-half the number entitling to a member, in which case a member shall be given for each such fractional part.

" That the number of members may at any time be increased by the Federal Parliament, regard being had to the proportionate rights then existing.

" That the Legislature of each province, in the Act consenting to the Union, shall divide such province into the proper number of constituencies, and define the boundaries of each of them.

" The local Legislature of each province may afterwards, from time to time, alter the electoral districts of the province for the purposes of representation in the House of Commons, and distribute the number of representatives to which the province is entitled in any manner such Legislature may think fit.

" That until provisions shall otherwise be made by the Federal Parliament, all the laws which at the date of the proclamation constituting the Union may be in force in the provinces respectively relating to the qualification and disqualification of any person to be elected, or to sit or vote as a member of the Assembly in the said provinces respectively, and relating to the qualification or disqualification of voters, and to the oaths to be taken by voters, and to returning officers and their powers and duties, and relating to the proceedings at elections, and to the period during which such elections may be continued, and relating to the trial of controverted elections, and the proceedings incident thereto, and to the vacating of seats of members, and to the issuing and execution of new writs in case of any seat being vacated otherwise than by a dissolution,—shall respectively apply to elections of members to serve in the House of Commons for places situate in those provinces respectively.

" Every House of Commons shall continue for five years from the day of the return of the writs choosing the same, and no longer, subject, nevertheless, to be sooner prorogued or dissolved by the Governor.

" There shall be a Session of the Federal Parliament once at least in every year, so that a period of 12 calendar months shall not intervene between the last sitting of the Federal Parliament in one Session and the first sitting of the Federal Parliament in the next Session.

" The Federal Government shall have power to make laws for the peace, welfare, and good government of the Federated Provinces (saving the sovereignty of England), and especially laws respecting the following subjects:—

" 1. The public debt and property.

" 2. The regulation of trade and commerce.

" 3. The imposition or regulation of duties of Customs on imports and exports, except on exports of timber, logs, masts, spars, deals, and sawn lumber, and of coal and other minerals.

" 4. The imposition or regulation of Excise duties.

" 5. The raising of money by all or any other modes or systems of taxation.

" 6. The borrowing of money on the public credit.

" 7. Postal service.

" 8. Lines of steam or other ships, railways, canals, and other works, connecting any two or more of the provinces together, or extending beyond the limits of any province.

" 9. Lines of steamships between the Federated Provinces and other countries.

" 10. Telegraphic communication and the incorporation of telegraph companies.

" 11. All such works as shall, although lying wholly within any province, be specially declared by the Acts authorizing them to be for the general advantage.

" 12. The Census.

" 13. Militia, military and naval service, and defence.

" 14. Beacons, buoys, and lighthouses.

" 15. Navigation and shipping.

" 16. Quarantine.

" 17. Sea fisheries.

"18. Ferries between any province and a foreign country, or between any two provinces.
"19. Currency and coinage.
"20. Banking and the issue of paper money.
"21. Savings-banks.
"22. Weights and measures.
"23. Bills of exchange and promissory notes.
"24. Interest.
"25. Legal tender.
"26. Bankruptcy and insolvency.
"27. Patents of invention and discovery.
"28. Copyrights.
"29. Indians and lands reserved for the Indians.
"30. Naturalization and aliens.
"31. Marriage and divorce.
"32. The criminal law (except the constitution of courts of criminal jurisdiction), but including the procedure on criminal matters.
"33. For rendering uniform all or any of the laws relative to property and civil rights in Upper Canada, Nova Scotia, New Brunswick, Prince Edward Island, and Newfoundland, and for rendering uniform the procedure of all or any of the courts in these provinces; but any statute for this purpose shall have no force or authority in any province until sanctioned by the Legislature thereof.
"34. The establishment of a general Court of Appeal for the Federated Provinces.
"35. Immigration.
"36. Agriculture.
"37. And generally respecting all matters of a general character not specially and exclusively reserved for the local Governments and Legislatures.

"The General Government and Legislature shall have all powers necessary or proper for performing the obligations of the province as part of the British empire to foreign countries, arising under treaties between Great Britain and such countries.

"All courts, judges, and officers of the several provinces shall aid, assist, and obey the General Government in the exercise of its rights and powers, and for such purposes shall be held to be courts, judges, and officers of the General Government.

"The Federal Parliament may also from time to time establish additional courts, and the Government may thereupon appoint other judges and officers, when the same shall appear necessary or for the public advantage, in order to the due execution of the laws of Parliament.

"The General Government shall appoint and pay the Judges of the Superior Courts in each province, and of the County Courts of Upper Canada, and Parliament shall fix their salaries.

"Until the consolidation of the laws of Upper Canada, New Brunswick, Nova Scotia, Newfoundland, and Prince Edward Island, the Judges of these provinces appointed by the General Government shall be selected from their respective Bars.

"That the Judges of the Court of Admiralty now receiving salaries shall be paid by the General Government.

"That the Judges of the Superior Courts shall hold their offices during good behaviour, and shall be removable only on the address of both Houses of Parliament.

"That for each of the provinces there shall be an executive officer, styled the Lieutenant-Governor, who shall be appointed by the Governor-General in council, under the Great Seal of the Federated Provinces, during pleasure, such pleasure not to be exercised before the expiration of the first five years, except for cause; such cause to be communicated in writing to the Lieutenant-Governor immediately after the exercise of the pleasure as aforesaid, and also by message to both Houses of Parliament within the first week of the first Session afterwards.

"That the Lieutenant-Governor of each province shall be paid by the General Legislature.

"That in undertaking to pay the salaries of the Lieutenant-Governors, the Conference does not desire to prejudice the claim of Prince Edward Island upon the Imperial Government for the amount now paid for the salary of the Lieutenant-Governor thereof.

"The local Government and Legislature of each province shall be constructed in such manner as the existing Legislature of such province shall provide in the Act consenting to the Union.

"After the Union the local Legislatures shall have power to alter or amend their constitution from time to time.

"The local Legislatures shall have power to make laws respecting the following subjects:—

"Direct taxation and the imposition of duties on the export of timber, logs, masts, spars, deals, and sawn lumber, and of coals and other minerals.

"Borrowing money on the credit of the province.

"The establishment and tenure of local offices, and the appointment and payment of local officers.

"Agriculture.

"Immigration.

"Education; saving the rights and privileges which the Protestant or Catholic minority in both Canadas may possess as to their denominational schools at the time when the Union goes into operation.

"The sale and management of public lands, excepting lands belonging to the General Government.

"Sea-coast and inland fisheries.

"The establishment, maintenance, and management of penitentiaries, and of public and reformatory prisons.

"The establishment, maintenance, and management of hospitals, asylums, charities, and eleemosynary institutions.

"Municipal institutions.

"Shop, saloon, tavern, auctioneer, and other licences.

"Local works.

"The incorporation of private or local companies, except such as relate to matters assigned to the Federal Legislature.

"Property and civil rights, excepting those portions thereof assigned to the General Legislature.

"Inflicting punishment by fine, penalties, imprisonment, or otherwise for the breach of laws passed in relation to any subject within their jurisdiction.

"The administration of justice, including the constitution, maintenance, and organization of the courts, both of civil and criminal jurisdiction, and including also the procedure in civil matters.

"And generally all matters of a private or local nature.

"The power, of respiting, reprieving, commuting, and pardoning prisoners convicted of crimes, and of remitting of sentences in whole or in part, which belongs of right to the Crown, shall be administered by the Lieutenant-Governor of each province in Council, subject to any instructions he may from time to time receive from the General Government, and subject to any provisions that may be made in this behalf by Parliament.

"That in regard to all subjects over which jurisdiction belongs to both the General and local Governments, the laws of the Federal Parliament shall control and supersede those made by the local Legislature, and the latter shall be void so far as they are repugnant to or inconsistent with the former.

"That both the English and French languages may be employed in the General Legislature and in its proceedings, and also in the local Legislature of Lower Canada, and in the Federal and local courts of Lower Canada.

"That no lands or property belonging to the General or local Government shall be liable to taxation.

"All bills for appropriating any part of the public revenue, or for imposing any new tax or impost, shall originate in the House of Commons or the local Assembly, as the case may be.

"The House of Commons or Legislative Assembly shall not originate or pass any vote, resolution, address, or bill for the appropriation of any part of the public revenue, or of any tax or impost to any purpose, not first recommended to the House or Assembly by message of the Governor-General or the Lieutenant-Governor, as the case may be, during the session in which such vote, resolution, address, or bill is passed.

"Any bill of the General Legislature may be reserved in the usual manner for Her Majesty's assent, and any bill of the local Legislatures may, in like manner, be reserved for the consideration of the Governor-General.

"Any bill passed by the General Legislature shall be subject to disallowance by Her Majesty within two years, as in the case of bills passed by the said provinces hitherto, and in like manner any bill passed by a local Legislature shall be subject to disallowance by the Governor-General within one year after the passing thereof.

"That, subject to any future action of the respective local Governments in respect thereof, the seat of the local Government in Upper Canada shall be Toronto; of Lower Canada, Quebec; and the seats of the local Governments in the other provinces shall be as at present.

"That the seat of Government of the Federated Provinces shall be Ottawa, subject to the Royal Prerogative.

"That the Confederation shall be vested at the time of the union with all cash, bankers' balances, and other cash securities of each province.

"That the Confederation shall be vested with the public works and property of each province—to wit:—Canals; public harbours; lighthouses and piers; steamboats, dredges, and public vessels; river and lake improvements; railroads, mortgages, and other debts due by railroad companies; military roads; public buildings, custom-houses, and post-offices, except such as may be set aside by the General Government for the use of the local Legislatures and Governments; property transferred by the Imperial Government and known as ordnance property; armories, drill-sheds, military clothing, and munitions of war; lands set apart for public purposes.

"All lands, mines, minerals, and Royalties vested in Her Majesty in the provinces of Upper Canada, Lower Canada, Nova Scotia, New Brunswick, and Prince Edward Island, for the use of such provinces, shall belong to the local Government of the territory in which the same are so situate, subject to any trusts that may exist in respect to any of such lands or to any interest of other persons in respect of the same.

"All sums due from purchasers or lessees of such lands, mines, or minerals at the time of the Union shall also belong to the local Governments.

"The several provinces shall remain in each vested with all other public property therein, except such as hereinbefore vested in the Confederation, subject to the right of the Confederation to assume any lands or public property required for fortifications or the defence of the country.

"The Confederation shall assume all the debts and liabilities of each province.

"The debt of Canada not specially assumed by Upper and Lower Canada respectively shall not exceed at the time of the Union 62,500,000 dollars; Nova Scotia shall enter into the Confederation with a debt not exceeding 8,000,000 dollars; and New Brunswick 7,000,000 dollars.

"But it is expressly provided that in case Nova Scotia or New Brunswick do not incur liabilities beyond those for which their Governments are now bound, and which shall make their respective debts at the date of Union less than 8,000,000 dollars and 7,000,000 dollars respectively, they shall then be entitled to benefit by the interest at 5 per cent. on the amount not so incurred, in like manner as is hereinafter provided for Newfoundland and Prince Edward Island. The foregoing resolution being in no respect intended to limit the powers now given to the respective Governments of those provinces by Legislative authority, but to limit the extreme amount of charge to be brought by them against the Confederation. Provided always that the powers so conferred by the respective Legislatures must be exercised within five years from this date, or will then lapse.

"Newfoundland and Prince Edward Island, not having incurred debts equal to those of the other provinces, shall be entitled to receive by half-yearly payments, in advance from the Confederation, the interest at 5 per cent. on the difference between the actual amount of their respective debts at the time of the Union, and the average amount of indebtedness per head of the population of Canada, Nova Scotia, and New Brunswick.

"In consideration of the transfer to the General Legislature of the powers of taxation, a grant in aid of each province shall be made, equal to an amount of 80c. per head of the population as established by the census of 1861; Newfoundland being estimated at 130,000 inhabitants. Such aid to be in full settlement of all future demands upon the General Legislature for local purposes, and to be payable half-yearly in advance to each province.

"The position of New Brunswick being such as to entail large immediate charges upon her local revenues, it is agreed that for the period of ten years from the time when the union takes effect, an additional allowance of 63,000 dollars per annum shall be made to that province. Provided that so long as the liability of that province remains under 7,000,000 dollars, a deduction equal to the interest on such deficiency shall be made from the 63,000 dollars.

"In consideration of the surrender to the Confederation by Newfoundland of all its rights in mines and minerals, and of all the ungranted and unoccupied lands of the Crown, it is agreed that the sum of 150,000 dollars shall each year be paid to that province by semi-annual payments; provided that the colony shall retain the right of opening, constructing, and controlling roads and bridges through any of the said lands, subject to any laws which the General Legislature may pass in respect of the same.

"All engagements that may be entered into with the Imperial Government for the defence of the country shall be assumed by the Confederation.

"That the Federal Government will secure without delay the completion of the Intercolonial Railway from the Rivière-du-Loup through New Brunswick to Truro, in Nova Scotia.

"The communications with the North-Western Territory, and the improvements required for the development of the trade of the great west with the seaboard, are regarded by this Conference as subjects of the highest importance to the Confederation, and should be prosecuted at the earliest possible period when the state of the Federal finances will permit the Legislature to do so.

"The sanction of the Imperial and local Parliaments shall be sought for the union of the provinces on the principles adopted by the Conference.

"The proceedings of the Conference, when finally revised, shall be signed by the delegates, and submitted by each deputation to its own Government, and the chairman is authorized to submit a copy to the Governor-General for transmission to the Secretary of State for the Colonies."

APPENDIX "B."

INCREASED PRODUCTION OF CULTIVATED PLANTS NEAR THE NORTHERNMOST LIMIT OF THEIR GROWTH.

Extracts from an Article upon the "Acclimating Principle of Plants," in the American Journal of Geology, by Dr. Forry.

The cultivated plants yield the greatest products near the northernmost limit in which they will grow.

I have been forcibly impressed with this fact, from observing the productions of the various plants which are cultivated for food or clothing in the United States. The following instances will go far to establish the principle—viz.:—

The cotton, which is a tropical plant, yields the best staple and surest product in the temperate latitudes. The southern parts of the United States have taken the cotton-market from the East and West Indies, both as regards quantity and quality. This is partly owing to the prevalence of insects within the tropics, but principally to the forcing nature of a vertical sun. Such a degree of heat develops the plant too rapidly—runs it into wood and foliage, which become injuriously luxuriant; the consequence is, there are but few seed-pods, and these covered with a thin harsh coat of wool. The cotton wool, like the fur of animals, is, perhaps, designed for protection; and will be thick and fine in proportion as the climate is warm or cool. Another reason is to be found in the providence of the Deity, who aims to preserve races rather than individuals, and multiplies the seeds and eyes of plants, exactly as there is danger of their being destroyed by the severity of the climate, or other causes. When, therefore, the cares and labours of man counteract the destructive tendency of the climate and guarantee their preservation, they are, of course, more available and abundant.

The lint plants, flax, hemp, &c., are cultivated through a great extent of latitude, but their bark, in the southern climates, is harsh and brittle. A warm climate forces these plants so rapidly into maturity, that the lint does not acquire either consistency or tenacity. We must go far north in Europe, even to the Baltic, to find these plants in perfection, and their products very merchantable. Ireland is rather an exception as to latitude; but the influence of the sun is so effectually counteracted there by moisture and exposure to the sea air, that it is always cool; hence the flax and potatoe arrive at such perfection in that region.

It holds equally true in the farinaceous plants. Rice is a tropical plant; yet Carolina and Georgia grow the finest in the world—heavier grained, better filled, and more merchantable, than any imported into Europe from the Indies. The inhabitants of the East Indies derive their subsistence almost exclusively from rice; they must be supposed, therefore, to cultivate it with all skill and care, and the best contrivances for irrigation. Such is, however, the forcing nature of their climate, that the plant grows too rapidly, and dries away before the grain be properly filled. Indian corn, or maize, if not a tropical plant, was originally found near the tropics; and, although it now occupies a wide range, it produces the heaviest crops near the northern limit of its range. In the West Indies it rises thirty feet in height; but, with all that gigantic size, it produces only a few grains on the bottom of a spongy cob, and is counted on only as rough provender. In the southern part of the United States it reaches a height of fifteen feet, and will produce thirty bushels to the acre; in the rich lands of Kentucky and the Middle States it produces fifty or sixty bushels to the acre; but in New York and New England agricultural societies have actually awarded premiums for one hundred and fifty bushels to the acre, collected from stalks only seven feet high. The heats of a southern sun develop the juices of this plant too quickly. They run into culm and blade, to the neglect of the seed, and dry away before fructification becomes complete.

Wheat is a more certain crop in New York, the northern part of Pennsylvania, and Ohio, and in the Baltic regions of Europe, than in the south either of Europe or America. In the north snows accumulate, and not only protect it from the winter colds, but from the weevil, Hessian fly, and other insects that invade it; and in the spring it is not forced too rapidly into head, without time to mature fully, and concoct its farina.

A cold climate also aids the manufacturing of flour, preserving it from acidity, and enables us to keep it long, either for a good market, or to meet scarcities and emergencies. Oats grow in almost every country; but it is northern regions only, or very moist or elevated tracts, that they fill with farina suitable for human sustenance. Rye, barley, buckwheat, millet, and other culmiferous plants, might be adduced to illustrate the above principle; for all their habits require a more northern latitude than is necessary to their mere growth.

The grasses are proverbially in perfection only in northern and cool regions, although they will grow everywhere. It is in the north alone that we raise animals from meadows, and are enabled to keep them fat, and in good condition, from hay and grass alone, without grain. It is there the grasses acquire a succulence and consistency enough not only to mature animals, but to make the richest butter and cheese, that contribute so much to the tables of the luxurious. The grasses, which often in the south grow large enough, are without richness and nutriment; in hay they have no substance, and when green are too washy to fatten animals; the consequence is, most animals in those latitudes browse from necessity, and are poor and without size or beauty. It is the same hot sun which forces them to a rapid fructification before they have had time to concoct their juices. The sugar-cane produces, perhaps, better where it never seeds than in the tropics; for the juices will never ripen so as to granulate, until checked by frost or fructification. In the tropics, the cane grows twenty months before the juices ripen, and then the culm has contracted a woody, fibrous quality to such a degree as to resist the pressure of the mills, and yields but little juice, and that to an increased effort. In Louisiana we succeed well with the sugar-culture, because, while the culm is succulent and tender, a white frost checks the growth, ripens the juices, and in five months gives us a culm, tender, full of juice, easy to press, and yielding much grain of sugar. When Louisiana, therefore, acquires all the necessary skill, she will most probably grow this article cheaper than the West Indies.

Tobacco is a southern plant, but there it is always light and chaffy; and although often well-flavoured, it never gains that strong narcotic quality which is its only peculiar property, unless you grow it as far north as Virginia. In the south the heat unfolds its bud or germ too soon, forces into full expansion the leaf, and drives it to seed before the narcotic quality can be properly elaborated. We may assert a general rule, applicable to all annual plants, that neither the root nor the leaf acquires any further size or substance after fructification.

The tuberose, bulbous, and other roots, cultivated for human and animal subsistence, are similarly affected by climate, and manifest habits in corroboration of the above principle. The Irish potato, although from or near the tropics, will not come to perfection but in northern or cool countries, or in moist, insular situations, as Ireland. It is in such climates alone, that its roots acquire a farinaceous consistence, and have size, flavour, and nutriment enough to support, in the eminent way in which they are susceptible, animal life. In the south, a forcing sun brings the potato to fructification before the roots have had time to attain their proper size, or ripen into the proper qualities for nourishment. In Ireland the plant grows slow, through a long and cool season, giving time for its juices to be elaborated and properly digested; hence that fine farina and flavour which characterizes them. The sweet potato produces larger, better flavoured, and more numerous roots in Carolina, where it never flowers, than in the West Indies. In the latter place this plant runs wild, covers the whole face of the earth with its vines, and is so taken up with making foliage, that the root becomes neglected, and is small and woody. In order to have the onion in perfection, it must grow through two years, swelling all the time its bulbs. In the south, however, it seeds in one year, and before it has made much bulb. Beets, carrots, parsnips, turnips, radishes, and other roots, are equally affected by a hot sun, and scarcely worth cultivating far to the south. They all fructify before they have formed perfect roots, and make foliage at the expense of their bulbs; hence they will always be articles of commerce. The south will have to depend upon the north for them.

The salad plants are in like manner affected by climate, and give further proofs of our assumption. Cabbages, lettuces, endive, cellery, spinage—plants whose leaves only are eaten—to protect their leaves from cold (through a kind of instinct), wrap them up in leaves, which form heads, and render many of their other parts tender and crisp for use. These leaves, thus protected, are not only tender, but more nutritious, because their growth has been slow and their juices well digested. In the south, a relaxing sun lays open the very buds of such plants, gives a toughness and thinness to the leaves, and they are too unsubstantial for animal support, because of such quick and rapid development.

The delicious and pulpy fruits are, in a still more striking way, illustrative of our principle. The peach, nectarine, plum, apple, cherry, currant, gooseberry, apricot, and many other such families, are not in perfection in the south. It is in Pennsylvania, Virginia, Maryland, Jersey, and in the north of Europe that we enjoy them, although, originally, they came from near the tropics. The peach of the Carolinas is full of larvæ, gum, and knots, and too stringy and forced to be juicy and flavoured. The apple of the south is too acerb to be either eaten or preserved. The plums, apricots, cherries, currants, gooseberries, &c., will not even mature until we go far north. All the trees which bear these delicious fruits will grow luxuriantly in the south, make much foliage and wood, with but little pulp, and that unsavoury. The kernel in the one-seeded fruit seems to be the first object of nature in southern climes; that becomes strong, oily, and enlarged; and one of the peach family has so entirely neglected the pulp, that it has only a husky matter around the kernel, as the almond. The changeableness of the weather in the south, in the spring season, throws plants off their guard; the frosts attendant on those changes destroy the young fruit; and it is only one year in three that the crop hits at all. The desiccated or dried state of these fruits enables us to enjoy them through the year; but in the south their acidity carries them into fermentation or decomposition before they can be divested of their aqueous parts. The climate of the south is equally against converting them into cider, or any other fermented liquor, because the heat forces their compressed juice so rapidly into an active fermentation, that it cannot easily be checked until it passes into vinegar. For the same reason distillation goes on badly in hot climates, and cannot be checked long at the proper point to give much alcohol; and whether we aim to enjoy the delicious freshness of these fruits themselves, sip the nectar of their juices, refresh ourselves with their fermented beverage, stimulate our hearts with their brandies and cordials, or feast through the winter upon the dried or preserved stores of their fruits, we are continually balked by the severity of a southern climate, and for such enjoyment must look to the north.

The melons are always affected by too great a degree of heat, even though their vines flourish so much in southern latitudes. The forcing sun hurries them on to maturity before they have attained much size, or acquired that rich saccharine and aromatic flavour for which they are so much esteemed. The cantelope-melon will rot, or have its sides baked by a hot sun, before it is fully formed; and the water-melon is always woody, dry, and devoid of its peculiar sweetness and richness in the south. Vines have been known to run 100 feet, and bear no melon. It is in Philadelphia and its neighbourhood, and in similar latitudes, that the markets are loaded with delicious melons of all sorts, whose flavour so much refreshes and delights us. It is there, near their northern limit, that we cultivate them with such uniform success.

The orange, strictly a tropical plant, is more juicy, large, and delicious at St. Augustine (Florida) than at Havana; and fruiterers, in order to recommend an orange, will say that it is from some place out of the tropics. In the West Indies, the pulp of the orange is spongy, badly filled with juice, and has too much of a forced flavour to be pleasant. The hot-house forcers of Europe, or at Rome, anciently at first produced bad fruit; too dry, too small, and without flavour; because they overacted. They have lately found out that fact, and now the productions of the hot-houses of London, Paris, &c., astonish and delight us with the quantity and excellence of the fruit. They have found out that gradual and uniform heat is the desideratum; countervailing the cold rather than imparting much heat. Fruit thus produced is pronounced better than any grown in the natural way, however perfect the climate.

The juices of the grape are best matured for wine near the northern limit of their growth. On the Rhine, in Hungary, the sides of the Alps, and in other elevated or northern situations, the wine is strongest, richest, and most esteemed. The French wines rank before the Spanish and Italian; and in no southern country of Europe or Africa, except Madeira, where elevation makes the difference, is the wine in much repute. The grapes of France are more delicious for the table than those of Spain or Madeira. In the northern part of the United States, the excess of heat and moisture blights the grape to such an extent that all attempts have failed in its cultivation. The grape-vine, however, whether wild or cultivated, grows there very luxuriantly. The vinous fermentation can also be best conducted in a climate comparatively cool; and all the pressing, fermenting, and distillation of the juice of this delicate fruit can be safer and more profitably managed in a mild region.

The olive, and other oleaginous plants, yield more fruit, of a richer flavour, and can be better pressed, and the oil preserved, in a mild climate. In France the tree is healthier, and the fruit and oil better than in Spain or Italy; and the Barbary States are known to import their oil from France and Italy.

Many other plants might be named, whose habits would equally support our position. It is presumed, however, that enough has been cited to call the attention of philosophy to this curious subject, and enable us to give proper attention to it, in all the practical operations of agricultural pursuit. Much time and expense might be saved, and profits realized, if this were more generally understood.

We have already observed, that the heat of the sun in southern climes forces plants to a false maturity, runs them on too rapidly to fructification, and renders dry and woody the culms, stalks, and leaves of the plants, where these parts are used. Hence the chaffiness of the leaf, the dryness of the culm, the lightness of the grain, and the unsavoury, spongy quality of the pulp of the plants in those latitudes. Hence the difficulty of fermenting their juices, distilling their essences, and preserving for use the fruit, juice, or blades of such plants. The prevalence of insects is another bar to the productiveness of southern plants; swarms of them invade and strip the leaves, bore the fruit, and lead to blight and decomposition; and just in proportion as the labours of man have rendered plants succulent, and their fruits and seeds sweet and pleasant, do these insects multiply on them, devour their crops, and defeat the objects of husbandry.

The labour of man, too, is more conservative in northern climates, because his arm is better nerved for exercise, his health and spirits more buoyant; and instead of saying, "Go and work," he says, "Come and work;" treads with a cheerful heart upon his own soil, and assists in the cultivation, collection, and preservation of his own productions. It is in temperate climates that man can be most familiar with nature; it is there he has the best opportunities of observing the guarantees which nature has for the preservation of her animals and plants against the devastation of the elements; he sees an occasional apparent neglect of individuals, but a constant parental care of races. In everything he sees the wisdom and benevolence of God.

APPENDIX "C."

PROF. M. F. MAURY AND PACIFIC RAILROADS—THE PHYSICAL, COMMERCIAL, AND MILITARY NECESSITY OF TWO RAILROADS, ONE NORTH AND ONE SOUTH.

At a special meeting of the Chamber of Commerce of the city of St. Paul, Minnesota, held on Saturday, Jan. 22, 1859, at the Room of the Chamber, Col. D. A. Robertson submitted a letter of Commander M. F. Maury, U. S. N. (Superintendent of the Observatory at Washington), upon the subject of Pacific Railroads.

On the motion of Gov. Alexander Ramsay, Col. Robertson was requested to furnish a copy of the same for publication, it being in the estimation of the Chamber the most able exposition of the subject treated upon ever written.

The request of the Chamber was complied with as follows:—

"DEAR SIR,   "St. Paul, Jan. 24, 1859.

"I venture to comply with your request in behalf of the St. Paul Chamber of Commerce, to furnish a copy of Commander Maury's letter of the 4th inst. for publication (striking out the portion of a private nature).

"In doing so, it is proper to remark that the letter was written in the course of private correspondence, yet, in furnishing it for publication, I confidently rely upon the acquiescence of its distinguished and patriotic author. Its contents, especially at this time, are of too much national value to be allowed to remain in the obscurity of any private hand. May I not say, with safety, that the scientific, geographical, and commercial facts therein presented, with such transcendent ability and high authority, settle the whole question so long debated about routes and roads to the Pacific?

"Yours truly,

"To Wm. R. Marshall, Esq.,   "D. A. ROBERTSON,"
"President St. Paul Chamber of Commerce."

"Observatory, Washington, Jan. 4, 1859.
"MY DEAR SIR,

* * * * * *

"I have often wished that the question, pure and simple, railroad or no railroad to the Pacific, could be put to the popular vote of the nation. Never, since the Memphis convention of 1849, should I have had any doubt as to the result. The vote would be largely for the road.

"While all admit the importance of one or more such railways, there has been such a diversity of opinion as to routes and plans, that no one route has as yet met with friends enough to carry it through in spite of its rivals, and I do not think that it ever will.

"Two roads at least are necessary. At least two roads—one at the north, the other at the south—are required for the common defence. At least two roads—one at the south, the other at the north—are necessary, socially and commercially; for by two roads so placed the markets of China, Japan, and the Amoor, will be brought nearer to us by many days' sail than it is possible for one road to bring them. This may sound paradoxical; yet I hope, before I am done, to explain the paradox to your satisfaction.

"Let us first consider the importance of two roads in their military aspect. Vancouver Island commands the shores of Washington and Oregon; and whether the terminus of the northern road be on Puget Sound or at the mouth of the Columbia River, the munitions sent there could be used for no other part of the coast, for Vancouver overlooks them.

"They could not, on account of Vancouver in its military aspects, be sent from the northern terminus to San Francisco and the south; nor could the southern road—supposing only one, and that at the south—send supplies in war from its terminus, whether at San Diego or San Francisco, by sea either to Oregon or Washington. Vancouver would prevent, for Vancouver commands their coasts as completely as England commands those of France on the Atlantic. So complete is this military curtain that you never heard of France on the Atlantic sending succour by sea to France on the Mediterranean, or the reverse, in a war with England. The Straits of Fuca are as close as the Straits of Gibraltar.

"In preparing for the national defences of the Pacific, this fact, and the fact that Vancouver Island is in the hands of a foreign power, are well calculated to impress peculiar features upon any system that may be adopted.

"But I promised to explain why two roads, one at the south, the other at the north, will bring the markets of Asia much nearer to us than either road, singly, would make them.

"Before, however, I go into that explanation, let us clear away some of the obstacles which error has placed in the way of a northern route to the Pacific.

"Most men of our age were educated under the belief that parallels of latitude and terrestrial climates are correlatives; that we might tell the temperature of any unknown country or region of country, if we knew its latitude.

"Humboldt and Dove exploded this idea with their isothermal lines. For example, they show that the mean annual temperature of North Cape, lat. 70° in Europe, is the same as that along the north shore of Lake Superior, in lat. 50°. Here is a difference of 20° of lat. without any difference in the average annual temperature of the two places.

"There is a difference in the length of day and night at the two places, and so far as climate is affected by difference in the length of day and night, climate is to that extent, and no farther, an affair of latitude. But with differences in length of day and night, the relations between climate and latitude cease. The thermometer and hygrometer then become the true exponents of climate. Every region, indeed, tells the whole story of its climates by its flora.

"Let us get rid, then, of our old notions concerning the relations of latitude to climate, and with unbiassed minds lay out this north temperate zone, which we inhabit, into thermal bands, and then study the flora of these bands. After we shall have done this, then I think we will be able to agree, at least among ourselves, as to the necessity of two routes to the Pacific. Moreover, we can select those routes that will be the best agriculturally and commercially; and when we shall finish with this investigation, you will find that these two routes lie exactly where the best plan of national defence requires them—the northern route commencing at the western boundary of Minnesota, and going to Puget's Sound, with a branch, in the course of time, to the mouth of the Columbia—the southern route commencing at El Paso in Texas, and going thence to San Diego and San Francisco.

"I speak of these routes as the routes which commerce and agriculture as well as war require. The elements indicate them. I place the climatology of these, the agricultural and commercial resources of the regions through which they pass, in the same catagory, because commerce is based on difference of agricultural productions, and difference of productions is an affair of climate altogether. Therefore, in studying climates and routes we study variety of production, and cannot help looking at them in their commercial aspects.

"The Army Meteorological Observations, Blodget's Climatology of the United States, and Dove's Isothermal Maps, enable us to divide that portion of the northern temperate zone occupied by the United States, into two grand and characteristic thermal bands.

"The fauna and the flora of these two bands differ. The people differ—their climates differ—the industrial pursuits in them differ—and, therefore, I call them grand and striking subdivisions.

"Speaking in a general way, the United States lie between the mean annual isotherms of 35° and 70°.

"Take a school map of the world and let us draw with a pencil these isotherms across Europe, Asia, and Africa also.

"Beginning on the west coast, with a pencil at Sitka, draw it with a free hand thence through the mouth of the Red River of the North, touching the north shore of Lake Superior, crossing the St. Lawrence below Quebec, and thence to St. John's, Newfoundland. Now beginning in Europe, near Christiana, drew your pencil up towards the Gulf of Onega; then draw through Orenberg to Kiachta, Marghen, and the mouth of the Amoor. You can now see sufficiently near for our present purpose how the isotherm of 35° runs. The mean temperature of all places south of this line is not more than 35°.

"In like manner we sketch off roughly the annual isotherm of 70° through the New World and the Old. It starts from San Diego, crossing the Colorado at its mouth, and then passing down through Chihuahua to Austin, in Texas, it goes by New Orleans and Pensacola to the sea. Striking the African coast near Mogador, it goes through Cairo, Ispahan, Delhi, to Canton. The mean temperature of all places to the north of this line is less than 70°.

"Now let us devide the belt included between these two isotherms into two nearly equal thermal bands, by tracing likewise with a free hand the isotherm of 52°, the mean (nearly) between 35° and 70°.

"Beginning near Cape Orford on the west coast, this isotherm passes up towards the Dalles, then down a little to the west of Salt Lake to Santa Fé; then up to Scott's Bluff, and then through St. Louis and Louisville to Baltimore. Taking it up in England, it passes through Belgium towards Zurich, then up towards Olmutz, and so on through Varna, Derbent, Kokan, and Pekin.

"This line divides this belt thermally and geographically into two bands of nearly the same size. They include the garden spots of the earth. In them man laid his first hearthstone, and from them the lights of civilization and Christianity have shed their first and their brightest rays.

"Let us, for the convenience of reference, call the northern band the upper band, and the southern one the lower.

"We are now prepared to cast the eye over them, and to generalize concerning the commercial and agricultural aspects of the two routes.

"The plants which give physiognomy to the fields and forests of these bands are, for the upper band, conifers, the willow, the beech, larch, fir, alder, elm, hickory, birch, cranberries, and pasture grasses. For the lower band, the characteristic plants are thick-leaved evergreens, and arborescent grasses, the cypress, cedar, ash, and magnolia, with roses.

"The chief commercial plants, besides the cereals—which are common to both—are, for the lower band, the orange, the vine, the fig, peach, date, pomegranate, citron, the melon, St. John's bread, the sweet potato, rice, indigo, tobacco, hemp, cotton, tea, sugar, and naval stores. For the upper band, buckwheat, hay, Irish potatoes, turnips, apples, pears, plums, herds, and flocks.

"Most of the railways, both in Europe and America, are in the upper band; so are the great centres of commerce, and the places for fairs in Europe and Asia—a sure sign that the occupations of the people in the upper band are not so exclusively agricultural as those of the lower. In other words, we are reminded by this division, that the people, in spite of legislative enactments, tariffs, and protection, have obeyed the laws enacted by nature as expressed for the geographical distribution of labour, and that man, though the same in both bands, has in each heeded those physical conditions by which he finds himself surrounded, and directed his labours to those pursuits which promise the best returns.

"This circumstance reminds us that railways in the upper bands should be much more apt to have full freights both ways than are railways in the lower band. The latter carry away tobacco, hemp, cotton, rice, sugar, &c., and may bring back, in a single car, the manufactured articles for which a whole train-load of cotton has been exchanged. Hence, as a rule, railroads in this band carry more than they fetch. The same raw and bulky articles go into the upper band to be manufactured, and when manufactured, they are put on the rails for distribution, and for market—thus increasing freights for this band both ways.

"Each one of these thermal bands in the United States wants its roads from sea to sea, and each must have it. Each wanted its system of roads between the Atlantic Ocean and the Mississippi River, and each has it, whether Congress would or not—and so it will be between the "Grand Ocean" and the Mississippi.

"Look at the steel engraved map in Putnam's Railroad Guide, and you will see how those systems of roads have been formed. Until last summer Virginia would stretch no railway line from any of her fine harbours into the Valley of the West. North Carolina had no harbours; hence, the blank space on that map between Ohio and Georgia.

"On the other hand, there was the great chain of lakes. Then there was the Baltimore and Ohio, and the Pennsylvania Central Railroads, which were commenced at a very early day, and pushed forward with vigour. Now, see what a net-work of roads these have called out, reaching to and beyond the Mississippi, and stretching due east to connect with these.

"While Virginia would not, and North Carolina could not, South Carolina and Georgia went to work with their system of roads, which has already stretched itself towards the setting sun far beyond the Mississippi.

"Texas has given a most magnificent grant of lands and loan of money to her southern Pacific Railway, which will extend the southern system as far as El Paso, within 600 miles of the Pacific.

"Roads from New Orleans, Vicksburg, Memphis, and other points are to join the Texas road. Memphis and El Paso are in the middle of the lower band. Hence, you perceive, this band has its roads well under way, and it is high time Uncle Sam should take hold and extend it westward.

"Unfortunately, this road has had troubles to an extraordinary degree—but it's a long night that has no day, and it now begins for the first time to see the light of real day. The dawn is promising.

"So, too, in Minnesota: St. Paul is in the centre of the upper band, and there is a railroad already under way from St. Paul to Pembina. A branch from this road leading to the Pacific will most fairly represent the system in the upper band. St. Paul is in the middle of it, and the distance by an air line from the western limits of Minnesota to Puget's Sound is, 870 miles; making only(say) 1500 miles of road to be provided for by the General Government, in order to secure both of these roads. Indeed, if the southern road be taken to the California line, California will take care of it thence to San Francisco. So that by providing for the construction of some 500 miles, Government can now secure one at the south. Ten years ago, when this question of a road to the Pacific began first to be agitated, Government would have had to provide for it all the way from the Mississippi to the Pacific—so it was held—and that would have required a single road about 2000 miles long. Now, Government aid along 1500 miles will give us two.

"These bands give a complete *quietus* to all objections to the northern roads on the score of climate. In other parts of the world roads abound in just such climates. The road from St. Petersburg to Moscow, and the Prussian roads, with others in the same bands in Europe, are even in a higher latitude than the St. Paul road will be; yet climate is no objection to them. Neither is it to the Canada railways, nor to any others as far north as the rails have been laid. We all expect to see the day when Russia will be extending her system of rails into Siberia, and none of us—for in that matter all of us have unbiassed minds—anticipate any difficulty on the score of climate.

"Rain maps for these bands show that the average annual amount of rain along this northern route and until you pass the Rocky Mountain range—after which the climate is mild, like that of England—is less than it is along any railway in the Atlantic States, or in the Mississippi Valley, or, indeed, in any part of the world. They show that the average amount of precipitation, both snow and rain, in winter, for that part of the route which lies between the Pacific range of mountains and St. Paul, is less than three inches!

"Thus, I think, the question of climate, of terrific snow-storms, and impassible drifts along this route, may be considered as disposed of.

"We return now to the paradox, that by these two roads to the Pacific, the markets of Asia will be much nearer to those of the Mississippi Valley than either road alone could bring them. To explain this it is only necessary to remind you how the winds blow and the current set that control the routes of sailing-vessels—the burden cars of the sea—between the eastern shores of Asia and our west coast.

"The route to Asia lies through the N. E. trade winds. These winds blow between the parallel of 30 deg. N. and the Equator; and vessels that take this route usually run across the broad Pacific between the parallel of 18 deg. and 25 deg. N. where the trades are strongest. Returning, they take the great circle route—the shortest distance—and keep well up to the north; for now the 'brave west winds' of those extra-tropical regions which would have been adverse for the outward voyage, are fresh and fair for the homeward run. So you perceive that a vessel trading under canvas between our Pacific States and China describes on every round voyage, an ellipse; coming out of the Straits of Fuca or the Columbia River, for instance, her course is first to the southward, as though she were bound round Cape Horn, and until she gets into the N. E. trade winds. Her course is then west until she enters the waters of the China Seas. She then hauls up to the northward and westward for her port. On the return voyage, her course, on coming out of her Asiatic port, is to the northward and eastward, until she gets fairly within the 'brave west winds.' With these she steers to the eastward, following the great circle route, gradually shaping her course to the S. of E. until she reaches our own shores again.

"If she be bound to San Francisco, her route, until she gains the offings of the Straits of Fuca, would be the same as though she were bound into Puget's Sound or the Columbia River.

"Thus you perceive that, on the outward voyage, San Francisco is on the way-side from Puget's Sound and Columbia River to China; whereas, Puget's Sound and Astoria are on the way-side of the route from China and Japan to California.

"To see how one road only would work, let us suppose it at the north—running from St. Paul to Puget's Sound. Let us now follow a package of merchandise—say of ginseng—that is sent over this road from Memphis to be bartered in China for tea. The ginseng would first go north up the Mississippi to get to the road. Thence it would cross to the Pacific; arriving at Puget's Sound, it would then be shipped for China. Now it must come *back to the South again to get into the trade wind region.* Thus, you observe, it would have to go more than a thousand miles up the Mississippi out of the way; and when it reaches the Pacific, it would have to return again as far to the south. Being exchanged for tea in China, it would be nearest for the tea to stop at

Puget's Sound, take the railroad and come south on the Mississippi, instead of coming south by sea along the Pacific coast.

"Now let us, in imagination, place the road at the south instead of at the north, and take a bale of furs to illustrate the route of trade and travel. The fur, we will suppose, is sent from St. Paul. It comes down the Mississippi to get to the road. That would not be out of the way for the *fur*, for it is bound south for the north-east trade winds at any rate; and it would be, in a national point of view, perhaps more desirable to have it go south by the Mississippi, than by sea in the Pacific. But when the silk for which it has been exchanged in China, on St. Paul account, arrives, on its return off the entrance of the Straits of Fuca, it has to turn out of its way. Instead of finding railway transportation to take it through from Puget's Sound across to Minnesota, it has to run away to the south. Perhaps a week after it might have been in St. Paul by a northern road, it arrives by sea in California, and is carried by rails to Memphis. Now it has to *double upon itself to go north, and recross every parallel of latitude that it crossed after turning out of its way from Juan de Fuca.*

"This doubling will require two or three weeks of time, besides risk and expense.

"With *two* roads there will be no *doubling*, hence two roads will bring China and Japan and Russia very much nearer to the Mississippi Valley than one can do. The distance saved will be, in furlongs, nearly twice the length of the Mississippi River, and in time some two or three weeks.

"Whether the Government, therefore, aids in the building of these roads or not, these circumstances will of themselves call for the construction of at least two roads to the Pacific—one at the north, the other at the south. Northern capital and southern capital will assist in both.

"I have thus endeavoured to make clear the paradox with which I set out, and I hope I have succeeded in showing to your satisfaction that at least two railways—one at the north, the other at the south—are required to the Pacific.

"There are no toll-houses on the lakes, and none on the Gulf of Mexico. The commercial voices of these two waters, could it be heard, would be raised, each trumpet-tongued, in favour of these two routes.

"The nearest way from Brazil and the Amazon, as well as from the West Indies to China, would then be by the South Pacific Railway.

"Yours truly,
"M. F. MAURY.

"D. A. ROBERTSON, St. Paul, Minnesota."

APPENDIX "D."

TABLE OF DISTANCES, FARES, &c., BETWEEN GREAT BRITAIN AND NORTH AMERICA.

Londonderry to	Belleisle	. . .	2260	miles.
Galway .	„ „	. . .	2280	„
Galway .	„ Quebec	. . .	2280	„
Cork . .	„ Quebec	. . .	2340	„
Galway .	„ Portland	. . .	2528	„
Cork . .	„ „	. . .	2460	„
Londonderry „	„	. . .	2525	„
Liverpool .	„ „	. . .	2750	„
Londonderry	„ Boston	. . .	2565	„
Cork . .	„ „	. . .	2508	„
Galway .	„ „	. . .	2565	„
Cork . .	„ New York .	. .	2698	„
Galway .	„ „	. . .	2768	„
Liverpool .	„ „	. . .	2980	„

Montreal Line to Quebec in summer and Portland in the winter from Liverpool. Fares—After cabin, 18 guineas; forward cabin, 15 guineas. Steerage passage-money to Quebec from Londonderry, 6 guineas.

From Glasgow to Quebec, by Allan or Anchor Line. Fares—Cabin, 13 guineas; steerage, 5 guineas.

Sailing ships to Quebec from Liverpool, Plymouth, Glasgow, Hull, or any English port, charge from £4 to £5; children under 12, half-price.

From Liverpool to New York, by Inman Line. Fares—Cabin, 15 to 22 guineas; steerage, 5 guineas.

From London to New York, by London and New York Steamship Line. Fares—Cabin, £15; steerage, 7 guineas.

DISTANCES TO CHICAGO, ILLINOIS.
FROM QUEBEC.

	1st Class.	2nd Class.	Emigrant.
Viâ Grand Trunk and Michigan Southern Railroads (1007 miles)	£4 0	...	£2 0

FROM NEW YORK.

	1st Class.	2nd Class.	Emigrant.
Viâ Hudson River, New York Central, Great Western (Canada), and Michigan Central Railroads (distance 950 miles) . . .	£4 12	£3 4	£2 0

Viâ Hudson River, New York Central, Buffalo and Erie, Cleveland and Erie, Cleveland and Toledo, and Michigan Southern Railroads (distance 963 miles).

Viâ New York and Erie, Buffalo and Erie, Cleveland and Erie, Cleveland and Toledo, and Michigan Southern Railroads (distance 960 miles).

Viâ Camden and Amboy, Pennsylvania Central, and Pittsburg, Fort Wayne and Chicago Railroads (distance 920 miles).
The fares in each case will be the same.

FROM BOSTON.

Viâ Boston and Worcester, Western, New York Central, Great Western (Canada), and Michigan Central Railroads (distance 1010 miles)

	1st Class.	2nd Class.	Emigrant.
	£4 16	£3 4	£2 0

FROM NEW ORLEANS.

Viâ New Orleans, Jackson, and Great Northern, Mississippi Central, Mobile and Ohio, and Illinois Central (distance 962 miles) . . } £6 0 none. none.

Viâ Steamboat to Cairo (1077 miles), thence by Illinois Central Railroad to Chicago (365 miles)—1442 miles . . . . . } £6 0 ... £2 4

Milwaukee is 85 miles by railroad from Chicago; Prairie du Chien, Wisconsin, is 200 miles by the Milwaukee and Mississippi Railroad from Milwaukee; La Crosse is united by means of the Milwaukee and Minnesota road which runs across the State of Wisconsin. To reach St. Paul, Minnesota, you may take the Galena and Chicago Railway from Chicago to the Mississippi, and thence by steamer; or the Chicago, St. Paul, and Fond du Lac Railway from Chicago to Prairie du Chien, on the Mississippi; or the La Crosse Railway, which is now finished to La Crosse, and will soon be to St. Paul.

TABLE OF DISTANCES AND FARES IN THE UNITED STATES AND CANADA, *VIA* GRAND TRUNK RAILWAY.

UNITED STATES.			From QUEBEC.			From PORTLAND.			
				FARES.			FARES.		
NAME OF PLACE.	NAME OF STATE.	DISTANCE.	1st Class.	Emigrant.	Extra Lugg. per 100 lbs	DISTANCE.	1st Class.	Emigrant.	Extra Lugg. per 100 lbs
		Miles.	£. s. d.	£. s. d.	s. d.	Miles.	£. s. d.	£. s. d.	s. d.
Boston	Massachusetts	423	1 14 10	0 17 5	..	..	..	..	..
BUFFALO	New York	573	2 7 0	1 3 6	1 6	697	2 17 2	1 8 7	2 0
Cape Vincent	New York	359	1 0 6	0 14 0	1 0	483	1 19 8	0 10 10	2 0
CHICAGO	Illinois	1007	4 2 10	2 1 5	6 3	1131	4 13 0	2 6 6	8 0
CINCINNATI	Ohio	1011	4 3 2	2 1 7	..	1135	4 13 4	2 6 8	..
CLEVELAND	Ohio	756	3 2 2	1 11 1	..	880	3 12 4	1 16 2	—
Dayton	Ohio	969	3 19 8	1 19 10	..	1093	4 10 0	3 4 11	—
Davenport	Iowa	1159	4 15 4	2 7 8	..	1283	5 5 6	2 12 9	—
DETROIT	Michigan	724	2 19 6	1 9 9	3 1	848	3 9 8	1 14 10	4 0
DUBUQUE	Iowa	1195	4 18 2	2 9 1	..	1319	5 8 4	2 14 2	—
Fond du Lac	Wisconsin	1176	4 16 8	2 8 4	..	1300	5 6 10	2 13 5	—
Galena	Illinois	1178	4 16 10	2 8 5	..	1302	5 7 0	2 13 6	—
Greenbay	Wisconsin	1094	4 10 0	2 5 0	..	1218	5 0 2	2 10 1	—
Indianapolis	Indiana	1036	4 5 2	2 2 7	..	1160	4 15 4	2 7 8	—
IOWA CITY	Iowa	1213	4 19 8	2 9 10	..	1337	5 9 10	2 14 11	—
Joliett	Illinois	1017	4 3 8	2 1 10	..	1141	4 13 10	2 6 11	—
Keokuk	Iowa	1227	5 0 10	2 10 5	..	1351	5 11 0	2 15 6	—
Lansing	Iowa	1352	5 11 2	2 15 7	..	1476	6 1 4	3 0 8	—
Milwaukee	Wisconsin	1092	4 9 10	2 4 11	7 4	1216	5 0 0	2 10 0	9 0
NEW YORK	New York	530	2 3 6	1 1 9	..	..	..	..	..
Ogdensburg	New York	281	1 3 0	0 11 6	..	..	..	..	..
Oswego	New York	456	1 17 6	0 18 9	..	580	2 7 8	1 3 10	—
Port Huron	Michigan	672	2 15 2	1 7 7	3 1	796	3 5 4	1 12 8	4 9
PRAIRIE DU CHIEN	Wisconsin	1282	5 5 6	2 12 9	..	1406	5 15 8	2 17 10	—
Rock Island	Illinois	1159	4 15 4	2 7 8	..	1283	5 5 6	2 12 9	—
St. Louis	Missouri	1292	5 6 4	2 13 2	..	1416	5 16 6	2 18 3	—
ST. PAUL	Minnesota	1555	6 7 10	3 3 11	..	1679	6 18 0	3 9 0	—
Toledo	Ohio	869	3 11 6	1 15 9	..	993	4 1 8	2 0 10	—
Watertown	New York	..	..	0 18 6	..	..	..	..	—
Zanesville	Ohio	958	3 18 10	1 10 5	..	1082	4 9 0	2 4 6	—

CANADA

NAME OF PLACE	NAME of COUNTY or DISTRICT	From QUEBEC				From PORTLAND			
		DISTANCE	FARES			DISTANCE	FARES		
			1st Class	Emigrant	Extra Lugg. per 100 lbs		1st Class	Emigrant	Extra Lugg. per 100 lbs
		Miles	£. s. d.	£. s. d.	s. d.	Miles	£. s. d.	£. s. d.	s. d.
Acton, West	Halton	536	2 4 0	1 2 0	3 1	660	2 14 2	1 7 1	4 2
Almonte	Lanark	385	1 11 8	0 15 10	2 1	509	2 1 10	1 0 11	2 6
Arnprior	Renfrew	402	1 13 0	0 16 6	3 1	526	2 3 2	1 1 7	4 2
Barrie	Simcoe	505	2 0 4	1 3 2	2 1	689	2 16 6	1 8 3	3 6
BELLEVILLE	Hastings	389	1 12 0	0 16 0	1 6	512	2 2 2	1 1 1	2 1
Berlin	Waterloo	564	2 6 4	1 3 2	2 1	688	2 16 6	1 8 3	3 1
Bowmanville	Durham	459	1 17 8	0 13 10	1 0	582	2 7 10	1 3 11	2 1
Bradford	Simcoe	544	2 4 8	1 2 4	2 1	668	2 14 10	1 7 5	3 1
Brampton	Peel	524	2 3 0	1 1 6	2 1	646	2 13 2	1 6 7	3 1
Brentford	Brant	631	2 12 0	1 6 0	3 1	754	3 2 2	1 11 1	4 2
Brighton	Northumberland	411	1 13 8	0 16 10	1 0	534	2 3 10	1 1 11	2 1
BROCKVILLE	Leeds	294	1 4 2	0 12 1	1 0	417	1 14 4	0 17 2	1 7
Bruce Mines	Lake Huron	881	3 12 4	1 16 2	4 2	1005	4 2 6	2 1 3	5 2
Carleton Place	Lanark	340	1 8 0	0 14 0	1 6	464	1 18 2	0 19 1	2 6
Chatham	Kent	680	2 16 0	1 8 0	3 1	804	3 6 2	1 13 1	4 2
Coaticook	Stanstead	143	0 11 10	0 5 11	1 0	174	0 14 4	0 7 2	1 6
COBOURG	Durham	432	1 15 0	0 17 9	1 0	556	2 5 8	1 2 10	2 1
Colborne	Northumberland	418	1 14 2	0 17 1	1 0	542	2 4 4	1 2 2	2 1
COLLINGWOOD	Simcoe	597	2 9 0	1 4 6	3 1	721	2 19 2	1 9 7	4 2
Compton	Compton	135	0 11 2	0 5 7	1 3	182	0 15 0	0 7 6	1 6
Cornwall	Stormont	237	0 19 6	0 9 9	1 0	361	1 9 8	0 14 10	2 1
Dickenson's Landing	Stormont	245	1 0 2	0 10 1	1 6	389	1 10 4	0 15 2	2 6
Dundas	Halton	546	2 4 10	1 2 5	1 0	670	2 15 0	1 7 6	2 6
Galt	Brant	572	2 7 0	1 3 6	2 1	696	2 17 2	1 8 7	3 1
Gananoque	Leeds	324	1 6 8	0 13 4	1 0	448	1 16 10	0 18 5	2 1
Georgetown	Halton	532	2 3 8	1 1 10	3 1	656	2 13 10	1 6 11	4 2
GODERICH	Huron	635	2 12 2	1 6 7	3 1	759	3 2 4	1 11 2	4 2
Guelph	Waterloo	549	2 5 0	1 2 6	2 1	673	2 15 2	1 7 7	3 1
Hamburgh	Perth	576	2 7 4	1 3 8	3 1	700	2 17 6	1 8 9	4 2
HAMILTON	Wentworth	541	2 4 6	1 2 3	1 0	665	2 14 8	1 7 4	2 1
Ingersoll	Oxford	597	2 9 0	1 4 6	3 1	721	2 19 2	1 9 7	4 2
Keene	Peterborough	452	1 17 2	0 18 7	1 0	576	2 7 4	1 3 8	2 6
Kemptville	Grenville	304	1 5 0	0 12 6	1 0	428	1 15 2	0 17 7	2 6
KINGSTON	Frontenac	342	1 8 2	0 14 1	1 0	466	1 18 4	0 19 2	3 1
Komoka	Middlesex	626	2 11 6	1 5 9	3 1	750	3 1 8	1 10 10	4 2
Lancaster	Glengarry	223	0 18 4	0 9 2	1 0	347	1 8 6	0 14 3	2 1
Lefroy	Simcoe	558	2 5 10	1 2 11	2 1	682	2 16 0	1 8 0	3 1
Lennoxville	Sherbrooke	123	0 10 2	0 5 1	1 3	194	0 15 8	0 7 10	1 6
LONDON	Middlesex	622	2 11 2	1 5 7	3 1	746	3 1 4	1 10 8	4 2
Matilda	Dundas	268	1 2 0	0 11 0	1 0	392	1 12 2	0 16 1	2 1
MONTREAL	Montreal	169	0 13 10	0 6 11	0 6	292	1 4 0	0 12 0	1 6
Mount Bridges	Middlesex	631	2 12 0	1 6 0	3 1	755	3 2 2	1 11 1	4 2
Napanee	Lennox	368	1 10 4	0 15 2	1 0	492	2 0 6	1 0 3	2 1
Newmarket	York	536	2 4 0	1 2 0	2 1	660	2 14 2	1 7 1	3 1
Niagara	Lincoln	587	2 8 2	1 4 1	3 1	711	2 18 4	1 9 2	4 2
Niagara Falls	Welland	584	2 8 0	1 4 0	1 0	708	2 18 2	1 9 1	4 2
Oakville	Halton	524	2 3 0	1 1 6	3 1	648	2 13 2	1 6 7	4 2
Osgoode	Carleton	312	1 5 8	0 12 10	1 6	436	1 15 10	0 17 11	2 6
Oshawa	Durham	469	1 18 6	0 19 3	1 0	593	2 3 8	1 4 4	2 1
OTTAWA	Carleton	336	1 7 8	0 13 10	1 6	458	1 17 10	0 18 11	2 6
Paris	Brant	568	2 6 8	1 3 4	2 1	692	2 16 10	1 8 5	3 1
Perth	Lanark	334	1 7 6	0 13 9	1 6	458	1 17 8	0 18 10	2 6
Peterborough	Peterborough	460	1 16 10	0 18 5	1 0	584	2 7 0	1 3 6	2 6
PORT HOPE	Durham	440	1 16 2	0 18 1	1 0	564	2 6 4	1 3 2	2 1
Prescott	Grenville	282	1 3 2	0 11 7	1 0	406	1 13 4	0 16 8	2 1
Preston	Waterloo	575	2 7 4	1 3 8	2 1	699	2 17 6	1 8 9	3 1
Princeton	Oxford	575	2 7 4	1 3 8	2 1	699	2 17 8	1 8 9	3 1
QUEBEC (Pnt. Lvi.)	Quebec	..	.. ..	.. ..	..	310	1 6 0	0 13 0	2 1
RICHMOND	Drummond	96	0 8 0	0 4 0	1 0	220	0 17 4	0 8 8	2 1
Richmond Hill	York	517	2 2 6	1 1 3	2 1	641	2 12 8	1 6 4	3 1
SARNIA	Lambton	671	2 15 2	1 7 7	3 3	794	3 5 4	1 12 8	4 2
Sault Ste. Marie	Lake Superior	900	3 14 0	1 17 0	4 2	1024	4 4 2	2 2 1	5 2
Shannonville	Hastings	383	1 11 6	0 15 9	1 0	507	2 1 8	1 0 10	2 1
SHERBROOKE	Sherbrooke	120	0 10 0	0 5 0	1 0	196	0 16 2	0 8 1	1 6
Smith's Falls	Lanark	319	1 6 4	0 13 2	1 6	443	1 16 6	0 18 3	2 6
St. Catherine's	Lincoln	560	2 6 0	1 3 0	1 6	684	2 16 2	1 8 1	2 6
STRATFORD	Oxford	589	2 8 4	1 4 2	3 1	713	2 18 6	1 9 3	4 2
Suspension Bridge	Welland	584	2 8 0	1 4 0	3 1	708	2 18 2	1 9 1	4 2
Thamesville	Kent	664	2 14 8	1 7 4	3 1	788	3 4 10	1 12 5	4 2
Thornhill	York	512	2 2 0	1 1 0	2 1	636	2 12 2	1 6 1	3 1
TORONTO	York	501	2 1 2	1 0 7	1 0	625	2 11 4	1 5 8	2 1
Trenton	Northumberland	400	1 12 10	0 16 5	1 0	524	2 3 0	1 1 6	2 1
Wardsville	Kent	653	2 13 8	1 6 10	3 1	777	3 3 10	1 11 11	4 2
Wellington Mines	Lake Huron	800	3 6 0	1 13 0	4 2	924	3 16 2	1 18 1	5 2
Whitby	Ontario	473	1 18 10	0 19 5	1 0	597	2 9 0	1 4 6	2 1
Williamsburg	Dundas	260	1 1 4	0 10 8	1 0	384	1 11 6	0 15 9	2 1
Windsor	Essex	732	3 0 2	1 10 1	3 1	856	3 10 4	1 15 2	4 2
Woodstock	Oxford	587	2 8 2	1 4 1	3 1	711	2 18 4	1 9 2	4 2

APPENDIX "E."

ITINERARIES OF ROUTES FROM ST. PAUL TO PEMBINA, FORT GARRY, FORT ELLICE, EDMONTON HOUSE, AND THE GULF OF GEORGIA, BRITISH COLUMBIA.

A.

Table of Distances from St. Paul to Pembina—Crow Wing or Woods Road.

I. ST. PAUL TO LAKE FLOYD.

United States Military Road Surveys, 1857.

FROM ST PAUL (FULLER HOUSE) TO	Miles.	Total
St. Anthony (opposite the Falls)	9	9
Manomin	7½	16½
Anoka (east of Rum River)	10	26½
Itasca	6½	33
Orono (Elk River)	7	40
Humboldt (Big Lake)	8½	48½
Marseilles (Bear Island)	9	57½
Boyington's Tavern	4	61½
Clear Lake	4	65½
East St. Cloud (Brantford post-office)	9	74½
Sauk Rapids	3	77½
Watab	5½	83
Langola	12½	95½
Swan River	10	105½
Little Falls	3	108½
Bell Prairie	5½	114
Olmstead's	8½	122½
Mouth of Nokay River (opposite Fort Ripley)	½	123
Crow Wing	7	130
Chippewa Agency at Gull River	4½	134½
Opposite mouth of Long Prairie River	12½	147
Commencement of Grand Marais—(*end of built road*)	5	152
Crossing of Crow Wing River—Wadena	8½	160½
Crossing of Wing River	9¼	169¾
Crossing of Bluff Creek	12¼	182
Commencement of Leaf Mountain	6	188
Outlet of Leaf Lake	5	193
Leaf City	2	195
Otter Tail City (to left of road)	5½	..
First crossing of Otter Tail River (Rush Lake)	7	202
Second " " " (*end of surveyed line*)	16	218
Third " " } *Odometer measurements.*	4½	222½
Detroit Lake—north shore } *Odometer measurements.*	10½	233
Lake Floyd (Eagle's Nest Lake) } *Odometer measurements.*	6	239

II. LAKE FLOYD TO PEMBINA.

Col. Nobles. 1859.

FROM LAKE FLOYD TO	Miles.	Total.
North end of Small Lake, to left of road	2½	241½
Timbered Lake, to left	5¼	246¾
Buffalo River, 10 feet wide, 1 foot deep	5¼	252
Dividing Ridge, lake and timber.	8⅓	260⅓
Junction of St. Cloud and Pembina trail	11⅔	272
Crossing of Wild Rice River, 35 feet wide, 2 feet deep	5	277
Crossing of Wild Rice Creek, 15 feet wide, 1 foot deep	5	288
Crossing of Sand Hill River, 30 feet wide, 1½ foot deep	19¾	301¾
Crossing of Sand Hill Creek (12 feet)	6	307¾
Bad marshes	1¾	309½
Stony butte and lake	11¾	321¼
Small creek, water in holes	3½	324¾
Crossing of Red Lake River, 175 feet wide, 3½ feet deep	4½	329¼
Small lake and marsh	11	340¼
Small lake	4¾	345
Coulee	12½	357½
Crossing of Snake River	4	361½
Crossing of Middle River, 20 feet wide, 6 inches deep	7	368½
Crossing of Pine River, 15 feet wide, 1 foot deep	6	374½
Bend of Pine River	4	378½
Small creek	6½	385
Big Point	15¼	400¼
South fork of Two Rivers	6¼	406½
Mouth of Two Rivers	5	411½
Pembina	12½	424

III. RED LAKE RIVER TO PEMBINA.

Col. F. L. Smith, 1856.

FROM ST. PAUL TO	Miles.	Total.
Red River		329¼
Small Lake	18	347¼
Middle River	17½	364¾
Tamarac River (Rivière aux Epines)	4	368¾
Small stream	16½	385¼
South branch of Two Rivers	11	396¼
North branch of Two Rivers	4¼	400½
Lac du Nord-Ouest	11½	412
Pembina, west side of Red River	¾	412¾

B.

Table of Distances from St. Paul to Pembina—plain trail.

I. ROUTE OF MAJOR WOODS AND GENERAL POPE.

June and July, 1849.

FROM ST. PAUL TO	Miles.	Total.
Crossing at Sauk Rapids		78½
Cold Water Creek	16	94½

	Miles.	Total.
Crossing of Sauk River (Richmond)	5	99½
David Lake (now Henry Lake)	14	113½
Lake Henrie (now Lake George)	7	120½
Crossing of Crow River	8	128½
Lightning Lake (now Grove Lake)	11	139½
White Bear Lake	14	153½
Pike Lake	13	166½
Main branch of Chippewa River	11	177½
Elk Lake	2	179½
Tipsina, or Pomme de Terre River	5	184½
Elbow Lake	10	194½
Rabbit River (W. branch of Pomme de Terre)	4	198½
Crossing of Otter Tail River	20	218½
Crossing of Red River (near Graham's Point)	22	240½
Crossing of Wild Rice River, west	13½	254
Crossing of Shayenne River	11	265
Crossing of Maple River	17	282
Rush River, turned it	18½	300½
" bend	9½	310
Point of Ridge	16	326
Main branch of Elm River	7½	333½
South branch of Goose River	8½	342
Salt Lakes	8½	250½
Main branch of Goose River	10½	361
Crossing of "	2½	363½
Turtle River	18	381½
Big Salt River	19½	401
Little Salt River	9	410
Little Hill River	12½	422½
Cart River (Rivière de la Charrette)	2½	425
Steep Hill River	2	427
Heartshorn River	3	430
Mud River and commencement of Poplar Islands	7	437
Branch of Tongue River	16	453
Mouth of Pembina River	10½	463½

II. ROUTE OF ELLIS SMITH AND PARTY.

August, 1858.

FROM ST. PAUL TO	Miles.	Total.
Crossing at St. Cloud, say		74.52
Sauk River bridge	6.83	81.33
St. Joseph	4.94	86.27
Cold Spring	9.88	96.15
Sauk River ferry, Richmond	5.57	101.72
Lake Henry	15.80	117.52
Lake George	5.66	123.18
Crossing of Crow River	10.27	133.45
Grove Lake	10.40	143.85
Chippewa River	5.23	149.08
White Bear Lake	6.11	155.19
Little Chippewa River	17.52	172.71

	Miles.	Total.
Lake	.84	173.55
Rapid River (main branch of Chippewa)	7.11	180.66
Lake (Pomme de Terre Lake)	8.07	188.73
Pomme de Terre River	1.41	190.14
Lake (Elbow Lake)	9.22	199.36
Lightning Lake	5.52	204.88
Crossing of Otter Tail River	15.42	220.30
Crossing Red River (near Graham's Point)	22.90	243.20
Crossing of Wild Rice River, west—bridged	11·39	254.59
Crossing of Shayenne River, bridged	14.82	269.41
Crossing of Maple River	18.49	287.90
Crossing of Rush River (creek only)	7.61	295.51
Bed of stream, water in pools (Rush River)	9.72	305.23
” ” ”	13.64	318.87
Hemlock River (main branch Elm River)	23.62	342.49
Goose River (south branch of [?])	5.07	347.56
Stream, 20 feet wide	11.79	359.35
Stream, 20 feet wide (Goose River, main branch)	5.97	365.32
Lake	4.61	369.93
Turtle River	17.39	387.32
Stream	4.97	392.29
Salt River (Little Hill River), bridged	32.98	425.27
Water in marshes	25.02	450.29
Crossing of Pembina River (ferry), Pembina	15.30	465.59

C.

Table of Distances of portions of various Routes between St. Paul and Pembina.

I. SAUK RAPIDS TO SIOUX WOOD RIVER.

Governor Stevens' Expedition. June, 1853.

FROM SAUK RAPIDS TO	Miles.	Total.
Cold Spring Brook	18	18
Sauk River Ford (Richmond)	6	24
Lake Henry	$19\frac{1}{2}$	$43\frac{1}{2}$
Branch of Crow River, 20 feet wide	19	$52\frac{1}{2}$
Lightning Lakes (Grove Lakes)	$9\frac{3}{4}$	$62\frac{1}{4}$
Branch of Chippewa River, 20 feet wide	$6\frac{1}{4}$	$68\frac{1}{2}$
White Bear Lake	5	$73\frac{1}{2}$
Tributary of South branch, 15 feet wide	$10\frac{1}{2}$	84
Swift Brook, 6 feet wide	$3\frac{1}{2}$	$87\frac{1}{2}$
Pike Lake	$1\frac{3}{4}$	$89\frac{1}{4}$
Chippewa River, 124 feet wide	$10\frac{1}{4}$	$99\frac{1}{2}$
Elk Lake	$\frac{1}{2}$	100
West Branch of Chippewa River (Pomme de Terre), 140 feet wide	$8\frac{1}{4}$	$108\frac{1}{4}$
Elbow Lake	$9\frac{1}{4}$	$117\frac{1}{2}$
Rabbit River (west branch of Tipsina)	6	$123\frac{1}{2}$
Small brook, 12 feet wide	$5\frac{1}{4}$	$128\frac{3}{4}$
Small brook (tributary of Rabbit River)	$11\frac{3}{4}$	$140\frac{1}{2}$
Bois des Sioux River, 8 miles above mouth	10	$150\frac{1}{2}$

II. ST. CLOUD TO GEORGE TOWN.

Stage and Mail Route.—Table prepared by Mr. B. C. Borden. 1859.

FROM ST. CLOUD TO	Miles.	Total.
St. Joseph	7	7
Cold Spring	10	17
Richmond	$4\frac{1}{2}$	$21\frac{1}{2}$
Oak Grove	$19\frac{1}{2}$	41
Sauk Centre	17	58
Kandotta	2	60
Osakis	10	70
Alexandria	12	82
Evansville	22	104
Dayton (Wascata P.O.)	27	131
Breckinridge	24	155
Graham's Point	12	167
Burlington } by land	26	193
Shayenne	20	213
Georgetown	4	217

III. ST. CLOUD, *viâ* SIOUX WOOD RIVER, TO GOOSE RIVER.

Col. C. F. Smith. August, 1856.

FROM ST. CLOUD TO	Miles.	Total.
First crossing of Sauk River	3	3
Cold Water Creek	14	17
Second crossing of Sauk River (Richmond)	5	22
Lake Henry	18	40
Lake M'Leod (Grove Lake)	15	55
Branch of Chippewa River, beyond White Bear Lake, which passed to left	$18\frac{5}{8}$	$73\frac{5}{8}$
Pipe Lake	$4\frac{1}{3}$	78
Tipsina, or Pomme de Terre River	18	96
Elbow Lake	13	109
Rabbit River	$10\frac{3}{4}$	$119\frac{3}{4}$
Bois des Sioux River, about 4 miles from mouth	$17\frac{1}{4}$	137
Graham's Point	17	154
Wild Rice River, west	$6\frac{1}{4}$	$160\frac{1}{4}$
Shayenne River	15	$175\frac{1}{4}$
Maple River	13	$188\frac{1}{4}$
Crossing of Maple River	$3\frac{1}{2}$	$191\frac{3}{4}$
Creek emptying into Maple River	7	$198\frac{3}{4}$
Rush River	$15\frac{1}{2}$	$214\frac{1}{4}$
Small branch of Elm River	15	$229\frac{1}{4}$
South branch of Goose River, here left road	$11\frac{1}{2}$	$240\frac{3}{4}$

IV. DETROIT LAKE TO GEORGETOWN.

By Mr. Borden.

Estimated 55

V.

Elbow Lake to Wascata, about 18
Wascata (Dayton), N., to forks of trail, about . . 80 98

VI.

From the Upper Sioux Agency (Yellow Medicine), on the Minnesota River, to Breckinridge, the distance by the land route is at least 125

VII. RAILROAD LINES.

1st. The length of the "branch" line of the Minnesota and Pacific Railroad from St. Paul to St. Vincent, as far as surveyed and located, to Crow Wing, is about 125 miles.

2nd. The length of the main line of the same railroad, as surveyed and located to a point on the Sioux Wood River within 8 miles of Breckinridge, is about 207 miles.

D.

Breckinridge to Pembina by the channel of the Red River of the North.

FROM BRECKINRIDGE (*mouth of Sioux Wood River*) TO	Miles.	Total.
Crossing of trail	11½	11½
Graham's Point	5½	17
Fort Abercrombie	6½	23½
Mouth of Wild Rice River West (Psihu River)	52½	76
„ Shayenne River	41¾	117¾
Village of Lafayette	¾	118½
„ Shayenne	2½	121
Mouth of Buffalo River (Georgetown)	7½	128½
„ Elm River	25¼	153¾
„ Wild Rice River East	6¼	160
„ Goose River	22¼	182¼
„ Rivière au Marais No. 5 (from Pembina) [Sand Hill Rivière (?)]	1	183¼
„ Sand Hill River [Rivière au Marais (?)]	23½	206¾
„ Coulée des Vaches	5¼	212½
„ Coulée de la Butte de Sable	1	213½
„ Coulée du Nez Rouge	4½	218
„ Rivière au Marais, No. 4	8¼	226¼
„ Coulée du Jeune Bauf	3	229¼
„ La Grande Coulée	3	232¼
„ Coon Creek	7¾	240
„ Red Lake River (La Grande Fouche)	4	244
„ Coulée de L'Anglais	4½	248½
„ Rivière au Marais, No. 3	7½	256
„ Turtle River	11¼	267¼
„ Rivière au Marais, No. 2	27¾	295
„ Salt River	3½	298½
„ Rivière au Marais, No. 1	13	311½
„ Park River	7¼	318¾
„ Rivière aux Epines	2¾	321½
„ Coulée du Bois Percé	26¾	348¼
„ Black River	3	351¼
„ Two Rivers	11¾	363
„ Pembina River	13½	376½

E.

Routes and portions of Routes to the North and North-west of Pembina.

I. PEMBINA TO THE FOOT OF THE MOUNTAINS.

W. E. Smith and G. C. Burnham. 1858.

FROM PEMBINA TO	Miles.	Total.
Fort Garry	70.23	70.23
Fort Ellice, ascending the Assiniboine	231.29	301.52
Touchwood Hills Fort . W.N.W. course	169.47	470.99
South branch of the Saskatchewan ,,	129.34	600.33
North ,, ,, ,, . ,,	54.88	655.21
Crossing the north branch, about a day and a half's journey west of Carlton, to Jack-Fish Lake (*per Odometer*)	105.10	760.31
Fort Pitt . . . . . estimated	70.00	830.31
Edmonton . . . . ,,	180.00	1010.31
The foot of the mountains . . ,,	180.00	1190.31

II. PEMBINA TO FORT ELLICE, viâ ST. JOSEPH.

Col. W. H. Nobles. 1859.

FROM PEMBINA TO	Miles.	Total.
St. Joseph by the south trail	31¾	
,, ,, north ,,	34¾	
St. Joseph to Oak Village . . . about	142	
Oak Village to Fort Ellice . . . ,,	61	
Whole distance to Fort Ellice . . . ,,		238

III. PEMBINA TO THE KOOTONAIS FORT.

Dr. A. J. Thibodo. 1859.

FROM PEMBINA TO	Miles.	Total.
Fort Ellice (viâ Fort Garry)	300	300
Fort Qu Appelle	126	420
The elbow of the Saskatchewan.	146	566
The entrance of the Kootonais Pass	546	1112
Kootonais Fort	105	1217

IV. PEMBINA TO MOUTH OF RED RIVER BY WATER.

FROM PEMBINA TO	Miles.	Total.
Fort Garry (confluence of Assiniboine) . estimated	100	
Lake Winnipeg beyond the Delta . . ,,	43	143

DISTANCE ACROSS THE ENTIRE CONTINENT.

Captain Blakiston, R.E. 1860.

	Miles.
Halifax, N.S., to Montreal	650
Montreal to Ottawa	100
Ottawa to Nipigon Bay, Lake Superior	650
Nipigon Bay to Red River Settlement	400
Red River Settlement to Rocky Mountains	800
Rocky Mountains to the Gulf of Georgia	400
Halifax, N. S., to Gulf of Georgia.	3000
Atlantic Summer Port of Montreal to Gulf of Georgia, B.C.	2350
Western extremity of Canadian Inland to Gulf of Georgia	1600

APPENDIX "F."

ST. PAUL AND PACIFIC RAILROAD.

STATEMENT.

Hon. EDMUND RICE *State Senator.*

By an Act of Congress, approved March 3rd, 1857, a grant of land was made to Minnesota to aid in the construction of a railroad from Stillwater, by way of St. Paul and St. Anthony, to a point between the foot of Big Stone Lake and the mouth of Sioux Wood River, and from St. Anthony, viâ St Cloud and Crow Wing, to the navigable waters of the Red River of the North, at such point as the Legislature might determine.

The land granted consists of every odd numbered section for six sections (or square miles) in width, on each side of said lines, being 3840 acres per mile, in length of road, and amounts in the aggregate to 2,457,600 acres.

By an Act of the Legislative Assembly of Minnesota, approved May 22nd, 1857, and amended March 10th, 1862, "THE ST. PAUL AND PACIFIC RAILROAD COMPANY" was incorporated, and all the abovementioned lands were granted thereto; and the terminus of the first named line was fixed at Breckinridge, on the Sioux Wood River, and of the other at St. Vincent, near the mouth of the Pembina River. The length of the former line is 222 miles, and of the latter, 428 miles, making in all 650 miles.

The line from Stillwater, viâ St. Paul to Breckinridge, has been accurately surveyed and located, as also from St. Anthony to Crow Wing; the maps have been filed with the Governor of the State, and with the Commissioner of the General Land Office; the locations have been approved by the Secretary of the Interior, and by his direction the lands have been alloted to the company.

The charter is liberal in all its provisions, and contains no restrictions as to the rate of tolls, speed, the mode or manner of connexions with other roads, &c., and requires no taxes to be paid; but in lieu thereof, 3 per cent. of the gross earnings of the road (deducting running expenses) is to be paid to the State annually.

In other respects it is all that could be desired.

It will greatly facilitate the object of this publication if the reader will consult recent maps of Minnesota and North America.

The great object proposed by the St. Paul and Pacific Railroad Company, and for which the grant of lands held by them will be a munificent endowment, is to connect, by railroad, the navigation of the Mississippi River, and its tributaries, at St. Paul, near the Falls of St. Anthony, and at Stillwater, on the River St. Croix, with the Red River of the North, and other navigable streams of North-West British America. While the road across the isthmus, between extensive river systems, is in course of construction, one arm of the railroad will, unquestionably, be extended to the head of Lake Superior, and another communication will reach an agricultural district west of Minneapolis of great natural advantages, and which is a favourite destination of emigrants.

Perhaps nowhere on the American Continent will such important commercial results follow as will be witnessed in Minnesota, when 6000 miles of steamboat navigation on the Mississippi and St. Lawrence Rivers, and ˙3000 miles of similar navigation on the rivers of Central British America, are joined together, mostly by the proposed routes of the St. Paul and Pacific Railroad, with a comparatively small investment of capital.

Fortunately for the accomplishment of this result, great inducements exist for the construction of the first eighty miles north-west of St. Paul. When completed, the loveliest and most fertile region of Minnesota, extending from St. Cloud to the Red River, will be tributary to its business. The valley of the Sauk River, already settled and producing large crops of grain; the beautiful lake region, of which Otter Tail Lake is the centre, as large as Massachusetts, and which, under the "Homestead Act," presents great attractions to the immigrant; and the valley of the Red River of the North, lying still further to the north-west, will depend exclusively upon the railroad communication from St. Paul to St. Cloud as their avenue to market.

An intelligent observer of the map and of the progress of western settlements can readily appreciate the probable extent of travel and transportation over the proposed line, looking solely to the internal movement of northern Minnesota. But this is far from a complete statement of the case. What may be called the freights, &c., *through Minnesota to the English settlements of Selkirk and the Saskatchewan* constitute an equally important fact for our consideration.

Selkirk settlement, north of Minnesota, and dependent on the route of the St. Paul and Pacific Road for their best and cheapest communication with the world, is a community of 10,000 souls, which will soon be the seat of government for a new crown colony of England, extending between Canada and British Columbia. For the present, Fort Garry, in this settlement, is the North American head-quarters of the Hudson Bay Company, the most powerful and sagacious commercial organization in the British dependencies. The posts of this company, more than fifty in number, occupy every commanding situation over the immense area bounded by Hudson's Bay and Lake Superior on the east, the Rocky Mountains on the west, and the Arctic Ocean on the north, with their admirable system of administration, now perfected during upwards of a century. The Indians are in complete subjection, and the fur trade of the immense interior of British America concentrates its annual product on the Red River of the north, at Fort Garry, from· which point, by the annual voyages of brigades of bateaux, merchandise and supplies are distributed to the most distant posts.

Prior to 1858, the imports and exports of the Hudson Bay Company were transported by the difficult and dangerous route of Hudson's Bay and Nelson River, or over the numerous obstacles intervening from Lake Superior to Red River, on the British side of the international line. In

1858, however, citizens of Minnesota interested themselves to transport material and construct a steamer on the Red River of the North, and now, in 1862, two such vessels navigate that stream. The trade previously existing between St. Paul and Selkirk has been greatly increased in consequence. The business of the Red River steamer, during the year 1860 and 1861, will illustrate this increase:

	No. lbs., 1860.	No. lbs., 1861.
Freight carried to Fort Garry	433,643	826,483
Freight brought from Fort Garry	89,306	91,576
Total Freight carried both ways	522,949	918,059
Number of Passengers	123	308

It will be observed that the transportation to Fort Garry has nearly doubled, while the number of passengers has increased 150 per cent. during the past year. Besides this, about 60,000 pounds were carried down the river in barges during 1861, making in all, 886,483 pounds, or 443 tons of merchandise carried to the settlement, and 46 tons brought from there. The imports from that country are almost wholly furs.

When it is considered, what no intelligent man now denies, that north-west of Minnesota the country, reaching from the Selkirk settlements to the Rocky Mountains, and from latitudes 49° to 55°, is as favourable to grain and animal production as Michigan, Wisconsin, and Minnesota —that the mean temperature for spring, summer, and autumn, observed on the 42nd and 43rd parallels in New York, Ohio and Michigan, has been accurately traced through Fort Snelling and the valley of the Saskatchewan to latitude 55° on the Pacific coast—and that from the north-west boundary of Minnesota, this whole district of Central British America is threaded in all directions by the navigable water-lines which converge from the south and west to Lake Winnipeg—no reasonable doubt remains that the colonization of the continent, even in its ordinary progress of agricultural settlement, will extend over the region here delineated. With such an extension of English policy and development, the railroad system of Northern Minnesota will connect near Pembina. These events of the near future will powerfully contribute to the construction of the line of the St. Paul and Pacific Railroad from St. Paul, by way of St. Cloud and Otter Tail Lake, to the international frontier.

A new event—a new and most influential element—has lately occurred to hasten a progress which might otherwise seem remote and speculative. The discovery of gold, in 1858, upon the Fraser River and its tributaries, was followed by the organization of British Columbia; and the fact is now fully ascertained, that the richest and most extensive gold-field of North-West British America—the Cariboo mines—is so far within the Rocky Mountains—so far up to the utmost sources of Fraser River—as to be practically more accessible from Minnesota and Selkirk than from the coast of Puget's Sound.

A propeller upon Lake Winnipeg, and two small river steamers on the Saskatchewan, combining with the steamboats now navigating the Red River, would constitute a line from Quebec, by way of St. Paul, which could accomplish the journey to the Cariboo district in thirty days, at an expense of 150 dollars. The summer of 1862 will doubtless witness the establishment of such a line of continental transit. An expenditure of 100,000 dollars, with present facilities, is more than would be necessary for the purpose. Once in successful operation, an overland emigration from England and the British Provinces alone would reach thousands annually. As it is, during the month of May, 1862, three hundred Canadians have passed through St. Paul to Fort Garry, expecting thence to make the journey overland to the Cariboo mines, prospecting at the sources of the Saskatchewan, where rumour indicates a counterpart of the surface diggings which have brought the Cariboo region, immediately over the dividing summits of the Rocky Mountains, so prominently before the world.

The Hudson Bay Company, with great sagacity, declines any struggle with such a march of events. The successor of Sir George Simpson as Governor of the Company, Governor Dallas, is understood to have proceeded to Fort Garry in the spring of 1862, fully authorized by the London Directors to co-operate in every possible way for the speedy colonization of Central British America. It would not be surprising if the additional steamers required in the speedy transmission of mails, freight, and passengers, to the gold region of British Columbia, were immediately constructed under the direction of the Hudson Bay Company. Their transportation on Lake Winnipeg and the Saskatchewan has reached a bulk which would fully justify the necessary investment.

The St. Paul and Pacific Railroad is indispensable to the development of Central British America. Its line from St. Paul to St. Cloud, and thence to the Red River, will be the trunk of transportation to the vast north-west, now revealing itself in such magnificent proportions. No prospect so favourable attended the first railroad project west of Chicago as now encourages the pioneer Minnesota Railroad from St. Paul, by way of St. Anthony's Falls, north-westwardly towards the Red River of the North.

The first division of the road, from St. Paul to Watab, a distance of 80 miles, has been placed under contract, and most of the right of way obtained; 10 miles of which, to St. Anthony, is in operation, and the balance will be completed as soon as the material can be delivered upon the ground. About 65 miles are already graded and bridged, and the balance will be graded by the time the iron is laid upon the portion already graded.

The company have executed a mortgage upon the first division of the road to Russell Sage, of the City of Troy, and Samuel J. Tilden, of the City of New York, trustees, to secure the payment of its first mortgage bonds for 700,000 dollars; and also its mortgage upon 307,200 acres of land, for the sum of 1,200,000 dollars, to Samuel J. Tilden, of the City of New York, and Edmund Rice and Horace Thompson, of St. Paul, trustees: about 1,600,000 dollars will be issued to pay for the completion of the 80 miles under contract, with the necessary buildings and machinery.

The present population adjacent to these 80 miles of road is estimated at 67,000. During the three years prior to 1858 it had increased tenfold. In Wisconsin, as appears by the then last census, the increase of population had been at the rate of 87 per cent. per annum; and taking this as a basis, the population upon these 80 miles of our road will be, in two years, 200,000. Emigration to Minnesota is rapidly increasing, and there is now every indication that in another year it will be greater than ever before; thus furnishing additional business for the road, and increasing the value of and creating a new demand for the Company's lands.

St. Paul has a population of 16,000; St. Anthony and Minneapolis (divided by the river only), 10,000; and the valley of the Mississippi to Crow Wing (128 miles) is lined with thriving villages and towns, and has business sufficient to sustain the road handsomely, if constructed at the present moment.

The traffic upon 80 miles of our road will be, for the first two years:—

1. The importation and distribution of manufactures, stores, &c., into the interior.

2. Indian annuity goods, provisions, &c., furnished by the Government to the Indians of Dakotah territory, amounting to the annual value of half a million of dollars.

3. Supplies (other than United States property) for Fort Ripley and Fort Abercrombie.

4. Supplies of goods, agricultural implements, &c., for Selkirk and Hudson Bay Company possessions.

5. Return products from these different points, consisting of cattle, furs, buffalo robes, hides, peltries, and horses; the trade of those places last year with St. Paul alone amounting to over a million of dollars; 140 reaping and threshing machines were taken to Pembina during last season.

6. The goods of the Hudson Bay Company, forwarded from England, amounting to about 1000 tons the present year.

7. Emigrants to and from the Cariboo and Salmon River gold-mines.

Estimated Income of Road for First Year.

	Dol.
45,000 tons merchandise from St. Paul to Minneapolis and St. Anthony, 1 dollar 50 cents	67,500
25,000 tons merchandise to points above St. Anthony, 3 dollars	75,000
100,000 barrels flour from Minneapolis and St. Anthony to St. Paul, 10 cents	10,000
80,000 barrels flour from points above St. Anthony, 15 cents	12,000
1,000,000 bushels wheat to St. Paul, 5 cents	50,000
10,000,000 feet pine lumber, 1 dollar per M.	10,000
Wool, hogs, cattle, &c..	5,000
200 passengers daily, each way, from St. Paul to Minneapolis and St. Anthony, 40 cents	29,200
40 passengers each way to terminus, 3 dollars	87,600
	346,300
Deduct 50 per cent. for Government tax and working expenses	173,150
	173,150
Interest upon first mortgage bonds 58,600	
„ „ real estate bonds 84,000	142,600
Surplus	30,550

Without resorting to sales of lands, which, by the terms of the mortgage, are pledged to pay interest and principle of the real estate bonds.

At St. Paul and St. Anthony this road will connect with three other railroads running easterly, southerly, and south-westerly.

To convince any one that the bonds issued by this Company should command a high price, and take their place as among the best upon the market, the following statement of cost of road, value of lands, &c., must be sufficient:—

1. The road, 80 miles from St. Paul to Watab, with a very valuable property at St. Paul, being about 30 acres water front, estimated at

100,000 dollars, with station-houses, engine-houses, shops, rolling stock, all complete (of which has been contributed by the State and stockholders over 800,000 dollars), costing about 2,700,000 dollars.

Is mortgaged, first, to secure the sum of 820,000 dollars.

2. The company own 307,200 acres of land, selected along and near the road in 1857, which, by the charter granted by the State of Minnesota, *are exempt from all taxation till sold and conveyed by the Company*, nearly all of which is very valuable; the average value of which is estimated by competent persons to be at least 10 dollars per acre, amounting to 3,072,000 dollars.

Upon which the Company have issued real estate bonds, and making them second upon railroad, for 1,200,000 dollars.

The Company, after paying for the entire cost of the road and equipments, will hold a surplus of over 400,000 dollars of its real estate bonds, and the surplus proceeds of the sales of the lands over and above the satisfaction of the bonds.

EDMUND RICE,

St. Paul, July 1st, 1862. *President.*

APPENDIX "G."

VALUE OF MONEYS.

THE following information will be found valuable to strangers visiting Canada, and particularly to emigrants bringing with them sterling money:

VALUE OF COLONIAL MONEYS.

The basis of the currency is the imperial gold standard, differing from sterling money in the different nominal value of the pound and its constituents.

The pound sterling is by law fixed at twenty-four shillings and four-pence currency. At this rate all large transactions are settled, and remittances, with the correction of the day for exchange, are calculated.

One pound currency contains four dollars.
One dollar ,, ,, five shillings.
One shilling ,, ,, two sixpences.
One sixpence ,, ,, six pennies.
One penny ,, ,, two coppers.

The value in sterling of the pound currency is rather over 16s. 5¼d.
The dollar currency rather over 4 1¼
The shilling ,, ,, ,, ... 0 9¾
The sixpence ,, rather under 0 5

But in retail transactions an approximation is made to the value of the coins current in Britain and the United States, and in small purchases the following are the rates at which such coins are usually paid away:—

BRITISH.

The sovereign	£1 4s.	6d.
The crown	0 6	1
Half crown	0 3	0½
Shilling, called *Trente-sous* . . .	0 1	3
Sixpence, ,, *Quinze-sous* . . .	0 0	7½

AMERICAN.

Eagle	£2 10s.	0d.
Dollar	0 5	1
Half dollar	0 2	6½
Dime, or ten cents	0 0	6
Real, or *York shilling* . . .	0 0	7½

A shilling sterling and a quarter of a dollar are taken in the stores as equal. The exchangeable value of the dollar, of course, varies with the course of exchange between the Provinces and the United States, which is principally ruled by that between New York and London. In general, its value is about 5s. 1d. currency, or 4s. 2d. sterling.

VALUE OF ENGLISH COIN THROUGHOUT CANADA.

STERLING.				CURRENCY.
£	s.	d.	Dols.	Cts.
0	0	1	0	2
0	0	6	0	$12\frac{1}{2}$
0	1	0	0	25
0	2	6	0	60
0	5	0	1	21
0	10	0	2	43
1	0	0	4	86
5	0	0	24	33
10	0	0	48	66
20	0	0	97	33
50	0	0	243	33
100	0	0	486	66

INDEX.

AFRICA, British possessions in, 2.
America, expeditions to, by—
  Almagro, 21.
  Balboa, Nunez, and Cabral, *ib.*
  Columbus, 19.
  Cortez, 21.
  De Hojeda, Alonzo, 20.
  De Solls, Sir Francis Drake, 21.
  Magellan, Orellana, Pizarro, *ib.*
  Sarmiento, Schonter, 22.
  Vespucci, Amerigo, 20.
America, discovery of, 15.
  In its primitive state, 10.
  Inducements to settle in, 198.
  Known to the inhabitants of Iceland and Norway anterior to the voyages of Columbus, 15.
  Scandinavian records, *ib.*
American Colonies, England's duty to her, 8.
  Railways, increase in traffic of, 131.
Arctic Ocean, expeditions to the, by—
  Back, Sir George, 23.
  Baffin, William, 22.
  Beechey, Behring, 23.
  Belcher, 24.
  Britton, Thomas, 23.
  Cabot, Sebastian, 22.
  Cook, Captain, 23.
  Davis, John, 22.
  Dease, Sir John Franklin, 23.
  Frobisher, Martin, 22.
  Hall, 24.
  Hearne, Samuel, 23.
  Hudson, Henry, 22.
  Inglefield, 24.
  Mackenzie, Alexander, 23.
  M'Clintock, M'Clure, 24.
  Parry, Sir Edward, 23.
  Penny, Rae, 24.
  Richardson, Sir John, 23.
  Ross, Sir John, Simpson, *ib.*
Asia, Western, migratory journeys of the people of, 13.
Astronomers, celebrated, 14.
Atlantic, speculations of Europeans as to a land peopled beyond the, 18.
Australia, statistics of, 2.

BENNETT, Mr. John, extracts from his Report on the Public Schools of New Brunswick, 52.
Blessings of peace, 142.

British Colonies, the, 1.
  Their extent, population, imports, and exports, 2.
British Columbia, boundary line of, 106.
  Cariboo gold river, 117.
  Discovery of the gold, 110.
  Early discovery of the colony, 106.
  Export of gold in 1863, 120.
  Fertility of soil in the gold neighbourhood, 121.
  Gold-mines, 108.
  Gold on Fraser River, 112.
  Lakes and Rivers, 107.
  Lillooett gold-mines, 117.
  Mines on Thompson River, 115.
  Progress of the colony, 121.
  Richness of the mines, 114.
  Rocky Mountains described, 105.
  State of labour in the colony, 119.
  Steele's company, 118.
  Testimony of Governor Douglas, D. G. F. Macdonald, Esq., and the *Times* correspondent, 111.
British Guinea, statistics of, 2.
British India, statistics of, *ib.*
British North America, its extent, population, imports and exports, 3.
  Its prospective wealth, 4.
British North American Confederation, proposed, 3.
  A means of security, 5.
  Duty of England towards the, 135.
  General review of the Confederacy, *ib.*
  Resolutions adopted at a conference held in Quebec as the basis of the, 205.

CANADAS, The, agricultural statistics of, 81.
  Colonization of, 29.
  Commerce of, 59, 60.
  Description of, 54.
  Farming interest of, 80.
  Kingston, Hamilton, and Cobourg described, 80.
  Lakes, rivers, and canals, 55.
  Mineral wealth of the great lakes, 59.
  Montreal and its trade, 77.
  Principal cities of Canada, *ib.*
  Quebec and its trade, 78—80.
  Shipping of Canada, 61.
  Tables showing the trade of, 83.
  Ten reasons for emigrating to, 67—77.
  The Pictured Rocks, 56.

Canada, the Rapids, 66.
 Trade of the colony, 62.
 Toronto and its trade, 78.
Canadian Almanac for 1864, extracts from the, 67—77.
Canadian Railways, 132.
 Buffalo and Lake Erie Railway, 133.
 Grand Trunk Railway, ib.
 Great Western Railway, ib.
 Cost of, 134.
Canadian song, 67.
Cariboo gold-mines, 117.
Charter, Royal, grant of a, by Charles II. to the Hudson's Bay Company, 85.
Chase, Hon. S. P., report by the, 59.
Chicago, shipping and trade of, 62.
Cities, principal Canadian, 77.
Cobourg described, 80.
Colonial moneys, value of, 239.
Colonization, the progress of, 25.
Colorado, area and population of, 184.
Confederacy, general review of the British North American, 135.
Confederation, the proposed British North American, 3.
Conference of delegates from the provinces of Canada, Nova Scotia, and New Brunswick, and the colonies of Newfoundland and Prince Edward's Island, resolutions adopted at a, 205.
Cultivated plants, increased production of, near the northernmost limit of their growth, 212—216.

DISTANCES and FARES, Table of, between Great Britain and North America, 223
Distances and Fares, Table of, in the United States and Canada, viâ the Grand Trunk Railway, 224, 225.
Distances to Chicago, Illinois—from Quebec and New York, 223; from Boston and New Orleans, 224.

EDMONTON, life at, 94.
Emigrant, homes for the, 98.
Emigrants, advice to, 120, 193.
Emigration from Germany to America, 195.
 General Progress of, to America, 193.
English appreciation of United States of America, and her sympathy, 140.
English coin, value of in Canada, 240.
Expedition, Franklin, loss of the, 23.
Explorer, geographer, and navigator, early efforts of the, 9.

"FERTILE BELT," the, 96.
Forry, Dr., on the "Acclimating Principle of Plants," 212.
Foster and Whitney, Messrs., their report of the geology of the Lake Superior District, extract from, 56.
Fraser River gold-mines, 112.
Fredericktown, the political capital of New Brunswick, where situated, 47.

GEOGRAPHERS, celebrated, 14.
Geology of the Lake Superior District, extract from report of the, 56.
Gibraltar, statistics of, 2.
Gold-fields, the Nova Scotian, 44.
Gold-mines of British Columbia, 108.
Gold, prospecting, panning, and washing, 124.
Great Salt Lake, settlements of the, 186.
Greenland, Eric the Red establishes a colony on the coast of, 16.

HALIFAX, description of, 43.
Hamilton described, 80.
Highway across the Hudson's Bay Territory, 99.
Highway between the Mississippi States and the Pacific coast, necessity of more than one, 183.
Honduras, statistics of, 2.
Hudson's Bay Company, Charter of the, 85.
 Definition of the, ib.
 Fur trade, extent and value, 86—88.
 Lands of, in the market, 101.
 Profits of the, 86.
Hudson's Bay Territory, American Trade, 98.
 Crossing the Rocky Mountains, 102.
 Government of, 88.
 Homes for the emigrant, 98.
 Minerals, vegetable productions, animals, fish, &c., 96.
 Physical features of, 89.
 Plains, lakes, and rivers, 90.
 Progress of the West, 103.
 Red River Settlement, 97.
 Report of the New York Chamber of Commerce, 92.
 Testimony as to the fertility of the territory—by Captains Blakiston and Palisser, 96, 149; M. Bourgeau, Sir George Simpson, Father De Smet, and Professor Hind, 91—95.
 The Railway Route, 95.
 The Saskatchewan Valley, 96.
Human race, the progenitors of the, 12.

ICELAND discovered by some Scandinavians, A.D. 861, 15.
Illinois, Agricultural progress of, 161.
 Area and population, ib.
 Railway system of, 163.
 Stock-breeding and raising in, 199.
 Valuation and taxation of, 162.
 Value of the lands of the Illinois Central Railroad, 182.
Immigration, comparative increase in, to America, from 1861 to 1864, 194.
Indiana, Agricultural products of, 152.
 Area, population, and progress, ib.
 Manufactures, 153.
 Railways and Canals, 154.

Inter-Colonial Railway, the, 134.
International Pacific Railway, testimony of Captains Palliser and Blakiston in reference to an, 187—191.
Iowa, Agricultural wealth of, 159.
  General description of, 158.
  Railway system, 161.
Itineraries of routes from St. Paul, Minnesota, to Pembina, Fort Garry, Fort Ellice, Edmonton House, and the Gulf of Georgia, British Columbia, 226.

KANSAS, statistics of, 185.
Kingston, description of, 80.

LABOUR in British Columbia, 119.
Letters to the Author, bearing testimony to the value of the lands situated in Central British America, 201, 202, 203.
Life at Edmonton, 94.
Lillooett gold-mines, 117.

MACDONALD, G. Forbes, F.R.G.S., on the discovery of gold in British Columbia, 111.
Maury, Professor M. F., on Pacific railroads, 217.
Mayne, Captain, R.N., on British Columbia, 124.
Michigan, cereal products and miscellaneous crops, 155.
  General statistics of, 154.
  Products of agriculture, *ib.*
  Railroads, 156.
Migration, laws of, 197.
Minnesota, agricultural productions of, 176.
  Extent of territory and population of, 165.
  Falls of St. Anthony and their water power, 169.
  Growth of property in, 179.
  Lands granted for railways in the State, 182.
  Mineral resources, sandstone, &c., 171
  Physical districts of, 166.
  Progress of population in, 180.
  Railway through the State of, 181.
  Rapid progress in cultivation, 175.
  Relations of, in reference to internal commerce, 173.
  Salt springs, 172.
  St. Croix Falls, the, 170.
  St. Paul, the capital of, 166.
  Superiority of Minnesota over New England, 170.
  The testimony of the Hon. W. H. Seward as to the future of Minnesota, 180.
Mitchell, Professor, his testimony as to the value of railroads, 130.
Montmorenci, the Falls of, 79.
Montreal, description of, 77.

NEBRASKA, statistics of, 185.
Nevada, population and progress of, 186.
New Brunswick, agricultural resources, 53.
  Capabilities of, 47.
  Census and militia, 53.
  Colonization of, 27.
  Commerce, 50.
  Description of, 46.
  Finances and government, 51.
  Fisheries, 49.
  Forests, 48.
  Minerals, fruit and vegetables, and manufactures, 49.
  Public schools, 52.
  Railway system, 132.
  Rivers and counties, 46, 49.
Newfoundland, agricultural statistics of, 31
  Colonization of, 25.
  Description of, 31.
  Fisheries and government, 32.
  Imports, exports, and shipping, 33.
  Population, 34.
New York Chamber of Commerce, report of the, 92.
New Zealand, statistics of, 2.
North America, the railway system of, 127.
"North Star" of the Western States, the, 181
Nova Scotia, agriculture of, 39.
  Botanical productions, seasons, 38.
  Colonization of, 28.
  Commerce and population, 41.
  Crown lands, 42.
  Description of, 37.
  Fisheries, 40.
  Gold-fields, 44.
  Government and education, 43.
  Minerals, 44, 45.
  Quadrupeds, birds, and fish, 42.
  Railway system, 132.
  Shipping, 39.

OHIO and MISSISSIPPI RAILROAD, opening of the, 129.
Ohio, description of, 150.
  Products of agriculture, *ib.*
  Railways, 151.
  Testimony of T. Addison Richards as to the fertility of her soil, 152.

PACIFIC RAILROADS, the physical, commercial, and military necessity of two, one north and one south, 217—222.
Palisser, Captain—his testimony as to the necessity of a railway route through the United States to the Red River country, 149.
Peace, blessings of, 142.
Peaceful relations between United States and Canada, 148.
Primary object of the book, 149.
Prince Edward's Island, colonization of, 27.
  Counties, towns, and population, 36.
  Description of, 34.

Prince Edward's Island—
  Education and government, 36.
  Imports and exports, 35
  Industrial resources of, *ib.*

QUEBEC, description of, 78.

RAILWAY, length of, in England, France, and the United States, 128.
  Must pass through the State of Minnesota on its way to the Pacific, 181.
  Route from the Atlantic to the Pacific, 6.
  System of Nova Scotia and New Brunswick, 132.
Railways of the United States, number, extent, and aggregate cost of all the, 163.
Reciprocity Treaty, the, 143.
  Increase of trade influenced by, 144.
  Increase of traffic on the American railways and canals, 145, 146.
  Leading features of, 143.
  Mutual advantages, 144.
Red River Settlement, account of, 97.
Rice, Hon. Edmund—his statement respecting the St. Paul and Pacific Railroad, 233—238.
Rice, Hon. Henry M.—his estimation of the State of Minnesota, 201.
Robertson, Col. D. A., letter of, to the President of the Chamber of Commerce of the City of St. Paul, Minnesota, 217.
Rocky Mountains, extent, altitude, and passes of the, 105.
Route to British Columbia wholly through British territory impossible, 149.

SASKATCHEWAN VALLEY, the, 90.
South Pacific Railway, estimated cost of, 187.
Speculations of Europeans as to a land peopled beyond the Atlantic, 18.
Steam a revolutionizer, 128.
St. John's, the capital of Newfoundland, described by Mr. Warburton, 34.
St. Lawrence, the rapids of the, 66.
  Superior Basin of the, 166.
Stock-breeding and raising in Illinois, 199.
St. Paul and Pacific Railroad, letters and papers concerning the, 200—203.
  Statement by the Hon. Edmund Rice in reference to the, 233—238.

St. Paul Chamber of Commerce, the, 217.
Swann, the Hon. Mr., on the construction of railroads, 130.

TABLE of distances and fares in the United States and Canada, *viâ* Grand Trunk Railway, 224.
Tables showing the trade and navigation of the canals of Canada, 83.
Tables showing the number of vessels (American and Canadian) engaged in the commerce of the lakes, 61, 62.
Territory, Hudson's Bay, 85.
Testimony of the Governor of Minnesota as to the fertile districts of that State, 200.
Toronto, description of, 78.
Travellers, celebrated, 14.
Travelling, early, 126.

UNITED STATES OF AMERICA, beauty of the lakes, rivers, prairies, and mountains, 139.
  English appreciation of America, and her sympathy, 142.
  Extent and progress of the States, 138.
  Exports and imports, 147.
  Increase of trade, 144.
  Peace and reciprocity, 142.
  Poets, orators, historians, &c., 140.
  Railway traffic, 145.
  Reciprocity Treaty, its leading features, 143.
  Traffic on the canals, 146.
Utah, population and progress of, 186.

VALUE of colonial moneys, 239.
Vancouver's Island, agricultural resources and coal-beds of, 122.
  Description of, 121.
  Importance of, as a naval station, 122.
  Imports and exports, 123.

WESTERN STATES OF AMERICA, wealth of the, 150—164.
West Indies, British possessions in the, 2.
West, progress of the, 103.
Wisconsin, agricultural progress of, 158.
  Income and expenditure, *ib.*
  Railroads and products of agriculture, 157.
  Topographical features, 156
  Valuation and taxation in 1863, 158.

www.ingramcontent.com/pod-product-compliance
Lightning Source LLC
Chambersburg PA
CBHW020801230426
43666CB00007B/799